ESSENTIAL

BUILDING BLOCKS
LIFE AND LEADERSHIP

DR. BOB TURNER

KAIO PUBLICATIONS, INC.

Bob shows the value of living like a leader, loving like a leader and truly leading like a leader. There is no single "one stop shop" for leaders, but this book comes very close. A must read for all leaders.

Wayne Roberts
Marriage Coach with His Shoes, Her Shoes
Director of the TRU Church Conference
Co-Director of the Mighty Men Leadership Conference

Bob Turner is a leader of leaders and an equipper of equippers. In this book, he draws from a deep well of learning and experience on the subject of leadership. Some of the best quotes, studies, and ideas from both secular and religious leadership books are masterfully curated and applied to Christian life and leadership.

Wes McAdams, Minister
McDermott Road Church of Christ

In Esssential: Building Blocks 4 Life and Leadership, readers will continuously be called back to Scripture, interact with materials from a number of works in the field, and be given general rules and specific tools to better assess how to come up with a vision, measure success, and continually call themselves back to the best practices for leading others.

Doug Burleson
Associate Professor of Bible
Director of the Annual Bible Lectureship
Freed-Hardeman University

Bob blesses us with outstanding insight from his research, but more importantly, everyone who reads *Essential: Building Blocks 4 Life and Leadership* will benefit from Bob's personal perspective as well as what he has gleaned from a lifetime of learning from other leaders.

Jeff A. Jenkins, Minister
Lewisville Church of Christ, Lewisville, TX

Bob Turner is a great resource for me when it comes to all things leadership related. From determining a vision, to setting and achieving goals, to building character, to developing passion, *Essential* is a holistic approach that includes the person, the personality, and the performance of an effective leader with God's holy Word being the basis for it all.

Chris McCurley, Minister
Oldham Lane Church of Christ, Abilene, TX

Bob Turner's book, *Essential: Building Blocks 4 Life and Leadership*, explores the concepts of effective leadership through a fluid combination of theory, practice, and most importantly, Biblical examples. Bob had a goal to write an effective, practical text that explores the characteristics of good leadership. *Essential: Building Blocks 4 Life and Leadership* accomplished that goal.

Richard England
Professor of Education and Music
Freed-Hardeman University

*Full reviews are located in the back of the book.

Table of Contents

Foreword by Jeremie Kubicek

What in your life is absolutely necessary? You can make the list high level and broad by stating the necessities of air, water, sun and more. Or you can go with the relational answer and state family, spouse, children and the like and they will all be correct until you begin to list a certain pair of shoes or a show you like.

Essentials, according to the dictionary, are the things that are absolutely necessary in our life. Bob Turner provides a thorough list of Essentials we need for Life and Leadership. Essentials like "Vision", "Goals", "Character" and "Passion" are absolutely necessary.

Imagine, for instance, ... a person or a leader without "Vision". We are told in Scripture that the people in that person's wake will perish without vision. It is essential to lead effectively.

What if someone doesn't have "Character"? Can any trust ever be built?

For something to be "Essential" means that it is of utmost importance, and that we can't live without it because it is absolutely necessary.

During the 2020 global pandemic, certain professions/jobs were deemed "Essential" for the economy amidst the Covid-19 storm – healthcare, construction, food manufacturing, real estate, etc. Without them, the lock downs would bring complete destruction for our economic and social engines. These are examples of "Essentials" in our daily lives and in our work.

So, what are the "Essentials" again of life and leadership? Bob highlights with excellent metaphor a mix of pragmatism and theology to make the "Essentials" real in your personal life and leadership.

If you are a young person or a new "leader", this book is a field guide for you to implement the "Essentials" into your everyday life.

If you have "been around the block" as an older leader, this book is a reflection to see what areas of the "Essentials" need to be fortified or optimized based on your situation.

In the end, I am certain that you will be encouraged and will take away a few nuggets either in metaphor or in practical idea to bolster your life and leadership. And, I am certain that you will give this book to any new leader just starting from scratch as they learn what is absolutely necessary in their life.

For me, I was encouraged to reignite my passion and my vision and the correlation of those two things together.

Let me encourage you to jump into this book with fervor and with a marker as you take notes to strengthen the "Essentials" in your life and in your leadership. You will be glad you took the time to devote to growth. I know I did.

Jeremie Kubicek
Founder & Executive Chairman, GiANT.TV
Best-selling author of *Making Your Leadership Come Alive*, *The 100X Leader*, *The 5 Voice*, and *The 5 Gears*.

Foreword by Neal Pollard

About halfway through this book, Bob shares two questions that epitomize how invaluable this resource is. The questions are, "If your church were to disappear tomorrow, would anyone in the community know?...Would anyone care?" If that does not fill our soul with convicting self-examination, it could be that we need to go deeper in our soul-searching! Having participated in many hours of strategic planning and vision meetings in churches in three time zones, I have seen the value of godly leaders daring greatly to do God's business. Often, churches flounder to form a plan to grow the church. More often, church leaders are making no plans at all, and, as Bob says, "Doing nothing is the biggest risk of all."

I am so thankful that I have read *Essential: Building Blocks 4 Life and Leadership* for at least five reasons.

First, it is eminently practical. It is a "how-to" process that carries leadership from start to finish in the effective establishment of vision, mission, and planning. There are so many examples of how to do, what to do, and why to do it which will empower the reader to put these principles to use. He is currently engaged in the very things he writes about, so it is fresh and relevant and is the fruit of so much interaction with churches and leaders wedded to his credibility and credentials. It is also practical in that it instills the truth that character and claims, instructions and influence, rise and fall together. Who we are as leaders is an integral piece of where we are going and leading others to go. Leaders must be growing if they expect their followers to grow. Practice is central to that.

Second, it is thoroughly documented and researched. You will come to appreciate Bob, as I do, as a diligent prospector who has found gems all over the place, has collected them into his bag of knowledge, and has given them to you as gifts to keep and use. He has done exhaustive study on the subject of leadership, and he competently distills the contents of tens of thousands of pages of material in hundreds of books to complement his superior grasp of the subject.

Third, it is based on proven principles. While there may be some processes and terminology you find less familiar, much of the content is the fruit of Bob's aforementioned, thorough study of the overall subject. Bob has built this approach through study and practice, going across the country and delivering the heart of this material to help churches implement a strategic plan for growth and development. He knows what churches are going through, and he has strategies that have been demonstrated to work.

Fourth, it is usable in format. I love organization, and Bob lays out his processes as logical roadmaps that build one upon another. The headings and sub points, adeptly situated in well-laid-out chapters, are veritable guides through his four essentials of vision, goals, character, and passion.

Finally, it is biblical in approach. This is no doubt the most important facet of this book's usefulness. With a theocentric worldview, I am most interested in what the Omniscient mind has to say. It adds strength to Bob's research that he fills each chapter with so many illustrations from Scripture to show how the need and the process are God-honoring and, so often, God-originating. Such will build your conviction to leave a spiritual legacy befitting such an awesome God.

You will find yourself convicted to live up to your potential as a leader. You will look closer at how you use your resources, your opportunities, and your challenges to glorify God through the stewardship of your life. Such personal persuasion can help you help the church where you attend be what God needs it to be in a lost and dying world. We are only here for so long, and that time is passing quickly (Jas. 4:13-15). We've excused ourselves for long enough! God needs us busy in His vineyard. *Essential: Building Blocks 4 Life and Leadership* is an essential tool in your hands to be effective in that eternal work!

Neal Pollard, Minister
Lehman Avenue Church of Christ
Bowling Green, KY

Preface

My journey began in 2000, when I started a research project concerning food. Odd place to begin, I know. But truth be told: I love to eat. (In fact, I'm eating while working on this preface.) While I was reading about the benefits of food, I came across this bit of information: there are four essential elements for life to exist on planet Earth—sun, air, water, and enzymes (food). Take away any one of these four elements, and life will cease to exist. I know this is not a revelation to you, but at that moment it became significant to me. Here's why.

Over the past thirty years, I have studied a number of areas related to leadership. For the last ten of those years, I became a bit obsessive about the subject. I read anything I could get my hands on related to leadership—and there's a lot to read. I am sure you've heard of several major authors on the subject, such as Dale Carnegie, Stephen Covey, John Maxwell, Warren Bennis, Simon Sinek, James Kouzes and Barry Posner, Brené Brown, Jim Collins, John Kotter, Andy Stanley, Angela Duckworth, Aubrey Malphurs, Jeremie Kubicek, Steve Cochram . . . and the list grows daily. Additionally, the number of biographies on great leaders throughout history is unending. Needless to say, the wealth of available information is mind-boggling. Type the word leadership into any search engine and you'll find more than two billion responses. Not all of these find their way into valuable research, but it does highlight the magnitude of the subject.

In an effort to grapple with this subject, I asked, "Is it possible to narrow the massive amount of material into a few key—or essential—components?" While contemplating the question, I realized there was a relationship between the essential elements of life and what I considered to be the essential components of leadership. As a result, I worked to develop and show the interrelationship between the four essentials of life and leadership.

The sun's light provides direction for each step in our daily journey through life, making life possible on every level. Vision illuminates direction for a leader's journey as they provide direction for those who follow. Air is the breath of life; inhaled into the lungs, oxygen strengthens every component of our existence. Goals breathe life into any organization, strengthening the purpose that supports where it is headed and why it exists. Water makes up the largest part of our body, the foundational building block and substance of life. Character is the building block of leadership, the foundational substance for success. Enzymes are nature's activists, the spark that drives energy into our lives. Passion is the spark that energizes our leadership, the compelling force to conquer and achieve.

I cannot overstate the value of every book or blog post I've read, all the lectures I've heard, or the classes I've taken on leadership. They provided a wealth of information I draw on to teach and now write. As you read through the sections and chapters of this book, please consider how these essentials of life and leadership can benefit you in your efforts to influence others for a greater cause.

What follows is an explanation of why this book focuses on life and leadership. I then embark on a journey to describe in four sections the relationship of these four essentials. Each section will highlight an essential element for life, providing background research to support why it is essential, followed by how that element connects to leadership. Thank you for taking time to read. I pray you benefit from the time spent.

Introduction

Essential: Life and Leadership

Life and leadership go hand in hand. On the surface, this may not seem to make sense. But trust me, one does not exist without the other. However, there's a burning question to consider: *Why?* Why write another book about leadership? Why discuss a subject that seems to have been adequately explored by numerous authors for centuries, if not millennia? Why connect the ideas of life and leadership? The questions are limitless. Perhaps a better question would be *"Why not?"* Allow me to share some context.

Several years ago, in preparation for a class on leadership, I spent some time researching a bit of national history. I considered the face of leadership over the past century. I examined the president who had served the longest during each decade, beginning with the 1920s. There were a few decades where several men served as president, but I only examined the one who served for the longest period of time. I took into consideration current events both nationally and internationally. The way I looked at it, these events had a bearing on the leadership of the time.

As I studied the lives of these leaders along with the events that occurred while they were in office, I also researched the definition of leadership as it existed in each decade. The revelation of this study was insightful, to say the least. I discovered that, along with the background of the president, current events played a major role in each decade's definition of leadership. Let me give you a few examples of what I'm talking about.

Although not every event during this time was bleak, the 1940s was a decade plagued by horrors, globally. It was a time of war and one of the darkest periods in world history. World War II dominated the scene, Hitler and his collaborators were responsible for the genocide of nearly six million Jews (the Holocaust), racial issues in the United States were digging deep roots, education gained greater emphasis, and as the United States emerged from the Great Depression, more women entered the work place. The world was introduced to television, which began to make its way into every home. This changed the way information was communicated, along with how American families saw and understood the world.

Harry S. Truman served as the president of the United States. As he led the country through these dark hours, a definition of leadership was presented that reflected the events of the time. Among several definitions that surfaced during the 1940s, Norman Copeland's military direct approach defined leadership as, "the art of influencing. . . people by persuasion or example to follow a line of action. It must never be confused with *drivership* . . . which is the art of compelling. . . people by intimidation or force to follow a line of action."[1] The use of such terms as *intimidation* and *force* indicate the influences of men such as Hitler and the desire to avoid such leadership styles. The use of such words as *persuasion* and *example* indicate a more servant—yet inspirationally oriented—approach to leading.

Skip ahead thirty years to the 1970s. The United States was experiencing growth in radical ideas. It's important to note how the 1960s introduced the world to mysticism, sex, drugs, and the age of rock-n-roll. Humanism and a move toward liberal ideology also impacted the mindset of the culture. Building on these influences, the world experienced an explosion in technology, space exploration, and advances in civil rights. Additionally, the women's movement gained a strong foothold in the culture, Roe versus Wade created a wave of controversy related to the rights of unborn children, and the homosexual movement became more prevalent. However, one of the most significant events that challenged our understanding of leadership occurred with the Watergate scandal that took place between 1972 and 1974.

Richard Nixon resigned as the president of the United States after two years of investigation surrounding the scandalous attempts by Nixon to cover up his administration's break-in of the Democratic National Committee headquarters. The investigation ultimately led to the indictment of sixty-nine people and conviction of forty-eight. Without a doubt, this changed our country's understanding of leadership. When such a major breech of trust occurs within the highest office of the country, people question every aspect of leadership and begin to doubt the security, stability, and wellbeing of the nation. We should not be surprised to see a change in the definition of leadership as a result of this. On the heels of this scandal, James MacGregor Burns wrote, "Leadership over human beings is exercised when persons with certain motives and purposes mobilize, in competition or conflict with others, institutional, political, psychological, and other resources so as to arouse, engage, and satisfy the motives of followers. . . . in order to realize goals mutually held by *both* leaders and followers."[2] Burns later discussed a definition of leadership from a moral perspective:

> The essence of leadership in any polity is the recognition of real need, the uncovering and exploiting of contradictions among values and between values and practice, the realigning of values, the reorganization of institutions where necessary, and the governance of change. Essentially the leader's task is consciousness-raising on a wide plane. . . . The leader's fundamental act is to induce people to be aware or conscious of what they feel—to feel their true needs so strongly, to define their values so meaningfully, that they can be moved to purposeful action.[3]

There are several key words throughout these definitions that highlight the moral element of leadership and the outcome in relationship to the events of the 1970s.

There's a wealth of information on the decades preceding and following the 1970s indicating the nature of leadership and how it has been defined. The challenge of settling on an objective definition of leadership that fits every generation, nation, culture, and people is enormous. While researching information on leadership through the decades and seeing the changes in the very definition of leadership, I was left to ask, "Does culture influence the direction of leadership and its definitio. Or does leadership influence the direction of culture and determine how leadership is defined?" On one hand, the answer is both. On the other hand, a thorough study of each decade reveals an answer that is subjective depending on the nature of the leader and the strength of the culture.

While I didn't conduct my historical research within the cultural contexts of other countries (and I'm certain that contextual elements factor into the study), the evidence that surfaced appears to be characteristic around the globe. Leadership is one of the most challenging subjects to tackle. Sadly, the majority of people in our world only know leadership by the specific styles they see in their own contexts, which may not always represent "good" leadership. I place quotation marks around *good*, because a descriptor of this nature is subjective. Regardless, we're left with the struggle of understanding how to define leadership, identify the characteristics of a "good" leader, and implement ways to develop the kind of leader worth following.

Based on this foundation, I want to return to answering the original question: *Why life and leadership?* As evidenced through the previous material, it is difficult to disconnect the two concepts. Life directly influences leadership, and leadership directly influences life. With this in mind, perhaps the answer can be found in a more spiritual location. Let me turn your attention to a biblical approach in order to find a clearer understanding of life and leadership.

Books have been written—and many more could be written—about the leadership styles and characteristics of biblical leaders. From Adam to Noah to Abraham to Joseph to Moses to Joshua to the judges to the kings to the prophets to Jesus and the apostles, the Bible provides everything we want and need to know about this amazing subject. Throughout the pages of each book or letter, we learn about leadership in the home, in the world, and among God's people. Each of these areas deserves a focus of its own, but that's not the purpose of this discussion.

I turn your attention to a period in time when Persia dominated the world. Here we learn about the captivity of Israel and the rise to influence of a courageous woman named Esther. Esther's position of influence with the king of Persia—which ultimately saved the nation of Israel—did not develop as one might imagine.

From the first to the last verse of the book, we learn about leadership on numerous levels. The book of Esther begins by introducing us to the king of Persia, Ahasuerus, and the scope of his rule in the world. During this time, the king hosted a banquet for the administration of leaders he had appointed throughout the land.

Unlike a typical banquet today, this one lasted seven days, and the consumption of alcohol during this time must have been immense, as the "royal wine was plentiful according to the king's bounty. The drinking was done according to the [Persian] law" (Esther 1:7–8). The king had consumed more than his share of alcohol and was "merry with wine," So he sent for the queen, Vashti, in an attempt to parade her before the leaders of Persia. Vashti refused. Not good.

The king sought counsel as to what needed to be done. Wisdom is attributed to the king in that he sought advice from "the wise men who understood the times" (Esther 1:13). After all, if word got out that the queen had gotten away with refusing the king, then all the women in the kingdom would "look with contempt on their husbands" (Esther 1:17). In order to prevent such disrespect, upon the advice of his counselors, the king issued a decree that Queen Vashti be removed and never again allowed in the king's presence.

This meant that another queen had to be selected. Here, the text introduces us to Esther. Following a one-year preparatory process of oil treatments, spices, and cosmetics, Esther was presented to the king. Imagine waiting a full year before such a presentation. As the account reveals, Esther's beauty of form and face found favor in the king's eyes and she became the next queen. I should probably mention at this point that Esther was an Israelite and a relative of a Jew named Mordecai, which was not revealed to the king at the time. Mordecai played a significant role in saving the king from an assassination plot, and the king subsequently sought to reward him.

At this point, we learn about the king's promotion of a prince named Haman. Haman was the epitome of how *not* to be a leader. His egotism was as extreme as his hatred for the people of Israel. Haman loved nothing more than to move through the city and have everyone bow and pay homage to him and his authority. However, there was one who would not bow: Mordecai. Isn't it interesting how someone can have 99.9 percent of the population's favor, yet that .1 percent against them overrules everything else? Such was the case with Haman. Mordecai was a burning thorn in the side of Haman—he was determined to destroy Mordecai and every Jew because of him. Haman approached the king with a plan to eliminate the Jews, and the king gave him his signet ring and the authority to do as he pleased (Esther 3:10–11).

A bit later, the king contemplated how he might honor one who showed him such favor as to save his life (Mordecai). He asked Haman what the king should do to honor such a worthy man. Haman mistakenly thought the king wished to honor him, so he laid out quite a ceremony. He suggested the king put a royal robe on the man, sit him on a horse the king had ridden, and then have one of the king's princes lead the man on the horse through the city saying, "Thus it shall be done to the man whom the king desires to honor" (Esther 6:9). The king loved the idea and instructed Haman to do so . . . for Mordecai. As you can imagine, this made Haman's hatred for Mordecai and the people of Israel even greater.

Haman ultimately constructed a gallows to hang Mordecai, and he established a day on which all Jews were to be killed. To give you a perspective of Haman's arrogance, the gallows were seventy-five feet tall. It seems he intended to make a point out of the situation. However, Haman did not count on what happened next.

Once word of Haman's plot circulated, Mordecai sent word to Queen Esther, seeking her assistance to prevent this horror. Esther expressed concern, because she was not allowed to enter the king's presence without a request—disobeying this could mean her death. The only exception rested on the king extending his scepter. Here's where Mordecai sends word to Esther in what has become the most famous section of the text: "Do not imagine that you in the king's palace can escape any more than all the Jews. For if you remain silent at this time, relief and deliverance will arise for the Jews from another place and you and your father's house will perish. And who knows whether you have not attained royalty for such a time as this?" (Esther 4:13–14). Providential? Mordecai thought so.

After three days of fasting and prayer, Queen Esther decided to seek a word with the king, which he quickly granted. She invited the king and Haman to a banquet, where she revealed Haman's plot. The king left the room angry. Upon his return, he found Haman "falling on the couch" near Esther. The king was so enraged that he sentenced Haman to hang on the gallows built for Mordecai. Mordecai was then elevated to second-in-command. Near the end of the account, we're told his leadership is noted in the "Book of the Chronicles of the Kings of Media and Persia" (Esther 10:2).

Where I'm headed with all of this is in the last verse of the book: "For Mordecai the Jew was second only to King Ahasuerus, and great among the Jews and in favor with his many kinsmen" (Esther 10:3). Mordecai was elevated to an amazing position of leadership. As we consider a definition of leadership and how to determine a leader, the last statement of the book provides an answer, for Mordecai was **"one who sought the good of his people and one who spoke for the welfare of his whole nation"** (Esther 10:3; emphasis mine). Life and leadership are connected in this powerful thought.

Go back and read it again. When looking for a definition of leadership or how to determine if someone is a leader, reflect on the thought expressed about Mordecai. Each individual has the right and ability to define leadership how they desire, and I'm confident there are numerous definitions that resonate with you in different ways. For me, a good leader will always be *someone who seeks the good of his people and speaks up for their welfare.*[4]

Building Block 1
Vision: The Inspiration of Life and Leadership

The Lead-In: Harnessing the Power of the Sun
In the center of all rests the Sun.
For who would place this lamp of a very
beautiful temple in another or better place than this
from which it can illuminate everything at the same time?
Copernicus (1473–1543)

In the spring of 1992, my wife and I traveled with some friends to Colorado Springs, Colorado. We spent the day touring the Cave of the Winds. As in many tours through caves or caverns, the guide described the formation of stalactites and stalagmites. We eventually came to a point where we were gathered in a small area surrounded by some of the most beautiful formations I have ever seen. All of a sudden, the tour guide turned off all the lights. To say it was dark does not come close to describing the nature of that moment. If you close your eyes and wave your hand in front of your face, you can still see some sort of movement, like a shadow. However, when the lights went out in that cave, I could not have seen a shadow of my hand in front of my face with my eyes open. My first thought was of the ninth plague in Egypt, when God brought three days of darkness on all the land. The text describes the darkness as something that could be "felt" (Exodus 10:21). Let me say, I *felt* it in that cave. If the darkness wasn't eerie enough, the tour guide began to explain that if someone remained in that type of darkness for thirty days, that person would go blind. She went on to say that if someone remained in that type of darkness for ninety days, they would go insane. At this point, I began thinking about God's pronouncement of judgment on those who would be cast into outer darkness, where there will be weeping and gnashing of teeth (Matthew 25:30). Needless to say, I was ready to leave that dark place.

Once we all had reached a point where we felt as petrified as the rock floor beneath us, the tour guide turned on a light in the far corner of the room. Like iron to a magnet, everyone in the room turned toward that light. There was an immediate sigh of relief. We could see a way out of this massive hole in the ground, where at one point we had wondered if we would ever see the light of day. In that moment, I realized the value of the sun in connection to our ability to see, and I was never more glad to feel the sunshine on my face as we walked out of the cave. I began to realize how essential vision is to leadership. Without vision, leaders will never see where they must go. Before I get to vision, however, I want to explore the essential nature of the sun to life.

Several sources list both beneficial and detrimental facts about the sun, including its distance from the earth, the size of the sun in contrast to the earth, the core and amount of heat transmitted, the orbit of the earth around the sun, and the sun's orbit around the Milky Way galaxy. National Geographic writer Michael Greshko claims the sun "holds the solar system together; provides life-giving light, heat, and energy to Earth; and generates space weather."[1] Finding these types of facts about the sun is not difficult. However, I sought to discover *why* the sun is essential to life on earth. The amount of scientific data available is unlimited, but in my research I discovered a few key factors that contribute to this discussion.

First, the distance between the sun and the earth is *just right*. The earth makes its journey around the sun once every year (365 days). This orbital journey is referred to as the "Goldilocks Zone." If you've never read "Goldilocks and the Three Bears," the story tells of young Goldilocks, who enters the home of three bears while they're away. She discovers an extreme contrast between Papa Bear, Mama Bear, and Baby Bear's food, chairs, and beds: Papa's and Mama's always have some flaw, but Baby Bear's are "just right." In application to the distance between the sun and the earth, the distance is "just right" for life to exist. According to Fraser Cain, "This means that [the earth] is in the right spot (neither too close nor too far) to receive the sun's abundant energy, which includes the light and heat that is essential for chemical reactions."[2] Cain goes on to explain that "these chemical reactions occur as a result of the sun's ability to create energy because it is essentially a massive fusion reaction." The energy created is called *solar energy*, which scientists continually strive to harness as a resource to benefit life. My former Christian Evidences professor used to say, "If the earth were 1/10 of an inch closer or farther away from the sun, life could not exist on this planet."

This Goldilocks Zone means that the earth's location and orbit is "just right" to sustain life on Earth.

Second, the sun provides life-giving energy. The depths of energy from this source are amazing. Wolfgang Berger, a professor with the University of San Diego, suggests this energy must be right for life to exist:

> The energy provided by the Sun has to come in the right amount, shape and form to be useful to Life on Earth. Life cannot use X-rays or radio waves as an energy source. Visible light is just right, the plants use it to make plant matter by photosynthesis, we and many other organisms use it to see by. Likewise, the amount of energy delivered by the Sun to our planet is just right for the hydrologic cycle to work, with water and water vapor changing back and forth, and some minor amount of ice (2 percent of the total water) collecting near the poles. Thus, the climate is between cold and warm, dry and wet, just about right.[3]

In an effort to further this study, a group of NASA scientists contributed to a historical discussion about the sun and its life-giving properties. The leading statement claimed, "Nothing is more important to us on Earth than the Sun. Without the Sun's heat and light, the earth would be a lifeless ball of ice-coated rock. The Sun warms our seas, stirs our atmosphere, generates our weather patterns, and gives energy to the growing green plants that provide the food and oxygen for life on Earth."[4] I do not explore each of these areas, but one specifically represents an essential element to life. The sun's ability to provide energy to the plant world is significant for two reasons: (1) Plants supply food for animals and humans, which also supports the essential nature of food that I discuss later, and (2) the supply of oxygen contributes to another essential element, which I discuss in the second section of this book. Neither would exist without the power of the sun. This life-giving source is essential to life.

Third, the sun improves mood. Those who live in areas with limited sunlight have been shown to have greater levels of anxiety and depression. Our family worked in an area of Northwest British Columbia that received approximately one hundred and fifty inches of rain each year. Sunshine was at a premium, and the lack of it produced ill-effects among the residents. The results led to unusually higher drug abuse and alcoholism, which contributed to domestic violence, crime, and immorality. People need sunlight. According to research conducted by Drs. Randy and Lori Sansone, "Empirical literature indicates that an association between sunshine and serotonin is likely. Given that the relationship between sunshine and serotonin is probably a multimediated phenomenon, one contributory facet may be the role of sunshine on human skin. Human skin has an inherent serotonergic system that appears capable of generating serotonin."[5] Dr. Timothy Legg adds further support of this theory:

> Decreased sun exposure has been associated with a drop in your serotonin levels, which can lead to major depression with seasonal pattern. The light-induced effects of serotonin are triggered by sunlight that goes in through the eye. Sunlight cues special areas in the retina, which triggers the release of serotonin. So, you're more likely to experience this type of depression in the wintertime, when the days are shorter.[6]

These studies point to the essential need of the sun for not only the physical element of life but also for the emotional. Consider the incredible life-giving source of the sun, which we tend to take for granted.

Fourth, the sun benefits vision. I understand the ability to see is not essential for life to exist. However, the relationship between the sun and vision supports the benefit of the sun. The American Academy of Ophthalmology referenced several studies indicating that children who spent more time outside in sunlight were less likely to develop nearsightedness. David Turbert says, "Although spending too much time outdoors without protection from the sun's ultraviolet (UV) light can damage eyes and skin, new studies show that natural light may be essential for normal eye development in kids."[7] In 2017, Gretchen Reynolds pointed to research suggesting that the "lack of direct sunlight may reshape the human eye and impair vision."[8] These studies linked claims with a strong correlation between eyesight and exposure to the sun.

An interesting relationship exists between the sun and our eyes, because the transmission of light through our eyes stimulates the brain, contributing to sight, color, and depth perception. While it's true that UV rays from the sun damage the optical lens and can result in blindness, the value of the sun cannot be overstated. Dr. Phil Maffetone says, "The human eye contains photosensitive cells in its retina, with connections directly to the pituitary gland in the brain. Stimulation of these important cells comes from sunlight."[9] The sun provides much more value to life than the ability to see. The cell stimulation Maffetone references contributes to our physical and mental health, as I previously mentioned.

This background leads to a consideration of the essential need for vision in leadership. As the sun benefits our vision—our ability to see—leaders with vision contribute to the ability to see a better future through the eye of faith. This ability is essential to leaders and the direction of their leadership, as I discuss throughout this section.

The sun is essential to all of life. The solar energy produced by the sun is essential for the agricultural development of land to produce crops. These plants require sunlight to grow. Additionally, animals and humans benefit from the food and oxygen produced. In an article for National Geographic, Kimberly Dumke writes, "The sun radiates light and heat, or solar energy, which makes it possible for life to exist on Earth."[10] Articles, books, and resources abound with information related to the essential nature of the sun. Ultimately, we discover a significant connection between the life-giving power of the sun and the life-giving power of vision for leadership. The next chapter focuses on answering the question *Why vision?*

Chapter 1
Why Vision?

The only thing worse than being blind is having sight but no vision.
Helen Keller

Few accounts are more challenging to understand and so inspirational to read than the life of Helen Keller. A few months before she reached the age of two, Keller contracted an illness (now believed to have been scarlet fever or meningitis) that resulted in the loss of both her sight and hearing. The inability to see and hear would cause many of us to give up and possibly blame God for our suffering. However, through the guidance of Anne Sullivan, a teacher gifted in working with those with disabilities, Helen Keller learned to communicate.

History records the early stages of her life, during which she was wild and uncontrollable. The difficulties Keller faced are unimaginable. Not only was she unable to see or hear anything, she was also unable to communicate until the arrival of Anne Sullivan, which Keller referred to as her "soul's birthday." Sullivan worked to develop avenues for Keller to communicate. The breakthrough moment occurred when Sullivan was able to sign the letters for the word water into Keller's palm, while running water over her other hand. When Keller realized that the letters spelled into her palm that day represented the cool liquid, she was frantic to learn more.

Over time, her other senses became heightened, and she learned to identify people by the vibration of their steps. She eventually gained an appreciation for music from the vibrations she felt with her hands. With patience and training, Keller learned how to speak and read lips with her hands. She was proficient in braille and went on to complete high school, and she became the first blind and deaf person to earn a bachelor of arts degree from Radcliffe College of Harvard University.

Her inability to see and hear did not deter her vision of what she could become. This vision provided direction for political and educational advances throughout her adult life. She became well known for her literary skills and motivational speaking. She advocated for the disabled and less fortunate. When leaders possess a vision for the future and can effectively cast that vision for those who follow, it results in security, stability, and confidence to support the direction ahead.

Throughout the next few chapters we'll focus on several areas connected to vision:

- *Why do I need vision?*
- *What hinders me from discovering and fulfilling my vision?*
- *How can the Bible help me in this journey?*
- *What benefits will vision provide?*
- *What exercises will help me discover this essential component of life and leadership?*

I can tell you up front that this is my favorite part of the journey. Nothing is more exciting than witnessing individuals, teams, and congregations come together with a vision for their future. As you strategically place each piece in this puzzle, the picture will become clearer and, hopefully, will motivate you to follow through on a personal vision and a vision for your church, team, community, etc. I also want to remind you, that although vision comes more naturally for some, it is not the result of a twenty-minute exercise. The journey is time-consuming and arduous, but it will make a difference in everything you strive to achieve in life and leadership.

Shall we begin?

As we embark on this journey, it is important to know the difference between vision, mission, and strategic planning. There are similarities, as all three are interrelated. However, they represent totally different concepts. A clear understanding of all three will help simplify the overall direction, purpose, and plan for the work ahead.

Simply defined, *vision* is "something that you imagine: a picture that you see in your mind."[1] In a spiritual context, "Vision is a clear, challenging picture of the future of the church, as leaders believe that it can and must be."[2] Thus, vision is a picture in our minds—a state that does not yet exist but is desired as the promise of a better future. The invitation to envision is the opportunity to dream of an incredible future. Consider this thought from pastor and author Mark

Batterson: "You are one idea, one risk, one decision away from a totally different life. Of course, it'll probably be the toughest decision you ever make, the scariest risk you ever take. But if your dream doesn't scare you, it's too small." Your vision must connect with something so big it can only be reached with God: "He does things we can't do so we can't take credit for them. God honors big dreams because big dreams honor God."[3]

Mission is defined as "a specific task with which a person or a group is charged, a preestablished and often self-imposed objective or purpose."[4] Thus, by definition, a *mission statement* expresses a plan for how to carry out a mission. Mission statements abound for secular and religious organizations alike. In missiological circles, mission is directly connected to the *missio dei*, or the "mission of God." Biblically, we understand the mission of God in relation to the salvific work of God in redeeming all of humanity to himself through Jesus Christ. The mission before His people today involves fulfilling that purpose.

Strategic planning is a construction of the specifics of how we will accomplish mission and vision. As I discuss in future chapters, goals are critical to leadership and strategic planning. According to businessdictionary.com, strategic planning "translates vision into broadly defined goals or objectives and a sequence of steps to achieve them. In contrast to long-term planning (which begins with the current status and lays down a path to meet estimated future needs), strategic planning begins with the desired-end and works backward to the current status."[5]

Based on these three definitions, I have come to identify vision, mission, and strategic planning as the who, what, and how of life and leadership. The vision refers to who we want to become in the future, mission is what we plan to do in order to achieve it, and strategic planning describes the specifics of how we take each step along the way. Making this distinction between vision, mission, and strategic planning keeps me from confusing the overlapping tendencies associated with all three. Since many claim that clarifying the vision is the first step in strategic planning, I turn your attention to the focus of this chapter: *Why vision?*

Over the years, I've collected a number of quotations from leaders who have challenged my thinking about vision. P. K. Bernard said, "A man without a vision is a man without a future. A man without a future will always return to his past." Consider the significance of this thought. Without a vision of the future, what do we have but the past? If we cannot move beyond the past, we'll never grow into something greater in the future. Kris Vallotton states this as follows: "When your memories are greater than your dreams, you are already dying."[6]

If your experiences are anything like mine, you've heard people wax nostalgic about their personal lives or their churches. It often sounds something like this: "Back when I was your age, I had to walk to school—uphill both ways!" or "You know, back in the 50s and 60s, we were the fastest-growing religious organization in the country."

I would never diminish the significant growth that occurred fifty, sixty, or seventy years ago. However, it sometimes seems as if we've forgotten that we no longer live in that time or culture. While I'm not—and never will be—in favor of changing the message of the gospel, I do believe we need to rethink our evangelistic methods, because cultures change. We see this demonstrated in the Bible. In Acts 2, when Peter preached on the day of Pentecost, more than 50 percent of his message was book, chapter, and verse from the Old Testament. He was speaking to a group of Jewish people who needed evidence that what they were witnessing was a fulfillment of prophecy, and that the man they had just crucified was Lord and Christ. However, in Acts 17, we see that a few years later, Paul spoke in Athens to a gathering of Greeks—here, he did not use a single quotation from the Old Testament. It was a totally different group of people, a different culture, and a different setting. In his attempt to reach these people, the message about the resurrection did not change—but how he presented the message did.

It's important to be aware of the culture in which you live and discover a vision of the future that will guide you to grow in your efforts to reach generations yet to come. For this reason, the question to ask is *Why do I need a vision?* The following are but a few reasons to consider.

To Properly Handle Change

Let's face it, most people fear change. Too many people believe that once any type of change is introduced, we're headed down a slippery slope. But change is part of life. From the day we are born, each breath brings change.

I find myself amused when I think about how averse to change religious people can be—despite the fact that *change* is preached every Sunday. It's just presented under a different name: *repentance*. Outside of religious circles, we typically don't use this word. I've never told my wife, "I was planning to go to the store, but I repented and stayed home." If you tell people they need to repent, they often can receive that, but when we instruct someone to change, it automatically has a negative connotation.

If we know that change is part of life, doesn't it make sense to guide that change with vision? When we have a vision for the future, it guides the decisions we make to achieve that vision. Without a vision, we're like the Israelites wandering in the wilderness—we wander around lost, doing everything we can to prevent change.

To Challenge the Status Quo

Status quo is "an emotional bias; a preference for the current state of affairs. The current baseline (or status quo) is taken as a reference point, and any change from that baseline is perceived as a loss."[7] The fear we encounter is really fear of loss. People are afraid that when change is introduced, they will lose something valuable—and this "something valuable" is often connected to traditions.

Perhaps you're familiar with the following definition of *insanity*: "To continue to do the same things in the same way yet expect different results." This is the direction so many have taken in their lives and in the church. We continue to do the same things in the same way, but we want different results. If the results aren't there, we fire the preacher and find another one—someone willing to hold on to the status quo and still help us grow numerically. If growth doesn't happen, something worse occurs and the church ends up closing their doors.

A vision changes everything—it moves us out of our comfort

zones and away from the status quo to achieve something different from what we've always done. You cannot remain in a holding pattern when you have a vision.

To Inspire Others toward a "Just Cause"

Leaders are known for their abilities to inspire others. In this case, it's about inspiring people toward a just cause. In his book *The Infinite Game*, Simon Sinek develops the concept of a "just cause" and the value it provides to the success of life and leadership. He defines a *just cause* as "a *specific* vision of a future state that does not yet exist; a future state so appealing that people are willing to make sacrifices in order to help advance toward that vision."[8]

Consider the impact of a vision that inspires people to the degree that they're willing to sacrifice whatever is needed to achieve the vision. I discuss this further in chapter 4, in which I explore a variety of exercises that will help you to achieve your vision. For now, remember that when you build your vision around a just cause, you will see amazing movement.

To Create a Better Future

I've been blessed far beyond what I deserve. I have a wife whom no words are adequate to describe—she is as beautiful on the inside as she is on the outside. We were blessed with three strong, gifted, and spiritually-minded children who all married above themselves. We were then given the most precious gift of ten grandchildren. Maybe I'll write my next book on lessons I've learned from them.

If that were not enough—and it is—I have a job working with some of the most wonderful people on the earth, doing work I love more than anything I've ever done in my life. As I make my way down my list of blessings, I'm thankful for my physical health and the material comforts I have that most do not enjoy. I know how much God has given me—and I'm thankful beyond words.

Whether or not you feel the same way about your life, don't we all want a better future? I want a better future for my children and grandchildren, and I want a better future for the church. But without a vision, the possibilities of a better future become limited, if not impossible. After all, when we cannot see something ahead that motivates us to work to make each area of life better, then we become comfortable with mediocrity. I can't imagine this is what you want for yourself, your family, or the church.

To Become All You Can and Should Be for God

Ultimately, this is what vision is all about: we desire to become all we can and should be for God. Everything we do is for the purpose of glorifying Him, because without God, nothing has value or meaning.

Solomon was clear in pointing out the vanity of life without God. Ecclesiastes is filled with accounts of Solomon's attempts to find value and meaning in life apart from God—he failed every time. Work, pleasure, achievement, and anything else we add to the list are worthless if God is not the focus—which summarizes our need for a vision. The task before you is not easy. You'll discover that a number of barriers can enter the picture and hinder you from discovering and fulfilling your vision.

Barriers to Discovering Your Vision

How you view obstacles when they arise can make a difference in your ability to move toward your vision or give up completely. There's a subjective nature to the list of barriers I've compiled below, and I'm sure you could add more.

After a few years of asking, I've learned that most everything falls under one of these seven general categories. The question I've asked numerous people is this: *What hinders people from discovering and fulfilling their vision?* Even though the responses vary, the overwhelming majority described the following obstacles.

1) Fear

The number one obstacle is fear. Some fear failure because they desire to succeed, so they work long hours and sacrifice time in other areas of life. However, many are equally afraid of success. They possess a fear of the unknown, fear of responsibility, fear of change, fear of what someone else might say, fear of death, fear of life. Fear can debilitate you, causing you to do things you would not normally do and hindering you from doing things you know you should do. When fear exists, faith is extinguished. The rumblings of fear among good-hearted brethren can hinder a vision faster than just about anything else.

2) Indecision

I remember my high school basketball coach telling me over and over, "Hesitation will cost you the game." Indecision and hesitation work the same way: When you're indecisive, you rob yourself of the opportunity to take intentional action. You float in a sea of doubt, tossed by the waves of others' decisions. You hesitate and fail to realize the cost. You can't make up your mind, so you choose to stay where you are—which is usually in the middle of nowhere.

I realize there are times when it's important to gather information and weigh out the pros and cons before making a decision, but to wait three, four, five, or six months will kill momentum. I've witnessed people leave congregations because leaders couldn't make a decision. Indecision will hinder the discovery and fulfillment of your vision.

3) Traditionalism

We all have traditions, whether in our families (Thanksgiving, birthdays, anniversaries, etc.) or in our churches (specific times of meeting, form and function of worship, casual or formal attire, translation, classes and curriculum structure, etc.). Traditions in and of themselves are neither good nor bad—they're just traditions.

Many of our traditions were established decades and sometimes centuries before us, and the practices we observe with friends and family have a special place in our hearts. However, we often fail to explore why these practices were established in the first place, how they became part of our traditional practices, and why we continue to engage them in the midst of cultural changes. These traditions quickly become part of the status quo, and we sometimes go so far as to find scriptural reasons to keep them, even when they weren't established by God. For example, why do we meet on Wednesday night at 7:00 for midweek Bible study? For most congregations, somewhere between 40 to 60 percent of the members participate in this midweek study. If you were to discover that 75 to 80 percent of people would attend if you changed the night from Wednesday to Thursday and held the study at 6:00 p.m. instead of 7:00 p.m., would you make the change? If the answer is no, this is where traditions become dangerous. If you're unwilling to challenge a tradition and discover why it was established, how it became a tradition, and why it's still observed, you become deadlocked into continuing a practice without a clear understanding— this ultimately becomes a barrier to vision and subsequent growth. When this happens, people experience frustration, lose focus, and often leave.

4) Risk Averse

This barrier is one that presents a challenge for me. I'm not one to take a lot of risks—and I'm not alone. Apparently, many around the world share this same aversion. Although I'm risk averse in some areas of my life, I'm not against taking risks. The challenge occurs when we become so risk averse that we're unwilling to advance toward a vision. When this happens, our lives and congregations become stagnant.

Batterson reminds us, "Until the pain of staying the same becomes more acute than the pain of change, nothing happens. We simply maintain the status quo. And we convince ourselves that playing it safe is safe. But the greatest risk is taking no risks at all."[9] In other words, extreme risk aversion can cause you to stall in one of the greatest needs of life and leadership. Imagine what can be accomplished if only you're willing to take the chance.

5) Apathy and Indifference

If I live to see my next birthday, I will reach fifty-nine years of age. Although my time on the earth has been limited, I've witnessed a number of incredible events in our history. However, in the midst of this journey we call life, I've become troubled by what seems to be humanity's biggest downfall. This doesn't apply to every single person—yet, generally speaking, the mindset of our world is one of apathy and indifference.

We tend to be unaffected by events—both good and bad—that occur outside of our own space. If it doesn't directly affect us, then we give little or no thought to it. Additionally, we fail to recognize the importance of changing the future. Our improvidence keeps us focused on right now—this moment, this place. This mindset not only infects the individual but filters into all areas of life, including spiritual focus. The result is that we're hindered from discovering and achieving our vision. People require leaders who move them beyond the apathetic and indifferent mindset of our world toward something greater than we can imagine—something only God can do through us to his glory.

6) Uncertainty

As I write these words, we're in the middle of the stay-at-home order issued by the government in response to the COVID-19 pandemic. Right now, on a global level, every person is plagued with uncertainty. We're uncertain about how this virus began, how someone becomes infected, the lethality of it, the length of the stay-at-home order, what will be the economic devastation, and the list goes on. This has been described as an "unprecedented time"—it is also an uncertain time.

Uncertainty can also become a barrier to vision. The future is uncertain: What will it look like? Who will be here? What resources will be available? Will we achieve success or failure? And so on. If you can be honest with yourself, there's uncertainty about whether you'll take your next breath. Instead of allowing uncertainty to hinder your vision, use your vision to challenge the uncertainty of the future. Use your vision to change the future in ways that your great-grandchildren will look back on and express gratitude for how you saw something better for them.

7) Building-centric versus People-centric

The contrast of these two ideas may not seem to challenge our thinking about vision, but history indicates otherwise. The emotional attachment to a building evidences itself constantly. When Christians become more concerned about the building than the people, we demonstrate a shortsightedness that leads down a destructive path. The church has never been about the building, yet our history points to the desire for bigger, better, and newer facilities in the right locations, because we're convinced this is what produces growth. We have somehow deceived ourselves into thinking that the right preacher in the right building will bring exponential growth. Do not misunderstand me: I know that a good preacher in a good location will bring a measure of growth. However, until the church turns its attention toward people and meets them where they live, growth will always be elusive. A building-centric mindset that avoids being people-centric becomes a barrier to vision.

I'm certain there are other barriers I could add to the list. Spend some time thinking through what yours are. When you know what hinders the discovery and fulfillment of your vision, you can begin the process of eliminating those areas. This will allow you to focus on what you need in order to move forward and achieve a vision that honors and glorifies God. Therefore, in the next chapter, I turn your attention toward some biblical thoughts about vision that will give a little spiritual credibility to this discussion.

Chapter 2
Biblical Thoughts about Vision

Where there is no vision, the people are unrestrained.
Proverbs 29:18

I've often heard Proverbs 29:18 quoted as biblical support for vision. The King James Version reads, "Where there is no vision, the people perish." While most English translations use the term *vision*, the idea represented by this word is not how we understand and communicate vision today. The Hebrew word that is used, *hazon*, is associated with a divine revelation from God, which often came in the form of a vision as opposed to a dream.[1] Where do we find information about a vision? God was clear on the mission, but where does God provide us with the vision? Where do we discover it? How do we discover a vision by which we use his mission to achieve that vision?

The Bible provides everything we need to know—if we know where to find it. While studying Scripture, I've come to use five words I believe represent the biblical components that contribute to understanding vision when we have the right F.O.C.U.S.: *Faith, Opportunity, Confidence, Unity*, and *Sacrifice*. In the following sections, I look at each component.

Faith

In Genesis through Revelation, we learn about faith. Abraham is known as the father of faith, and from Genesis 12 through 22, we see the development of his faith. While the concept of faith appears throughout the Bible, when we want to learn the definition of faith, we usually turn to Hebrews 11. In the first verse, the author of Hebrews defines faith as "the assurance of things hoped for, the conviction of things not seen" (Hebrews 11:1).

I could write pages and pages on these two aspects of faith alone. However, for the purpose of this discussion about vision, I focus on the last part of the verse: "things not seen." When we dive into a discussion about faith, we dive into a discussion about the unseen. If we can see it, then it's not faith but fact. Read through Hebrews 11—

highlight the phrases that relate to what is seen or visible and underline what is unseen. See the examples I've provided below:

1) Hebrews 11:3: "By faith we understand that the worlds were prepared by the word of God, so that what is **seen** was not made out of things which are **visible**."

    Even though we were not present when God created the universe, by faith we understand that God spoke and brought into existence something from nothing. The first word is *blepo*, which refers to what a person sees with their eyes (fact).[2] The second word is *phaino*, which means "to shine or to produce light."[3] Therefore, by faith we understand that God created what we see, but not with things seen or produced in light.

2) Hebrews 11:5: "By faith Enoch was taken up so that he would not **see** death; and he was not found because God took him up; for he obtained the witness that before his being taken up he was pleasing to God."

    Enoch is one of two men who did not experience death. The other was Elijah (2 Kings 2:11–12). With both men, we see a beautiful relationship of faith in God.

3) Hebrews 11:7: "By faith Noah, being warned *by God* about things not yet **seen** [unseen], in reverence prepared an ark for the salvation of his household, by which he condemned the world, and became an heir of the righteousness which is according to faith."

    If Noah never saw it rain or experienced a flood, the point is the same. By faith he built an ark, even though he had never before seen anything like what he experienced 120 years after it was completed.

4) Hebrews 11:10: "For [Abraham] was **looking** for the

city which has foundations, whose architect and builder is God."

Abraham's faith sits at the heart of this chapter in Hebrews and the history of God's people. He obeyed God by leaving his country to go to a place that God would show him. He did not know where he was going—he went because he trusted God to deliver on His promise. Ultimately, Abraham knew that God's promise extended far beyond a piece of land where his children and grandchildren would live.

5) Hebrews 11:13: "All these died in faith, without receiving the promises, but having **seen** them and having welcomed them from a distance, and having confessed that they were strangers and exiles on the earth."

By faith, Abel, Enoch, Noah, Abraham, and Sarah were able to see God's promises—even though they did not receive them in their lifetimes.

6) Hebrews 11:23: "By faith Moses, when he was born, was hidden for three months by his parents, because they **saw** he was a beautiful child; and they were not afraid of the king's edict."

Because the biblical account of Moses takes place in a chapter about faith and the concept of what is seen and unseen, I'm convinced that Amram and Jochebed did not simply gaze at their son and think he was a mighty handsome lad. By faith, they saw something in their son beyond what the physical eye could see, which moved them to act in defiance of Pharaoh. Ultimately, this act provided deliverance for Israel.

7) Hebrews 11:27: "By faith [Moses] left Egypt, not fearing the wrath of the king; for he endured, as **seeing** Him who is unseen."

The faith of Moses's parents must have influenced him, because in Moses, we see faith demonstrated through endurance. He could see the one who is unseen. This path of faith provides an example for each of us. Your vision needs to keep you focused on the one who is unseen. When it is, you'll make bigger plans than you can achieve on your own. Moses led a multitude of people from more than four hundred years of enslaved oppression to the mountain of God, delivering the law that would guide the nation for approximately one and a half millennia.

The word used throughout the majority of the text is *horao*, which implies perceiving, noticing, or catching sight of something.[4] The writer wanted us to understand that faith is more than what we see with our physical eyes—it's what, or *who*, we see through the eye of faith. When you lay a foundation of faith for your vision, you are then ready to take the next step: opportunity.

Opportunity

At its core, opportunity is simply circumstances presenting possibility, either to be gained or lost. How many opportunities have we missed because we did not see the possibilities? In reality, if we are unable to see possibilities, we will never take advantage of opportunities.

No one demonstrated this better than Jesus did. Throughout the Gospel of John, Jesus engaged people to help them see Him differently—to see Him for who He really was. One of the best examples of this is Jesus's encounter with the Samaritan woman, through which we learn several lessons about vision and opportunity. I've read John 4 many times over the years. Recently, I noticed something I never had before. The text says, "And He had to pass through Samaria" (John 4:4). As I read this verse, I thought, *No, He didn't*. Jesus did not have to pass through Samaria. In fact, Jews usually did everything in their power to avoid passing through Samaria. But Jesus knew the possibility and, as a result, seized the opportunity. His vision was not for one group of people or one nationality. Through Him, all the nations of the earth would be blessed.

Jesus and the apostles had been traveling for several hours, and they were approaching the hottest part of the day: the sixth hour, around noon. The Bible tells us that Jesus, "being wearied from His journey, was sitting thus by the well" (John 4:6). The apostles left to purchase food, and while they were away, a Samaritan woman came to draw water. From this point, the account in John 4 focuses on the discussion, discovery, and direction that influenced the way the Samaritans and the apostles saw Jesus.

Although we never learn the Samaritan woman's name, the discussion between this woman and Jesus highlights a powerful truth about who Jesus is. The discussion began with a simple request for a drink of water. We may not fully understand the racial tension between Jews and Samaritans, but the concept is evident from her reaction. She responded, "How is it that You, being a Jew, ask me for a drink since I am a Samaritan woman?" (John 4:9). John's parenthetical statement reveals the reason for her reaction: "For Jews have no dealings with Samaritans."

I will not dig into the specifics of the entire chapter. However, it is critical to note how this woman saw Jesus as an ordinary Jew making an unusual request. As the discussion continued, Jesus explained, "If you knew the gift of God, and who it is who says to you, 'Give Me a drink,' you would have asked Him, and He would have given you living water" (John 4:10). We can see the change in the way the woman saw Jesus as she inquired if He is greater than their father, Jacob, who gave them the well. Jesus pointed out that the water He offers will quench one's thirst in such a way that those who accept it will never thirst again. Emphatically, she said, "Sir, give me this water." Her motives lacked proper priority, because she didn't fully understand what Jesus was expressing.

Jesus asked her to get her husband; to which she responded, "I have no husband." I would love to know what she thought when Jesus said, "You have correctly said, 'I have no husband'; for you have had five husbands, and the one whom you now have is not your husband" (John 4:17–18). Talk about a mic-drop moment. Can you imagine the shock on her face? We see an immediate change in the way she saw Jesus: "Sir, I perceive that You are a prophet."

In this moment, we move from a simple discussion to discovery. Once the Samaritan woman discovered that Jesus was more than an ordinary Jew, she inquired about the contrast in the locations of worship of her people (in the mountain) and the Jews (in Jerusalem). A major discovery unfolded. She acknowledged that the Messiah was coming, and that "When that One comes, He will declare all things to us," (John 4:25). In one of the few times that Jesus specifically identified Himself as the Christ, He told her, "I who speak to you am *He*."

The woman left her water jug and went to her people to convince them to come meet this man who told her *all things* about herself. I emphasize *all things*, because she identified the Messiah to be the one to declare all things to them. Regardless of what she might have known that to mean, she connected it to Jesus revealing her life. Ultimately, this led the people of Samaria to confess their faith in Jesus as the "Savior of the world" (John 4:42).

Volumes have been written about the discussion and discovery in these forty-two verses. The direction of the chapter, however, has an essential underlying message. In the middle of this section, Jesus used the opportunity to teach the apostles a lesson they needed to know in preparation for the kingdom work ahead.

The apostles were astonished that not only was Jesus speaking to a woman, He was speaking to a Samaritan woman. It would have been taboo for a Jewish man to speak to her. However, Jesus was no ordinary Jewish man. Just as the Samaritan woman's view of Jesus changed, the apostles' perception also needed to change. Jesus directed the apostles to consider the need for all people—including the Samaritans—to know Him as the Messiah. He used an analogy of the harvest to help them see that people were ready and that the need was great for all nations. Their understanding of Jesus would shape the way in which they approached others.

I pray we all learn the value of this powerful lesson: *How we see Jesus changes how we see others*. Only when we see Jesus as the one true Savior of the world will we have the vision needed to see people differently. It is not about race, gender, age, educational level, or anything else. Only through the eyes of Jesus can we clearly see the opportunities before us. But remember: if we cannot see the possibilities, we will never see the opportunities. The vision of Jesus guided His encounters with others and helped them see Him differently. Our task must be to help the world see the church differently. As long as the world sees the church as any other religious group, then one religion will always be as good as another. The concept of "organized religion" does not appeal to many. As we will discuss, discover, and direct, our vision of Jesus and the church changes everything. In addition to faith and opportunity, vision must be based on confidence.

Confidence

One of my favorite Bible characters is Caleb. (If you're not familiar with Caleb, take a look at Numbers 13–14 and Joshua 14.) Caleb's story begins with Moses selecting twelve men—one from each of the sons of Israel. These men were appointed to spy out the land where Moses was leading this massive group of people. Moses told the twelve men to scout out the land and report back. Were there giants in the land? What were their cities like? Were they fortified? Then, oddly enough, he asked them to bring back some fruit.

I remind myself these people had been slaves for more than four hundred years. They had been holding onto a promise that described a land flowing with milk and honey. Think about how they might have imagined this place. Consider the stories told from one generation to the next. The reality of the situation can be hard for us to grasp. We live with such abundance, and we have the ability to visit places with the most beautiful scenery in all of God's created Earth. With such comforts available to us in this life, it's no wonder we struggle to imagine what heaven is like. Yes, we quote from Revelation, and intellectually we know heaven is a place far better than where we live now, but we do everything in our power to live as long as possible on this earth. Perhaps if we were to live through a period of slavery such as Israel experienced, we would be a bit more anxious to know what this place looks like and get there as quickly as possible. With this in mind, I am confident they wanted to know if this promised land produced anything like what they had imagined. Bring back some fruit.

The spies did, indeed, return with fruit. In fact, the first thing they did was show the fruit of the land and say, "It certainly does flow with milk and honey, and this is its fruit" (Numbers 13:27). Remember, this fruit was a "single cluster of grapes; and they carried it on a pole between two *men*, with some of the pomegranates and the figs" (Numbers 13:23). After showing off the abundant fruit of the land, ten of the spies dropped a bombshell: giants were in the land, and they lived in fortified cities—there was no way Israel could achieve victory. To provide Israel with perspective, they said, "We became like grasshoppers in our own sight, and so we were in their sight" (Numbers 13:33). Talk about a vision problem. They lost confidence in themselves, but more importantly, they lost confidence in God to deliver on His promise.

For years, I quoted this verse as, "We were as grasshoppers in their sight, and so we were in our own." I reasoned that the way other people saw us influenced the way we saw ourselves. While this may be true, this is not what the text says. Read it again. The problem was the way they saw themselves, which directly affected the way the people in the land saw them. I wonder sometimes if we think about the significance of this. How often do we limit our vision of who we can become because of the way we see ourselves? And—as stated in the text—how are others influenced by that limited vision? Perhaps we need to start dreaming bigger dreams.

Back to Caleb and confidence. Caleb was one of two spies who did not see the situation in the same way as the ten spies who delivered the bad report. Caleb and Joshua stood up and pointed to God: "If the Lord is pleased with us, then He will bring us into this land." They wanted everyone to know that the "protection [of the people in the land] has been removed from them, and the Lord is with us; do not fear them" (Numbers 14:8–9). But the people listened to the ten spies, not to Joshua and Caleb. Their choice would cost them forty years in the wilderness—one year for every day the spies were in the land. Not only did the ten spies die, but everyone over the age of twenty also suffered the same fate over the next forty years. The consequences for their lack of confidence in God were severe.

We learn from the end of Deuteronomy and the first half of Joshua that Moses died before entering the promised land. Joshua was selected to lead the next generation of Israel into the land, but the journey would not be easy. Many battles were fought before the Israelites were able to possess the land God promised to them—another great lesson about faith. Believing that God will deliver us doesn't mean we're exempt from fighting the battles before us. Forty-five years after the Israelites came to possess most of the promised land, Caleb approached Joshua and said, "Behold, I am eighty-five years old today. I am still as strong today as I was in the day Moses sent me; as my strength was then, so my strength is now, for war and going out and coming in. Now then, give me this hill country . . . I will drive them out as the Lord has spoken" (Joshua 14:11–12).

I'm currently fifty-nine years old. Mentally, I really don't feel any different than I did forty-five years ago. But when I try to accomplish physical activities like I did in my late teens and early twenties, I'm quickly reminded of how much time has passed. Mental fortitude can override physical capabilities, but we don't know whether or not this was Caleb's situation. At eighty-five, did he feel the same way he had at forty? Or did he actually have the same physical strength he had at forty? Regardless, Caleb was confident in his physical capabilities. He had a confidence built on faith, and he was confident God would help him achieve his vision of taking down the giants who lived in that hill country. This type of confidence is exactly what you need when you discover your vision for the future. You must never fear the giants before you, because God is with you. When God is on your side, you can achieve whatever you focus your heart, mind, and ability to achieve. *This* is confidence. And when we have confidence, those who follow gain confidence in their leaders.

But faith, opportunity, and confidence are only the first three pieces of our biblical vision puzzle. Vision promotes and directly impacts the nature of unity.

Unity

The most-cited biblical leadership text is probably Nehemiah. Throughout this book, we learn about the power of prayer, evaluation, decision-making, determination, and *unity*—or working together.

Before we focus on the key biblical thought of unity, I want to consider the vision of Nehemiah and how his ability to communicate the vision united people to achieve it.

Nehemiah demonstrated great concern for the nation when he learned about the dire situation of Jerusalem. The walls of the city were broken down, the gates had been burned, and there was no protection for the people in Jerusalem. Nehemiah wept, mourned, fasted, and prayed. He continued praying throughout the entire journey and influenced others to do the same. When King Artaxerxes saw Nehemiah, he asked why Nehemiah's face was sad. After Nehemiah explained what had happened to Jerusalem, the king asked what Nehemiah would request of him. Note that the first response of Nehemiah was again to pray.

The king granted the request of Nehemiah to return to Jerusalem and rebuild the walls, and he provided letters to the governors of the provinces beyond the river to secure necessary materials. Nehemiah arrived and evaluated the situation, inspected the walls, and gathered the people together. I initially believed his vision was to rebuild the wall, but after studying the text, I learned his vision was greater. We might say the *mission* was rebuilding the wall— but the *vision* was much bigger. Once the people were assembled, Nehemiah said, "You see the bad situation we are in, that Jerusalem is desolate and its gates burned by fire. Come, let us rebuild the wall of Jerusalem so that we will no longer be a reproach. I told them how the hand of my God had been favorable to me and also about the king's words which he had spoken to me" (Nehemiah 2:17–18a).

Four thoughts stand out here. First, Nehemiah *defined the problem*: "You see the bad situation we are in, that Jerusalem is desolate and its gates burned by fire." Even though it was evident to everyone, Nehemiah wanted publicly to define the magnitude of the task. If you plan to unite people, you can't neglect, deny, ignore, or assume that people are aware that the problem exists. In fact, even if people do know the problem, it's still important to define it clearly.

Second, Nehemiah *offered a solution*: "Come, let us rebuild the wall of Jerusalem." The only way to address the problem was to communicate how they could overcome it. I'm sure the people who lived in Jerusalem were aware of the need to rebuild the wall, but it took a leader to stand up and challenge them to get the job done. In leadership terms, the same need exists today. People often are aware of the work that needs to be done, but it takes a leader willing to challenge them and work alongside them to achieve the task at hand.

Third, Nehemiah *presents the reason*: "So that we will no longer be a reproach." Remember, at one time Israel was the great nation of God—a light to the world. People feared Israel because of their great and holy God. However, because the Israelites had sinned against God, He allowed them to be taken captive by the Babylonian nation, and the city was destroyed. The result was a nation in reproach. Nehemiah's vision was not to rebuild the wall—his vision was to make Israel the great nation of God it had been once before. Leaders today must know their purpose and communicate it well. When people understand the purpose behind the vision, people will follow and sacrifice to achieve it. You'll read more on this in later chapters.

Fourth, Nehemiah *inspired them with hope*: "I told them how the hand of my God had been favorable to me and also about the king's words which he had spoken to me." Imagine the scene: Nehemiah gave an update on the situation—of which everyone is aware. Perhaps they were thinking, *Sure, we know we need to do this . . . but how can we get this job done when we have no protection from our enemies?* Nehemiah wanted them to know that God was with him and would continue to also be with them. The evidence was based on the support of King Artexerxes. When leaders know that God is with them and they communicate the evidence of God's work in their lives, people develop a confidence in their leaders to take them to any destination. Confidence is the power of a leader's vision.

Notice the mindset of the people once Nehemiah expressed these four thoughts. Their immediate response was, "Let us arise and build." As we continue to read through the text, we find people united. Even when the people were challenged by enemies, the text tells us, "We built the wall and the whole wall was joined together to half its *height*, for **"the people had a mind to work"** (Nehemiah 4:6; emphasis mine). Later, we read about the intensity of their situation and the unity required to rebuild the wall:

> When our enemies heard that it was known to us, and that God had frustrated their plan, then **all of us returned to the wall, each one to his work.** From that

day on, half of my servants carried on the work while half of them held the spears, the shields, the bows and the breastplates; and the captains *were* behind the whole house of Judah. Those who were rebuilding the wall and **those who carried burdens took their load with one hand doing the work and the other holding a weapon**. . . The work is great and extensive, and we are separated on the wall far from one another. At whatever place you hear the sound of the trumpet, **rally to us there.** Our God will fight for us. **So we carried on the work** with half of them holding spears from dawn until the stars appeared. (Nehemiah 4:15–17, 19b–21; emphasis mine)

The people were united around a vision that inspired them to make whatever sacrifice was necessary to achieve it. They had a leader who was willing to stand alongside them to work and fight for the just cause. Keith Kasarjian, a good friend of mine, once shared a powerful message to show the nature of unity as described in the text of Nehemiah 3. Keith's main points are below. Note how the nation not only rebuilt the wall, but also achieved the vision:

1)   *Leaders set the example* (3:1): One of the primary functions of leadership is to set an example. We learn here that "Eliashib the high priest arose with his brothers the priests and built the Sheep Gate; they consecrated it and hung its doors." Priests were recognized as leaders in Israel and— along with Nehemiah—provided an example.

2)   *Families did the work* (3:3, 12): The work was not limited to a few people or even to leaders within the household—families worked together. "The sons of Hassenaah built the Fish Gate . . . Shallum the son of Hallohesh, the official of half the district of Jerusalem, made repairs, he and his daughters."

3)   *Some people will not work* (3:5): When the vision

is clear, the majority of people come together to achieve the work. But there will always be those who are unwilling to get involved, which we can see when we read, "Their nobles did not support the work of their masters."

4) *Some do more work* (3:5, 27). The beauty of unity is witnessed when people recognize that others aren't helping to carry the load, so they step up and contribute more. This was the case with Israel:

"Moreover, next to him the Tekoites made repairs . . . After them the Tekoites repaired another section in front of the great projecting tower and as far as the wall of Ophel."

5) *God uses the gifts of everyone* (3:8): God has always given people a variety of talents, but even so, people aren't always gifted in the work that needs to be accomplished. However, a great vision unites them in the work, as we learn: "Next to him Uzziel the son of Harhaiah of the goldsmiths made repairs. And next to him Hananiah, one of the perfumers, made repairs, and they restored Jerusalem as far as the Broad Wall."

6) *Some work with passion* (3:20): I love people who have a deep passion for the work at hand. We see this zeal in one man identified in the text: "After him Baruch the son of Zabbai zealously repaired another section." The church needs more who work with zeal, because people with passion and less ability will always outwork those with ability but no passion.

These examples demonstrate the significance of unity. However, we have one last piece that is required for vision: sacrifice.

Sacrifice

As we have witnessed throughout history—even recent history—no vision is ever achieved without sacrifice. When we look at the first settlers of the United States, we see lives scattered across the battlefields of this land. Men and women made great sacrifices in their efforts to secure freedom. Whether the Revolutionary War, War of 1812, Mexican-American War, Civil War, Spanish-American War, World War I and II, Korean War, Vietnam War, Gulf War, or the war in Afghanistan, these events demanded great sacrifice on the part of those who fought for the vision of freedom we enjoy and celebrate in this country. This is the same story in many other countries.

Throughout the Bible, we also see many with this same sacrificial nature, including our God. The New Testament reveals the incredible sacrifice of God coming in the flesh. I'm incapable of capturing the truly immense power and significance of this event. Paul said it this way: "Have this attitude in yourselves which was also in Christ Jesus, who, although He existed in the form of God, did not regard equality with God a thing to be grasped, but emptied Himself, taking the form of a bond-servant, *and* being made in the likeness of men" (Philippians 2:5–7). This thought highlights the sacrifice Jesus made when He left his existence as God to become a man. But not only did He become a man, He became a bond-servant. He did not have to come, but He did, and He willingly emptied Himself to take on this form. He thus provides us with an example of how to live a sacrificial life of service.

I must also acknowledge Jesus's sacrifice at the cross. If you've ever seen Mel Gibson's movie *The Passion of the Christ*, you can better understand the horrific nature of what Jesus endured. The humane efforts of our current culture prevent us from a complete comprehension of such treatment. We can only imagine the brutality of the event—the visuals provided in this movie may be as close to what actually happened as anything I can communicate. The sacrifice Jesus willingly made in laying down His life for us on that cross demands our attention and devotion.

Other stories in the Bible demonstrate the willing sacrifices of those who were dedicated to the purposes of God. Hebrews 11 lists many who suffered beyond our understanding. According to the writer, the "world was not worthy" of them (Hebrews 11:38). The apostles also provide examples of those who sacrificed. On one occasion, Peter said, "Behold, we have left everything and followed You" (Mark 10:28). Near the end of His time with the apostles, Jesus expressed that He was going away and that where He was going they could not come (John 13:33). Peter wanted to know where Jesus was going and why he could not follow right away. Peter then made this bold proclamation: "I will lay down my life for You" (John 13:37). As the words fell from his lips, Peter did not know how this would play out in his life . . . but he would soon learn.

One of my favorite studies in Scripture comes from the questions throughout. From the beginning of Genesis where God asks Adam and Eve, "Where are you?" (Genesis 3:9) to the questions asked by and of Jesus, each time I come across a question, I try to consider how I would answer. Give it a try! Read through the gospel accounts of Jesus and highlight the questions. Then ask yourself how you would answer. As an example, Jesus asked the apostles, "Who do people say that the Son of Man is?" (Matthew 16:13). (We can read their response in Matthew 16:14.) How would you answer the question today? Who do people in your generation say Jesus is?

Jesus then directed the question on a more personal level: "Who do you say that I am?" (Matthew 16:15). Again, how would you answer today? There are hundreds more of these questions to consider.

Let's look back at John 13: Once Peter made his declaration of sacrificial commitment, Jesus asked, "Will you lay down your life for Me?" (John 13:38). Whenever I speak on this passage, I never ask for a show of hands in response to this question. I think that—like Peter— in the moment, we would all raise our hands and say we were willing to die for Jesus. However, there's another question I think must be asked: *Am I willing to live for Him?* The reason for this question may seem obvious, but if not, consider this thought: If you're not willing to live for Him, you would never be willing to die for Him.

When we think about sacrifice, there's much on the line in Christianity. As you discover your vision, you need to know that while it takes faith, opportunity, confidence, and unity, you must also be willing to make whatever sacrifice is necessary to achieve it, because no vision is ever achieved without sacrifice.

When the Bible becomes a foundational piece to your vision,

victory is inevitable—even though you may not see this victory in your lifetime. Hopefully, your vision is so great that it will guide future generations to greater achievement for the Lord. May it be a light that guides all who follow behind you. Abraham understood this concept, as we learn in Genesis 13.

Abraham brings us full circle in this biblical discussion. In Genesis 12:3, we read God's promise to Abraham: "And in you all the families of the earth will be blessed." God made good on this promise, but Abraham did not see it during his lifetime. In fact, Paul reminds us that the promise was fulfilled in Christ (Galatians 3:15–16). Can you imagine receiving a promise that would not be fulfilled for thousands of years? After God made this promise, a conflict arose between Abraham's herdsmen and the herdsmen of Lot (Abraham's nephew). Both men had become so prosperous the land could not adequately sustain them: "They were not able to remain together" (Genesis 13:6). In order to resolve the conflict, Abraham suggested that Lot look out over the land and select where he wanted to go; Abraham would go the other direction.

I love what happens next: As soon as Lot selected the well-watered land near Sodom and Gomorrah and left, God showed up to talk with Abraham. God told him, "Now lift up your eyes and look from the place where you are, northward and southward and eastward and westward; for all the land which you see, I will give it to you and to your descendants forever" (Genesis 13:14–15).

Four thoughts stand out in this instruction. First, God told Abraham to lift up his eyes and *look*. We find Jesus instructing the apostles to do the same in John 4:35. In that context, Jesus referenced the work ahead of the apostles in sharing the promise of a greater inheritance through the gospel. God wanted Abraham to lift up his eyes and look on the inheritance he was promised. I can't help but wonder how much we miss today because we're unwilling to lift up our eyes and look. Maybe we have our heads in the sand, are wearing blinders, or are just covering our eyes because we don't want to see the needs of the people around us. Regardless, the fulfillment of our vision rests on lifting up our eyes and looking.

Second, God wanted Abraham to look from the place "where you are." I've had the privilege of traveling with Christians from the United States to work alongside other Christians in numerous countries. I know the benefits that come to those who travel outside of their own contexts and cultures to share the gospel, and I know the benefit to recipients. What challenges me is how much time, talent, energy, and money is spent to travel across the planet to share Jesus with people we do not know when we will not walk across the street to share the message with people we do know. I remember my dad saying, "Sometimes, you just need to drop your bucket in your own back yard." I now know what he meant. For Abraham, the promise started by looking from where he stood. We need to do the same. Look from the place where you live.

Third, God wanted him to look northward, southward, eastward, and westward. Have you ever considered why God had Abraham look in every direction? I have a theory. For Abraham to not look in a specific direction was to miss what God had promised. The early church began in Jerusalem but then expanded to "Judea and Samaria, and even to the remotest part of the earth" (Acts 1:8). Imagine what can happen when we begin where we are and then branch out in every direction. The promise God makes is one that ushers in kingdom growth of seismic proportions, but we must look northward, southward, eastward, and westward.

Fourth, God promised to give the land to Abraham and his descendants forever. The faith of Abraham was connected to this promise. The writer of Hebrews pointed out that he did not receive God's promises, but saw them and welcomed them from a distance. He was seeking a city whose architect and builder is God (Hebrews 11:10–13). Immediately following the promise of land, God reiterated and expanded on the promise He made in Genesis 12: "I will make your descendants as the dust of the earth, so that if anyone can number the dust of the earth, then your descendants can also be numbered" (Genesis 13:16). This promise was completed in Christ.

The Bible introduces us to a foundation for *vision* built on *faith* followed by *opportunity*, the power of *confidence*, working together, united in one purpose, and a willingness to *sacrifice*. We find that God gives a victory that can only be measured in eternity. Moving forward, we learn that with vision come several benefits. These I discuss in the next chapter.

Chapter 3
Benefits of Vision

*If you are working on something exciting that you really care about,
you don't have to be pushed. The vision pulls you.*
Steve Jobs

The biblical concepts from chapter 2 provide a guiding light for a vision essential to leading God's people. Over the past ten years, I've learned and shared how vision benefits leaders and congregations alike. However, listing the benefits of vision is one thing—it's quite another to understand how these benefits become a driving force that connects to the reasons for vision. Below, I share six benefits with you.

Vision Informs Decision-Making

Hands down, the number one benefit of having a vision is this. With a vision in place, every decision can be made with clarity and greater ease. Leaders are often approached by people who lobby to begin various programs. Because leaders want to encourage involvement—and because churches are constantly looking for ways to grow—these programs are added to long lists of current programs. In time, leaders may discover they have more programs than they have people to adequately operate them. Leaders must learn how to evaluate the effectiveness of their programs and how to cut loose programs that are no longer effective.

A vision makes all the difference. Once a vision is in place, you can evaluate the current programs and make a decision about whether to keep or cut them. You make these decisions based on how a program contributes to your vision. If a program contributes to the vision, then you keep it—if it doesn't help you achieve the vision, you cut it. The process can be time-consuming and painstaking, but it's much easier than the previous approach of accepting any and all programs. When considering whether or not to add a new program, ask yourself if the program will help you achieve the vision. If the answer is no, then don't add that program. If a program will help you achieve the vision, then add it. The same process can be used for other aspects of church operations. Once others recognize that the decision-making process is connected to the vision, they learn to self-evaluate programs before presenting and lobbying for them. The entire strategic-planning process proceeds more smoothly when a vision exists.

Vision Promotes Greater Unity

Unity is a primary goal for any congregation or ministry. As long as I've been a Christian, every congregation I've encountered has made some kind of effort to achieve unity either internally or externally. Within a congregation, the desire is to have 100 percent of the congregation united in word and work. In relationship to the greater family of Christ, the focus must be the same. My intent here is not to dig into the biblical foundations of unity or evaluate the boundaries by which we determine unity. We read that Jesus prayed for unity (John 17), the early church practiced unity (Acts 2), and the apostles pleaded for unity (1 Corinthians 1). It only makes sense that our current focus be the same.

As I've worked with and learned from congregations across the country, I've seen what happens when there's no vision. (I'm sure you know where I'm going with this.) Without a vision, people have no direction and, as a result, lack purpose. Leaders are frustrated at the lack of participation in potlucks and programs. Active members tend to see less active or inactive members as lacking spiritual commitment. What happens? A divisive spirit develops. No harmony. No love. No peace. No unity.

I've also witnessed the opposite. When leaders cast a vision before the congregation, everything changes. Everyone knows what they're striving to achieve and who they want to become. Do you want to promote unity? The choice is yours.

Vision Kick-Starts Momentum

In 2009, John Maxwell introduced us to the "law of the big mo,"[1] which refers to the critical role momentum plays in leadership. When momentum exists, people change in at least three ways:

1) *Momentum energizes people.* A level of excitement occurs, and it becomes infectious through out the larger group. When momentum takes hold, step back and watch how powerful the movement becomes.

2) *Momentum encourages involvement.* Once people are excited about the vision, they want to be involved. A shift in thinking occurs when people believe they're contributing to something great.

3) *Momentum eliminates negative thinking.* This is huge. I realize there will always be people who express negativity. For some reason, these individuals feel it is their role to shoot down anyone who has enthusiasm and stop anything that people are excited about. However, momentum tends to prevent the naysayers from getting traction. If nothing else, the people involved will stop the negativity.

I know we could include more than three benefits of momentum, but the point would be the same. Vision kick-starts momentum, and momentum changes people. Therefore, vision just makes sense.

Vision Motivates the Actions of Life and Leadership

What gets you up in the morning? Your first response may be the alarm clock or your children . . . or maybe you can't wake up without coffee. I'm not opposed to people drinking coffee. I know people who love it. I know people who apparently are unable to function without it. But I've never even tasted a cup of coffee. As a child, I ate one piece of coffee-flavored candy, and that's all it took to convince me that flavor was not something I ever wanted to experience again. Regardless of where you stand on the subject of coffee, what motivates you?

Motivation is different for everyone. But I want to believe that life is more than just getting up, going to work, coming home, eating supper, visiting with the spouse, playing with the kids a bit, watching a little television, then going to bed. Are you living for the weekends so you can sleep in, lie around most of the day, take a trip to the lake, or participate in some other recreational activity? This seems to fall short of a purposeful life. If you have nothing to look forward to but retirement and death, then it's time for change.

Vision gives you a reason to get up in the morning. It's impossible to function without it. When you clearly see who you want to become in the future—whether five, ten, fifteen, or twenty years down the road—you become motivated. Suddenly, life and leadership have purpose. There's a reason for your actions. Discovering how to motivate the unmotivated is time well spent, and one step in that direction is vision. I cannot count the number of studies, blog posts, books, and videos I've encountered that discuss the factors that motivate people, characteristics of motivated people, how to achieve and maintain motivation, and more. As far as I could tell, none of these mention vision. This is a gap that must be addressed. Vision motivates our actions. Believe it. Live it.

Vision Creates Meaning

What creates meaning in your life? Family? Friends? Career? Recreation? Experience? This list could be much longer—we all have specific areas in our lives that create meaning. Meaning relates to how individuals look at specific areas of their lives. First, meaning gives us a sense of purpose. Second, meaning provides value by which we make decisions.

I can't tell you what does or will create meaning in your life—I only know what does so in my own. However, a glance back at the thoughts concerning motivation and momentum lend to this discussion, because purpose and meaning are two sides of the same coin. A vision based on a just cause creates meaning. I introduced the concept of a just cause earlier, and I dig more deeply into this area in the next chapter.

Vision Challenges Us to Do Something Great

If you're like me, you've heard hundreds or thousands of sermons, read more books than you care to mention, watched tons of videos, and listened to motivational speeches for your job on an annual basis. It's entirely likely that most of these provided valuable information yet little to no application. We live in a culture that stresses the value of information; however, guidance on how to apply the information is missing. Why? Because application is more difficult. This is why vision is so essential to leadership. A confidently communicated vision moves people to action. Remember, a vision reflects a potential future that is appealing, exciting, motivating, and challenging. It does this because vision is supposed to represent something greater than what exists now. A vision that does not challenge us to do something great needs to be discarded and replaced—because it is not really a vision.

These six benefits highlight the value of vision for life and leadership, but there's more. I've examined a number of key thoughts about the importance of vision, but how do you actually discover your vision? What steps will help you on this journey? The next section lays out a plan, with exercises that will guide you or your organization in the direction of discovering your vision.

Chapter 4
Exercises for Discovering Vision

The vision must be followed by the venture.
It is not enough to stare up the steps—we must step up the stairs.
Vance Havner

Bill, Kevin, and Leon are three men who serve as shepherds for a local congregation in the Midwest region of the United States. When I was first introduced to these men, I learned about an event the church hosted each year to encourage and equip shepherds in their work. After a short visit about the dynamics and demographics of the church, I emphasized the need for their leadership team to start with discovering a vision for the congregation. I advised them that this first step was essential to anything else they felt was needed, and we arranged a time for me to conduct a vision workshop.

The leadership team gathered to explore the possibilities a vision would provide for the congregation. While these men were hopeful, they possessed a sense of skepticism. I emphasized the benefits of a vision—described in the previous chapter—but then the real work began as the participants engaged in exercises designed to walk them step-by-step through the process of discovering a vision. I ensure every group I meet with that by the end of the day they will have all the "nuts and bolts" to discover their vision. I made that same promise to Bill, Kevin, and Leon.

When we reached the end of the day, ideas were flowing. But the process was not over—a final vision statement does not usually evolve out of one meeting. The group needed time to work on specific ideas and words to frame exactly what their vision needed to say. Once the process was completed, the atmosphere changed and these men were transformed. They were no longer skeptical of the purpose, process, and power of a vision. The result is transforming the entire congregation. Communication improved between the leadership and the congregation. Members are now excited about the direction ahead. Leadership became more involved in member's lives. Unity increased and a laser-like focus on their vision helped inform every decision made.

I've been blessed to work with numerous individuals and churches. The opportunity to discuss vision and witness the transformation of leaders and churches as they move toward their vision thrills me. Bill, as a representative of the leadership, has expressed numerous times that having a vision changed everything. On one occasion, he wrote, "We looked internally as individuals and as shepherds and have grown because of this process. Our shepherds are closer and have a better understanding and respect for one another because of the time we have to focus on God and our vision."

Bill, Kevin, and Leon's story is one of several that demonstrate the incredible transformation that occurs when a vision exists. Before I outline specific exercises for discovering your vision, I share Andy Stanley's six steps for creating a powerful vision statement, from his book Making Vision Stick.[1] The material provided in this quick read is significant for anyone considering their vision.

1) *A vision statement must be memorable.* Long vision statements are forgettable and cumbersome. A vision statement must be short, memorable, and visible. Some congregations display their vision statement on a banner above the pulpit, include it in the bulletin, or use it as part of their email signature.

2) *A vision statement should be simple.* The goal is to have everyone excited and talking about the vision. If a vision statement is complex, then it's unlikely that anyone will share it with others.

3) *Leaders must cast a vision convincingly.* If you want buy-in from others, you must communicate the vision with confidence and conviction, which will engender the same in others.

4) *A vision statement must be repeated regularly.* I'm convinced that people need to see and/or hear the vision weekly, monthly, and yearly. Observing the Lord's Supper on a weekly basis serves as an example of the vision Christ set before us in this feast.

We should learn from his example and repeat our vision regularly.

5) *Take time to celebrate.* Stanley says, "What gets celebrated gets repeated." Every step along the way to achieving your vision is a step that must be celebrated. Celebrating even the little things excites people to do even more.

6) *A vision must be embraced personally.* Before the vision is cast before others, you must embrace the vision on a personal level. When this happens, others will follow.

These six steps provide a backdrop for discovering your vision. Through research and personal experience, I developed the following exercises to help leaders sort through each necessary piece of the puzzle to discover their own vision.

Step #1—Discover the Why

Simon Sinek's book *Start with Why*[2] provides invaluable material on successful leadership. From his concepts, I share a few thoughts to help you discover the *why* behind your vision. There are two major components: past and present.

The why begins with going backward, looking to the past. Sir Winston Churchill said, "The farther back you can look, the farther forward you are likely to see." What exactly should you look for when looking backward? Look for the purpose for which your organization or church was established. How long has the organization been in existence? Why did the founding members believe it was a good idea? Many of the congregations I've worked with over the years have a document that describes the historical details of the congregation. These documents reveal information about the purpose, cause, and beliefs of these founding members. Here's where you can begin to discover a part of the *why*.

As you consider the foundational information from these documents, you need to remain true to the purpose, cause, and beliefs upon which your church or organization was started. You may discover that the purpose goes back even farther than fifty, seventy-five, or one hundred years ago. Your *why* may go back to a biblical foundation established in the early days of the church in the first century. A study of the Gospels and Acts is a great place to start to learn about God's *why*. Remember, your *why* must remain true to your purpose, cause, and beliefs.

Your *why* must be authentic. Our current culture longs—in fact, *screams*—for authenticity. People can spot fake Christianity a mile away. Anytime you build relationships around an ulterior motive, the relationship will not last long. Either you grow tired of waiting for someone to respond in connection to your motives and you move on, or they discover that the only reason for the friendship was to get them to respond and they move on. You must build relationships that are genuine—where you actually love the individual regardless of what they have done in the past, what happens in their life currently, or how they respond. They need to know that you're a friend no matter what. At some point in their life, they'll experience an event that alters their thinking, and they'll need to know you're there. Who knows—in that moment you may have an opportunity to share your faith. Be patient.

Your *why* must be balanced. Our culture suffers from extremism, and balance can seem to be elusive. We experience daily the labeling of left or right, liberal or conservative, Democrat or Republican, black or white, functional or dysfunctional, passive or aggressive, introvert or extrovert, and the list goes on. I'm constantly amazed at how many people politically, socially, and religiously have been influenced by the mindset that if a person is on one side, then they automatically must be against—even to the point of hate—those on the other side. My friends, it doesn't need to be this way. We need balance based on good judgment, not the direction of social, political, or religious winds that blow and change on a daily basis.

To discover your *why*, ask as many people within your organization as possible, "Why would anyone choose to come here?" Why would anyone want to visit and be part of this group? In early 2013, I began an educational journey that has helped and challenged me in many ways. In one of my early intensive courses, a professor asked two questions that shook me to the core. He asked, "If your church were to disappear tomorrow, would anyone in the community know?" He paused and followed up with the second question: "Would anyone care?" Take a few moments to really consider these two questions and answer them honestly. Then think about the question I began with: *Why would anyone choose to come here?*

I've witnessed participants of my workshops wrestle with this question. I usually allow small groups to spend ten to fifteen minutes working on answers, and then I ask them to share their responses. After listing all of the responses, I encourage everyone to focus on the threads that surface. These threads usually come together to provide a strong foundation for developing their *why.*

About ten years ago, a good friend agreed to teach one class period on leadership; and his corporate background was invaluable for these students. During the class, he introduced us to material from Simon Sinek and the concept of the "golden circle." (If you're unfamiliar with this concept, check out Sinek's TED talk.[3]) The golden circle represents three questions connected to organizational success and longevity. Sinek discusses how many corporations know *what* they do and even *how* they do it. The problem is they don't always understand *why* they do it. This same mindset exists in churches today. Have you ever considered why you meet on Sunday night to worship again? If your congregation is like most I know, about 40 to 50 percent of the people return from the Sunday morning attendance. Please do not misunderstand me here—I'm never in favor of meeting less. In fact, I would prefer we meet more, but my point is the same. We have not done a good job communicating why we meet twice on Sunday. If younger generations are asking why, and the only response we have is, "because that's the way we have always done it," we should not be surprised that our attendance suffers. I've heard people respond to the question in several ways. One, it was started during the early agricultural days of this country to give people a chance who worked in the mornings to attend. Two, it started during the Industrial Revolution when shift workers could not get off for the morning service. Three, a well known restoration preacher felt everyone needed to hear him preach, so he started a second service in order for people to listen to him more. Four, leaders years ago decided that it was best for people to have more teaching, so they started an evening service and we are to submit to the leaders. Maybe you've heard these or others, but here are my questions: "Do the same reasons for which an evening service was started still exist in our current culture?" "Do we really know why we continue a practice that has no biblical command, example, or inference?" Again, I'm not saying it cannot or should not be done, but do we know *why*? Why is essential, if we plan to impact any generation with our message and practices.

In *Start with Why*, Sinek discusses how the brain works when making decisions. The brain is made up of two major parts. The outer part—the *neocortex*—is where we process facts and figures. We would understand this as the analytical part of the brain. The inner—or *limbic*—part of the brain is where we experience emotions. The majority of people make decisions from this emotional part of their brains. The *what* is developed from the neocortex. The *how* and *why* are developed from the limbic part of the brain—emotions move us and others to commit.

While walking students through an exercise to answer the question, "Why would someone choose to come here?" our guest teacher tied everything together and shared two words that provided a *why* so profound we were all moved: *eternity matters*. Let these two words sink in for just a moment. From a Christian worldview, the reason we live a Christian life, share the gospel of Jesus with others, worship our God, encourage each other day after day, and do *anything* is based on these two words.

This may or may not be the *why* for your organization. I share it as an illustration of how the process works. In order to discover your *why*, I suggest you gather leaders and members to discuss the following. Start by listing out as many reasons as possible why someone would choose to visit the congregation where you attend. List all of the responses on a white board for everyone to see. Once the responses are listed, begin sorting through each and look for threads. Circle, or write separately, the words with common themes. These words provide a foundation for discovering your own why. Discuss how these themes relate and ask the group: "What is the overarching narrative that connects all of them together?" Once that's determined, you're well on your way to the next step.

Step #2—Identify Your "Just Cause"

As with the previous step, Simon Sinek provides guidance for this one. This time the information comes from his book *The Infinite Game*.[4] In this book Sinek uses the term "just cause," which he defines as "a *specific* vision of a future state that does not yet exist; a future state so appealing that people are willing to make sacrifices in order to help advance toward that vision." Your *why* comes from your past; it's your origin story—it's who you are. A just cause is your *why* projected into the future.

How does one identify or understand this idea of a just cause? By way of example, Sinek refers to the Declaration of Independence: "We hold these truths to be self-evident, that all men are created equal, that they are endowed by their Creator with certain unalienable Rights, that among these are Life, Liberty and the pursuit of Happiness." Based on this example, Sinek lists five components of a just cause:

1) *A just cause stands for something*—it is affirmative and positive in nature. Sinek writes, "While being against something may be effective in rallying people, it doesn't inspire and it won't last. A Just Cause is what you stand for, rather than what you stand against." As we think about the church today, what is that affirmative and positive cause for which we stand?

2) *A just cause is inclusive*—it is open to all to contribute. According to Sinek, "It inspires all to make their worth while contributions and feel valued for it." How do you make it possible for everyone to contribute, and how do you make them feel valued for their contribution?

3) *A just cause is service-oriented*—it benefits others. I don't know how this could have a more biblical intent. From the example and teaching of Christ to the instruction given by the apostles, the Christian life is one of service and love—putting the needs of others above our own. How does your just cause serve and benefit others?

69

4) *A just cause is resilient*—it is enduring. As Christians, our just cause must endure beyond our generation and the next and the next and so on. Sinek says, "It must endure political, technological, and cultural change." As the title of Sinek's book suggests, our pursuit of a just cause must be infinite.

5) *A just cause is idealistic*—it's big, bold, and unachievable. As you look to determine your just cause, you must push yourself to think bigger and bolder. When a just cause is idealistic, people are drawn to it. They want to share in the effort and they are willing to make sacrifices toward it.

Working on a just cause takes time. I suggest getting everyone involved in the discussion. Ask each person to list three ideas related to the story connecting their church to the past, what they want the congregation to achieve, and who they want to become. Spend the necessary time to look over and discuss specific threads to help unite these ideas into a core theme. Consider how they relate to the five areas identified above by Sinek. Make adjustments. Rework or reword the thoughts expressed. Understanding everyone's perspective of these five areas will benefit the development of a just cause upon which your vision can be constructed.

Step #3—Ask Evaluating Questions

Before digging into details of this section, a short exercise will help. Take a few minutes and write down three responses to the following questions. The first is *How do you see yourself?* The question is intended to explore how you see yourself as a person, but more importantly, how you see the congregation. Give specific details to the description. The second is *How do you see God?* This question is a little more challenging. Consider how you would describe God and list your responses. Share your responses in a group discussion to see how others responded. Once completed, continue the discussion based on the ideas that follow.

Correctly discovering your vision requires you to ask two evaluating questions. The first is *Do I see myself correctly?* Ten years ago, I watched a video clip of Henri Nouwen[5] as he discussed most of what I share with you now. I have modified the material to fit the direction of this book, but Nouwen gets the credit for the meat of this piece.

Between the time we are born and the time we die, we live to answer one question: *Who am I?* From the perspective of the world, we usually answer this question in one of three ways. One: *I am what I do.* The reason we strive for success or do good for others is because it makes us feel good about who we are. Two (in some ways, this one is more significant than the other two): *I am what others say about me.* Often, the reason we strive for success and do good for others is because we want others to speak well of us. When people speak well of us, we fit in, we belong, and we feel accepted—this makes us feel good about who we are and how we answer the question. Three: *I am what I have.* I have a good family, good health, material possessions, and so on. Again, when these exist we feel good about who we are.

There's a fatal flaw when we answer the question I've described by these three answers: life becomes a giant zigzag in which we make every effort to stay above the line. What happens when we experience failure and we don't do good for others? What happens when people speak ill of us? What happens when we don't have a good family, our health is poor, or we lack the material possessions of this world? We tend to retreat into dark places. We get discouraged at best and depressed at worst. We fail to realize the lie. It *is* a lie, because the answers to this question does not determine who we are.

Take a moment and open your Bible to Matthew 4. Read through the temptations experienced by Jesus. After you read the first eleven verses, go back and look at each temptation separately and consider how they align with the discussion above. Satan told Jesus, "If you are the Son of God, command that these stones become bread" (4:4). In essence, Satan was saying, "Do something." Next, he took Jesus up to the pinnacle of the temple and said, "If you are the Son of God, throw Yourself down; for it is written, 'He will command His angels concerning you'; and 'On their hands they will bear You up, So that you will not strike Your foot against a stone'" (4:6). Have you ever considered why Satan took Jesus to the temple? The temple is where people were gathered. What would people have said about Jesus? Think about what people will say about you. How does this affect how you see yourself? Lastly, Satan showed Jesus all the kingdoms of the world and their glory and says, "All these things I will give You, if You will fall down and worship me" (4:9). Essentially, Satan said, "Look at all you will have, Jesus."

Each time, Jesus responded by saying, "It is written" and then quoting from a specific place in the book of Deuteronomy. But I think Jesus was basically telling Satan, "It's a lie—that's not who I am." Look at the last verse of Matthew 3: upon the baptism of Jesus, a voice out of heaven said, "This is My beloved Son, in whom I am well pleased" (3:17). Jesus knew He was the beloved of God, and He held on to that truth throughout his life. Regardless of what He did, what others said about Him, or what He had, He knew that He was the beloved child of God. Sadly, so few people today realize this truth—even Christians. We get sucked into the culture around us, and we think the way to answer the question is how the world would have us answer it. Throughout the New Testament, Christians are identified as God's "beloved." It's time to start recognizing who you are. When you do, you can then focus on how to answer the next question.

Do We See Our God Correctly?

The second question is *Do I see my God correctly?* The discussion is incomplete if we only answer the first question. Do we know who our God is, really? Perhaps you've seen the movie *Aladdin*. The song "Never Had a Friend Like Me" that the Genie sings could easily represent the way some people view their relationship with God. They want to rub a magic lamp and have God pop out to get them out of trouble or give them what they want. Let me burst your bubble if you think this way—this is not who our God is.

Take some time to read through Genesis—look at all the ways God reveals His nature to us through the names He uses. In Genesis 1:1, we read, "In the beginning God created the heavens and earth." The name translated "God" in this verse is *elohim*, which references God's power and strength—the kind of power and strength that could speak and bring into existence something out of nothing. From the root of this name, we also learn that He is the one who is to be feared: if He can bring life into existence, he has the ability to take it out of existence as well.

In Genesis 2:4 we read, "This is the account of the heavens and the earth when they were created, in the day that the LORD God made earth and heaven." The name translated "LORD" is *yhwh*, which is often translated as *Jehovah*. We find in *yhwh* the personal name of God. In a beautiful description of the sixth day of creation, when God created Adam and Eve, we're introduced to this personal name of God. How fitting that since Adam and Eve were made in the image of God (1:27), He reveals His personal name! This indicates the intimacy God desires with the pinnacle of His creation, which He made in His own image.

Later, in Genesis 16:13, Hagar called "the name of the LORD who spoke to her, 'You are a God who sees'; for she said, 'Have I even remained alive here after seeing Him?'" The phrase "you are a God who sees" comes from the name *elroi*. Hagar recognized that the Lord saw her affliction and helped her. Every time I think about this name for God, I find comfort in knowing that God sees. He sees my struggles. He sees my weaknesses. He sees my afflictions. He sees it all. This is our God.

In Genesis 17, we're given another name for God—one He ascribes to Himself. Let me share a little background: In Genesis 12, God made a promise to Abram that through his seed all the families of the earth would be blessed (12:3). Throughout the text, from chapter 12 to chapter 17, we see this promise reiterated on several occasions. The problem is that Abram's wife, Sarai, was barren. She couldn't have children, which we read in Genesis 11:30, prior to God making this major promise. As time goes along, God tells Abram, "Your reward shall be very great" (15:1), but Abram reminds God that he is without child.

In chapter 16, we find Abram and Sarai implementing a way to help God make good on his promise. This is where Hagar comes into the picture. One of the cultural practices of the day was for a woman who could not have children to give her servant, or handmaid, to her husband as a wife. The purpose was for the servant to bear children on the wife's behalf. This is what Abram and Sarai did, and Hagar became pregnant with Ishmael. In Genesis 17, God renamed Abram and Sarai as Abraham and Sarah, and He reminded Abraham that God had promised him a son—Isaac—through Sarah. Think about this for a moment. By this time, Abraham was one hundred years old and Sarah was ninety. The Bible emphasizes that she was past the age of bearing children. How is it remotely possible that such a thing could happen? I'm certain they'd never heard of any other woman becoming pregnant at this age. As we begin Genesis 17, God reveals Himself as "God Almighty": *el-shaddai*. I like to think of this as God's way of reminding Abraham what my grandson often reminds me: "I got this, Papa." God wanted Abraham to realize there was nothing impossible for Him to accomplish.

There are only three men to whom God ever revealed Himself as *el-shaddai*: Abraham, Isaac, and Jacob. Each time, this revelation was related to the promise God made to Abraham about his seed through whom all the families and nations of the earth would be blessed. We need to know that if God had the power to bring life to the deadness of Sarah's womb, He had the power to bring about the birth of His son through a virgin named Mary, and He had the power to raise that son from the dead after He was crucified. *This* is our God!

You'll find other names for God throughout Genesis that powerfully reveal more and more about our God. And you could study the New Testament and learn even more. For example, read Ephesians 3:20 and reflect on the thought expressed by Paul: "Now to Him who is able to do far more abundantly beyond all we ask or think, according to the power that works within us." How big can you think? I'm sure you can think pretty big—because I can think pretty big. Isn't it amazing to realize that our God dwells in a realm beyond the biggest thing we can think? Perhaps the problem is we think too small. We fail to ask. Somehow, we believe God won't do something because we've convinced ourselves it can't be done.

During my first year in Colorado, I was driving on a side road when I saw a neon sign in front of a church building. The sign asked, "What would you do if you knew you could not fail?" What *would* we do? I ask, because we cannot fail. If our God is who He claims to be and is with us, there's no physical or spiritual force on this earth that can stop us. Be convinced of that truth, and remind yourself of it over and over as you discover your vision.

74

Step #4—Know What Success Looks Like

I begin here with the words of Mark Batterson: "Mismanaged success is the leading cause of failure. Well-managed failure is the leading cause of success."[6] Defining success might be one of the most subjective tasks I know. How do we define success? If we cannot define success, then how will we know what success looks like? I approached several people to share their definition of success. Perhaps the following list will illustrate the dilemma we face.

Moving even the smallest portion of what is currently impossible into the realm of possibility.

—Tony Raburn, President and CEO of
Omada [7]

Success is the realization and acceptance that whether you are leading an organization, leading in your congregation, leading within your family or simply trying to encourage and inspire others through the construct of your life, your sincere, informed and thoughtful best efforts...are enough.

—Dean Murphy
Past President Monarch Landscape Companies

Success is...knowing who you are and loving it.

—Doug McNary
Faithful Servant of God
President of Western Union North America (retired)

To have the will and fortitude to keep trying in this life and to know my children for an eternity!

—Jack Hoagland
Developer, Manager of Cool Water Land and Cattle Investments

Success is about context. If I measured it with material objects or the balance in my checking account, I think later in life I would reflect back on the lost opportunities to live a meaningful life along the way. I would argue that success has many definitions, but for me it's simple. Define it by what brings you happiness, not other's perception of what happiness is.

—Michael Castenada
Captain, Combat decorated Marine Corps Veteran

To leave a legacy of faithful children and grandchildren. Always strive to "Make Heaven Crowded".

—Carla Hoagland
Realtor, Managing Broker

It's very rare that I feel I have achieved success at any point. Maybe they are only milestones I've attained. Success is a destination and I'm still on that journey reaching for that immaculate finish line. So I say, do this! Do this and let them come up and tap you on the shoulder and say, "Hey you scored the winning run! You've tapped your mission goals. You've crossed that finish line." You want them to come tell you, "You can go home now." That'll be when I find my success. Until then, the journey continues. I seek success in the constant journey of self-evaluation for the best me.

—Eugene Thompson
Owner and President of Ionic Dezign

Success is the ability to inspire others to be better in their home, church, community, and on the job by talking about my mistakes, ways I have been inspired, people who have inspired me, doors that were opened by God, and how He has worked in my life. Success involves having someone who can inspire you in some way to be better in life.

—Dave Miller
Police Department Operations Sergeant
SWAT team Commander

I believe you see my point. Let's back up for a minute and look at a technical definition. Merriam-Webster's Dictionary defines success as a "favorable or desirable outcome, also: the attainment of wealth, favor, or eminence."[7] Based on this definition, it's still difficult to determine what we mean by success and the specific areas of application. What does success look like in your home? What does success look like in your community? What does success look like in your job? What does success look like in your church?

Go back and reread the definitions above. You'll find a few commonalities—the most significant of which is that most of these definitions are *others-focused*. Most spoke of success in terms of amazing change and adding value to the lives of others. Note some of the key words: *inspire, loving, moving, legacy, happiness, family, journey, will, quality, possibility*, and **context**. While these terms and others can help clarify the idea of success to some degree, you still need to consider what success looks like in your specific context. As stated, context is critical to defining success. What does success look like in your context? Andy Stanley claims, "In leadership, *success* is *succession*.[8]

Too often we find ourselves determining the outcome of success in terms of numbers. I've spoken with numerous leaders from countries around the globe. Sadly, the majority of these leaders state that the problem of defining success is a continued focus on numbers. How many people were brought to the Lord? If the number is high, the work is seen as successful. Churches from across the United States will send money to support the places they see as successful in this regard. Many ministries struggle to survive with limited funds because churches do not see the work as fruitful.

I understand that each congregation has a difficult challenge when determining where they use their budgeted funds for any work. I simply encourage you to step back and consider how you define success. Strictly from a church perspective, consider this important question: *Have we been successful?*

Through the work of the church, if a man is a better husband to his wife and a woman is a better wife to her husband, has our work been successful? If parents grow in parenting their children, has our work been successful? If employees shine in their jobs as greater examples of Christ to their coworkers, has our work been successful?

If an employer treats employees better because of faith, has our work been successful? If each individual becomes a more active part in the community as an influence for Christ, has our work been successful?

I know we would all answer yes! So when you consider how to discover your vision, first take enough time to define success. This definition may change your vision.

You can do this exercise alone or, preferably, in a group. Write out your own definition of success. The best approach is to define success for the church. Ask each person in the group to share their definition. Then, list out the commonalities within those definitions and discuss how the definition of success will help with your vision. In *Chase the Lion*, Batterson states, "In God's book success is spelled *stewardship*. It's making the most of the time, talent, and treasure God has given you. It's doing the best you can with what you have where you are."9 Success is far more than the number of people who sit in the pews and the size of your budget. The bottom line is that success is about changing people's lives, eternally. When this factors into your vision, people will commit their lives to it.

Step #5—Be Concise and Avoid Vagueness

In a book I read to prepare for writing my doctoral dissertation, there's the following phrase: "Vagueness breeds vagueness."10 Vision must be concise. When it's vague, people cannot see where they're going—everything appears foggy. Anytime you have to define words for people, there's a better than average chance your vision is vague or possibly abstract. Consider a few ways to determine if your vision is concise and avoid the vague plague.

1)   Does your vision statement use subjective terms? For example, "We want to be a great organization." *Great* is subjective and vague. How one person defines great will differ from the way another person defines it.

2)   Does your vision statement use figurative or symbolic language? For example, "We want to be a beacon of light for souls searching for the shore." While

you probably understand the idea I've presented here, the figurative use of terms such as *beacon, light,* and *shore* have the potential to leave people confused.

3)   Does your vision statement use uncommon or unfamiliar language? For example, "We want to be an egregious organization." You might think this isn't good because *egregious* has to do with being extraordinary in a bad way. However, an ancient use of the word involves something distinguished or eminent—but will people know that? Or will you have to define it every time?

4)   Does your vision statement use complex sentence structure? For example, "We want to be a place where Jesus, working through us, can help the suffering, the lonely, and the broken to find love, acceptance, help, hope, forgiveness, and encouragement." All the ideas represented in this statement are good, but the structure is so complex it can leave people wondering what it means.

In and of themselves, these vision statements aren't bad. They may need a little tweaking, but the ideas behind them demonstrate a thought process moving in the right direction. As you think about developing your own vision, let me share a few vision statements that demonstrate simplicity and conciseness:

We want to be a church that unchurched people love to attend.

—North Point Community Church

We want to be the end of your search for a caring church.

—Submitted during a workshop by
a ten-year-old in Carlisle, Pennsylvania

We want to become a harmonious bridge between recovery and the church.

—Southside Recovery Mission

We want to be a trusted and unified family of God that brings every soul into a relationship with Him.

—Mannford Church of Christ

We want to be a family that grows, serves, and loves together.

—Forsythe Avenue Church of Christ

These statements represent something that does not yet exist but is so appealing that people want to achieve it. What does your vision statement look like? Assemble the leaders and members of the congregation together and divide everyone into groups of four. Discuss a vision statement for the church. If you want, use pieces of the vision statements above. However, your vision statement should reflect your context and desire for your church. Once written out, ask each group to share and discuss how to wordsmith a final draft of your vision statement to present to the congregation.

Step #6—Challenging, Energizing, and Meaningful

This final exercise can be the most difficult, because here's where the honing process begins. Let me encourage you up front: do not be married to your initial attempts at a vision statement. I've witnessed small groups work on vision statements where someone else in the room may have something good to contribute, but the group can't seem to see anything outside of their own vision. Step back and realize this isn't about any one person or group—it's about a vision for the whole body. A vision is most effective when it's produced by assembling the collective thoughts of a group in order to achieve something great. With this in mind, write out your vision statement on a whiteboard so everyone can see it and ask the following questions as you rework the wording for your vision.

Question #1: How Does the Vision Statement Challenge Us?

Your vision must challenge you to do something great. Examine your vision statement carefully. How does it challenge you? My experience has been that people have a tendency to write a vision statement that describes who they already are—not who they desire to become. By way of example, consider this vision statement from a church in the Midwest: "We are a gospel-centered, city-focused church community." If your vision describes who you are now, it will not challenge you to reach something greater in the future. Here's an example from a church in Arizona: "We are committed to helping every person believe in Jesus, belong to a family, become a disciple, and build His kingdom." The thoughts expressed in this vision statement are encouraging, and I hope these words can be said of every congregation. However, notice again the terminology of the vision statement. The message conveys who they are and what they're committed to rather than speaking to the future and who they will become.

Remember, your vision statement needs to challenge you beyond who you are now and what you currently do for the cause of Christ. Your vision must challenge you to do greater things than you can imagine—with God's help. If you can accomplish it on your own, scrap it and start over.

Question #2: How Does Our Vision Energize Us?

Every congregation of the Lord's people I know desires to have energy. They want a spark to get everyone engaged and involved in the work of the church. Vision should provide exactly that: energy. One of the reasons I encourage congregations to develop their own vision statement is because what energizes one group of people may not energize another. In most of my vision workshops, I present several vision statements developed by other congregations. The attempt serves to kickstart the creative juices for those present in the workshop. However, I make it clear they should not look at someone else's vision statement and settle on repeating it simply because they don't want to take the time to develop their own. The process of developing a vision statement can be arduous and usually takes time, energy, and thought. Unfortunately, this type of commitment can be difficult, because we live in a culture that prefers to have someone else do the work for us and tell us what we need to do.

But if this is your approach, you will not produce a vision that energizes the people you lead. Think about the people who make up your church or organization. What are their likes and dislikes? What do they need? What are some of their favorite activities? What gets them up and moving? What do they love most about your church or organization? Answering a few questions can help you formulate thoughts that connect to what energizes them.

Let me share a few examples. The first is a vision from a church in the northern United States: "To be a biblically functional community of believers so Christ's redemptive purposes can be accomplished in the world." A number of good thoughts are found in this vision statement. The concept of being "biblically functional" is wise for any community of believers, and accomplishing Christ's redemptive purposes in the world should be the engine that moves every Christian. But when you read the vision statement, *does it energize you?* For some, the answer is yes. For others, it might not resonate.

A second vision comes from a church in the southeastern United States, "A gospel-centered church that equips culture-shaping Christians." Again, there are two powerful thoughts about this vision. First, every church needs to be gospel-centered. Without this core, we have to wonder what we seek to accomplish. Two, equipping Christians to shape the culture rests at the heart of our work. It's vital to prevent culture from shaping Christians and instead reverse the shaping process. *But, does this vision energize you?*

Studying others' vision statements can get your creative juices flowing, but someone else's vision will not work for you. You need to carefully consider your own community. What energizes you? Once the initial vision statement is placed on the table, you need to ask, "How does our vision energize us?"

Question #3: How Does Our Vision Create Meaning?

This question is also subjective. What creates meaning for one person may be different for another. Nonetheless, is it your intent that the vision connect with everyone?

A good place to begin is to list out common elements that create meaning, such as family, community, love, belonging, etc. These and more provide meaning for most of us. When you examine your initial vision statement, look for words that convey meaning to those who belong to your organization. Your vision statement must be meaningful for each person. A congregation in Oklahoma wrote this vision statement: "To make a lasting difference in your life, in our community, and in the world." From this statement, we find meaning expressed by the phrase "make a lasting difference." Even though the type of difference is not specified, the implication is something positive that people desire. Then notice the three areas described: home, community, and world. If people make a difference in all three areas of life, they find meaning.

Another vision statement comes from a church in the western part of the United States: "A place where faith and real life intersect." While this statement may not overtly describe a future state, the implication is that they desire to become this place. Either way, the meaning expressed here is on the heart of every Christian. I have yet to meet a Christian who does not desire to know how to put their faith into practice on a daily basis. How does your faith help you in your home as a husband, wife, father, or mother? How does your faith guide your decisions at work? How do you demonstrate your faith at the grocery store, bank, post office, or sports arena? The list goes on, but I believe you get the point.

When you look at your initial vision statement, consider: *How does our vision create meaning?* You could add to that by saying, *for everyone.* You want the vision to create meaning for each person in your church or organization. If it does, you'll find more people connected, engaged, and involved in helping achieve the vision.

Every individual connects somewhere along the way in this journey of life. When we come together in a community, such as in the church, we find our lives intersect on a much deeper and more spiritual journey. With this in mind, doesn't it make sense that we have a vision of who we can become together? The sun makes it possible for each of us to physically see where we are headed and so it is with vision. We need a vision of the future—something so appealing that people are willing to make sacrifices in order to achieve it. In order for that to happen, your vision must be built around your *why*, a just cause, an understanding of who you are and who God is, and what success looks like. In addition, your vision must be concise, challenging, energizing, and meaningful. However, this is only the first step in your journey. The first essential step of life and leadership is vision, but the second essential takes us to another level.

Building Block 2
Goals: The Initiative of Life and Leadership

The Lead-In: I Need a Breath of Fresh Air
Goals are as essential to success as air is to life.
David Schwartz

Our family moved to the northwest corner of British Columbia in 1993. We were just ninety miles south of the tip of Alaska and as far north and west as you could get and still be on dry land. During our tenure in the "Rainbow City" of Prince Rupert, I enjoyed several beautiful and unique experiences. One of these unfolded in the summer of 1995, when I decided to enroll in a scuba-diving course. The design of the course was to equip and certify the students to participate in open-water diving. The thought excited me beyond words. At the time, I was unaware of what was involved, but I—pardon the pun—jumped in with both feet.

The course required both book and practical, experiential learning. I was much more excited about the latter, but studying the book came first. I guess they figured this part of the course would separate the wheat from the chaff before they invested their time and equipment in the practical experience of diving. I dove in (sorry, I couldn't resist), studied hard, and passed all the exams. The only thing left to pass was the open-water test. I wasn't worried.

Before we experienced the open water of the Pacific Northwest, we were taken to a pool to learn how to use the mask, air tanks, and fins. What followed this was the open-water experience. I use the term *experience*, because that is what it was: an experience I will not soon forget.

I should lead with the fact that the water temperature in the Pacific Ocean ninety-five miles south of the tip of Alaska is not the same as in a heated swimming pool. I began to realize this when they had us put on wetsuits. I felt like the creature from the Black Lagoon. Regardless, I was excited—at least for the moment. Our first exercise was to experience what it felt like to run out of oxygen. I fully understood the purpose of this exercise, but I felt like I could learn this better on land than I could at a depth of thirty-five feet. However, I was unable to convince the instructor of my logic in this.

Once we arrived at the ocean floor, the instructions were to have our dive buddy stand behind us and turn off the oxygen to our breathing apparatus. A strange and rather deceptive thing occurred when my dive buddy turned off my air. I was holding his hand and could feel him turn off the valve to my oxygen. For a few seconds, I could still breathe. In my mind, I began to think I was Aquaman. I told myself that I would just take a couple of deep breaths and then hold my breath for a bit. If you've ever done this exercise, you know it doesn't work that way. I tried to take my next breath, and the air was gone—there was nothing. It felt as if someone had put their hands around my throat. I thought death was imminent. I squeezed my buddy's hand, and he turned the air back on, and I once again took in the life-giving oxygen from my tank.

In that moment, I had a clear picture of how essential air is to life. I've grown accustomed to being a land dweller. In fact, I've not done any open-water diving since that day. I'm not sure what I thought was in the Pacific Ocean, but at thirty-five feet I couldn't see much, and what I could see didn't excite me about being in the water. Let me say, there are reasons why humans and the creatures of the deep do not exist in the same environment. Beyond that, I need fresh air!

A late professor of mine taught Christian Evidences during my years of theological training. Not only was he a wonderful teacher, he was a dear friend. I always loved the way he would talk about the fragile nature of life and the evidences of God in relationship to that life. He frequently reminded us that you don't need much scientific evidence to prove that oxygen is essential for life. He would often say, "All God has to do is shut off our air for about five minutes and we're all gone." I only had to experience that for a few seconds to have a whole new appreciation for his sentiment.

Air, oxygen, and breath are words we associate with life. Kim Rutledge et al. for National Geographic writes, "Air is the invisible mixture of gases that surrounds the Earth. Air contains important substances, such as oxygen and nitrogen, which most species need to survive. Human beings, of course, are one of those species."[1] While the word *important* is used, I would argue that *essential* is a more accurate assessment, because our survival is 100 percent dependent on the mixture of oxygen and nitrogen we breathe into our lungs.

88

But air contributes more to life than the oxygen we take into our lungs. Kevin Lee for the Sciencing website identifies at least three key reasons air benefits life:

> Eliminate air, and nobody will ever hear sounds that move between locations. Because air molecules cause violet and blue wavelengths of sunlight to scatter, the sky appears blue. With no air, the sky would always be black. You can also thank air for rain, snow and tornadoes, because air helps create weather. Storms, for example, often occur when a cold air mass collides with a warm air mass. An air mass is a body of air that acquires the temperature of the area over which it resides.[2]

The benefits of air fill volumes of online and printed sources. Air—also identified as the earth's atmosphere—consists of elements essential to life. Without this atmosphere, life does not exist. For our distinct purposes, I focus on the essential element of this life-giving source we breathe: oxygen.

In her response to why breathing oxygen is so important, Lina Begdache, research assistant professor at Binghamton University said,

> When we breathe, atmospheric oxygen is taken to our lungs. From there, it diffuses through tiny ballooned structures called alveoli into tiny capillaries within the lungs that carry blood throughout the body. Oxygen is transported within a blood protein called hemoglobin and is taken to cells to start a process called cellular respiration. . . . Once oxygen gets into the cell, it further diffuses into the mitochondria, which is the powerhouse of the cell. Oxygen plays a vital role in energy production via a system called electron transport chain (ETC), which is an important component of cellular respiration."[3]

Imagine this powerhouse at work in our bodies every second of the day—with every breath we take, it gives us life.

At the risk of sounding redundant, I need to mention the multiple life-giving qualities oxygen provides. The essential nature of oxygen is clear, but oxygen does more than just fill our lungs. Consider why our bodies rely on oxygen, as contributed by Burt Cancaster for the Vitality Medical website. Cancaster not only discusses the nature and benefit of oxygen, he also shares three life-giving qualities that oxygen brings to our bodies.

1) Oxygen fuels our cells and helps provide the basic building blocks our bodies need to survive.

2) Oxygen is a particularly important part of our immune system. It is used to help kill bacteria, and it fuels the cells that make up our body's defenses against viruses and other invaders.

3) The human eye is in particular need of oxygen to function well. Our eyes absorb much of the oxygen they need directly through the cornea.[4]

As I wrote this paragraph, I took a deep breath and contemplated the wonder of oxygen. How often do we breathe in and breathe out so involuntarily that we never consider this amazing function? If you're like me, you've never thought about it before. Honestly, I never gave it much thought until I researched the subject. I think we all understand air is essential, yet we rarely give it much consideration.

Breathing air into our lungs gives us life and so much more. Air is the breath of life. The oxygen breathed into our lungs strengthens every component of our existence. In the same way, goals and plans breathe fresh air into the lungs of our leadership. Our goals and plans give life to the body of people we lead, strengthening the purpose that supports where we are headed and why we exist. When leaders build on their vision by setting goals and establishing plans, this fresh air is taken into the lungs of the people who follow, which sparks life. As you read through the four chapters of this section, you'll learn about goals and gain useful tools to set your own goals and establish the plans needed to achieve them.

Chapter 5
Goals and Planning

It must be borne in mind that the tragedy of life doesn't lie in not reaching your goal. The tragedy lies in having no goals to reach.
Benjamin E. Mays

From about kindergarten, our son has established goals and made plans. Rarely has he experienced any curveballs, because he always knew where he wanted to go, and he set goals to help him get there. His goals were well-rounded in nature: physical, financial, relational, and spiritual—what we might refer to as *holistic*.

One of his goals—which I found intriguing—was to meet the person he wanted to marry before completing his college degree, get married after graduation, and begin his family. As parents, we were all in favor of him getting married at some point and starting a family, but we were not always impressed with the young ladies he brought home.

Near the end of his junior year, he was dating a nice girl he met while in school. We were wondering if she might be "the one," since they seemed pretty serious at the time. The best laid plans of mice and . . . parents. A curveball was headed his way, or so we thought.

His plans for the summer before his senior year involved a twelve-hour Spanish-immersion course in Mexico City. Not long after he arrived in Mexico, his girlfriend sent an email suggesting they take a break from the relationship. When we heard the news, we figured he would be devastated, and—as any good parents—we were ready to console him. Instead, he said something to the effect of, "If that's the way she feels, she's not the right girl for me."

We had no idea how God was at work in what would be the greatest goal-honoring plan in our son's life. A young lady from Findlay, Ohio, just happened to be enrolled in the same twelve-hour Spanish immersion course in Mexico. If it couldn't get any better, the same day our son received his Dear John email from his girlfriend, this young lady from Findlay received a similar message from her boyfriend back home. We have to stand in awe of how God works. Any other time, this situation would be disastrous, but such was not the case. All this happened on Monday. On Tuesday, as fate would have it, these two young people met for the first time.

Upon returning home, our son informed us he had met the girl he wanted to marry. Again, as any good parents would be, we were a bit skeptical. I mean, they had just met. And how would this long-distance relationship work during their last year of college—one in Tennessee and the other in Ohio? But we trusted our son's judgment, and I'm so thankful we did, because once we met this young lady, we understood exactly why he loved her.

These lovebirds married the summer after graduation, and I was privileged to perform their wedding ceremony. Now, almost fourteen years later, we've been blessed with four amazing grandchildren from this union. If you don't believe that God honors goals and planning, you might want to rethink that position.

There are two types of people: those who have goals and those who do not. Statistics suggest a significant contrast between goal-setters and non-goal-setters. Professors from Arizona State University researched the relationship between goals and retention factors among first-year university students. The results of the study were significant. In the discussion of their findings, they concluded the following:

> First-semester freshmen without an identified career goal made less positive persistence decisions than did those with a defined job-related career goal. . . . It is likely that without defined goals, students lack the motivation to make and follow through with persistence decisions. . . . Clearly, having an identified goal that is dependent on successful completion of an education facilitates decisions to remain in school. Such a goal is likely to motivate students to continue in the face of daily challenges.[1]

The findings concur with research conducted by others. The significance of having goals directly contributes to the persistence needed to achieve those goals. This is true regardless of the type or nature of the educational, professional, religious, political, or personal goal.

Finding an individual or organization that has achieved success by luck or chance is difficult, if not impossible. Goals are the reason for their successes, because when goals exist, people establish the appropriate plans and persist in achieving those plans to reach their goals. There is truth found in the old saying "Those who fail to plan, plan to fail."

Narrowing down the significance of goals in leadership is an incredible task. Goals are more than a dream or wish. Goals are objectives stemming from leadership vision, which is why I follow the section on vision with one focused on goals. Goals serve to provide purpose and direction. Goals establish priorities, unity, efficient use of time, and aid in charting the future. Throughout the chapters in this section, I examine these areas and more. For our purposes, I begin with looking at how the Bible addresses goals.

Biblical Context of Goals

Goals are a key component of strategic planning, and strategic planning is a biblical concept. Let's take a few moments to look at a few passages that demonstrate this.

I begin with one of the most evil and corrupt times in history. Certainly, we all remember times in history when evil was rampant. Perhaps we think about Hitler and the Nazi party, Stalin or Lenin and the growth of communism, Mussolini and the development of fascism, or Pol Pot and the Khmer Rouge regime. But I want to take us back to another time when the world was wicked. The Bible says that during this time, "the LORD saw that the wickedness of man was great on the earth, and that every intent of the thoughts of his heart was only evil continually" (Genesis 6:5). The evil of mankind was so great that "the LORD was sorry that He had made man on the earth, and He was grieved in His heart" (Genesis 6:6). In the midst of this evil and wickedness, one man found favor with God: Noah. The text of Genesis 6 outlines God's plan for building a boat the size of three football fields, which would save Noah and his family along with specific numbers of clean and unclean animals. It's estimated to have taken 120 years to build the ark, and Noah could never have accomplished this feat without a strategic plan, which God provided in amazing detail.

In another biblical account of strategic planning, King David was credited with uniting the nation of Israel after the self-centered and rebellious Saul failed God. David fought many battles and shed much blood during these wars. David's heart was set on building a house for the Lord rather than keeping the vessels of the tabernacle in a tent. However, even though David was identified as a man after God's own heart (Acts 13:22), God prevented him from building the temple because David had shed so much blood (1 Chronicles 22:8). God sent word through Nathan the prophet that David wouldn't construct this sacred edifice for the Lord—instead, the task would be given to his son Solomon (2 Samuel 7:4–17).

When Solomon ascended to the throne, David passed along "the plan of the porch of the temple, its buildings, its storehouses, its upper rooms, its inner rooms and the room for the mercy seat; and the plan of all that he had in mind for the courts of the house of the Lord" (1 Chronicles 28:11–12). When we read about the dedication of the temple and Solomon's prayer (1 Kings 8), we can see that when plans are followed, the outcome is beautiful and magnificent. The temple's glory and splendor is highlighted only by its comparison with future attempts to reconstruct the temple after its destruction. When Israel returned from captivity, the first order of business was to reconstruct the temple, yet "the old men who had seen the first temple, wept with a loud voice when the foundation of this house was laid before their eyes" (Ezra 3:12). Nothing compared to the beauty of the temple constructed by Solomon.

Solomon certainly understood the value of planning. He wrote in Proverbs 20:5, "A plan in the heart of a man is *like* deep water, but a man of understanding draws it out." He followed this up in the next chapter: "The plans of the diligent *lead* surely to advantage, but everyone who is hasty *comes* surely to poverty" (Proverbs 21:5). Both of these passages indicate there is much wisdom in establishing and implementing plans. In fact, goals and plans are essential to success. Think about it from God's perspective.

I believe we would all agree that God establishes goals and implements plans. While it is greatly misused in application for today, Jeremiah wrote, "'For I know the plans that I have for you,' declares the Lord, 'plans for welfare and not for calamity to give you a future and a hope'" (Jeremiah 29:11). Sounds like God had a vision too. In this verse, God wasn't promising Christians today that He would provide us with wealth and protect us from harm in order to secure for us a future of hope—this promise was made to Israel once the seventy years of captivity were completed. Knowing the context makes a big difference. The point to remember is that Scripture shows us that God has goals and makes plans.

In fact, wasn't the death, burial, and resurrection of Jesus part of the "predetermined plan and foreknowledge of God" (Acts 2:23)? Another New Testament passage indicates that God had a plan from before the creation of the world to provide an opportunity for us to be His adopted children through Jesus (Ephesians 1:4–5). If God has goals and set plans in place before the world was created, and if we see the benefit of goals and plans throughout Scripture, does it not seem essential that we develop goals and plans today while seeking God's blessing of them?

God establishes goals and makes plans to achieve them. The essential nature of these goals and plans cannot be emphasized enough. Before we dive into the specifics, let me back up and define goals and consider two major types of goals. Merriam-Webster provides a concise definition of goals as "the end toward which effort is directed."[2] In a 2002 article, Edwin A. Locke and Gary P. Latham defined goals as "the object or aim of an action, for example, to attain a specific standard of proficiency, usually within a specified time limit."[3] Twelve years earlier, in *Theory of Goal Setting and Task Performance*, Locke and Latham provided another definition: "A goal is an idea of the future or desired result that a person or a group of people envision, plan and commit to achieve."[4] Additional research reveals many technical and practical definitions that further clarify the meaning and implications of this four-lettered word: *goal*.

In addition to the challenge of defining goals, we find an unending list of categories of goals. Although we cannot examine every type of goal, we'll look at a few that provide good foundations. Based on research by Heidi Grant and Carol Dweck, there are two major types of goals: performance and learning. I discuss each of these and consider a few additional thoughts as they relate to other types of goals connected to this study.

Performance Goals

Performance—or sometimes referred to as achievement—goals "validate one's ability or avoid demonstrating a lack of ability."[5] According to Grant and Dweck, performance suffers when individuals lack faith in themselves to accomplish the goal. Ultimately, this lack of faith prevents growth and development. Performance goals factor into areas that include production and sales, process improvement, and decision making—the list grows from the corporate world into our everyday lives. Any area that requires performance requires a goal in order to achieve success.

Learning Goals

Learning goals are associated with desired outcomes within an educational environment. Teachers provide these outcomes as part of their syllabi and class structures. Grant and Dweck identify learning goals as an effort to acquire new knowledge or skills. In an earlier study, Dweck and E. S. Elliot reveal, "Learning goals, with their emphasis on understanding and growth, were shown to facilitate persistence and mastery-oriented behaviors in the face of obstacles, even when perceptions of current ability might be low."[6] Learning goals provide value regardless of performance ability and can be applied to any area of life one desires to improve.

Developmental Goals

While the two categories above are inclusive of most areas in life, there are other types of goals within the broader scope of this topic. Developmental goals are usually associated with learning. Therefore, they often fall into the category above. At the same time, developmental goals can also be related to performance, because they involve management processes, production, and other areas of life. Developmental goals can be personal (improving ourselves by learning new skills or abilities) or others-centered (improving the skills or abilities of others, teaching or coaching them to learn). Leaders benefit from these types of goals, as they're holistic in nature.

Relational Goals

Another category addresses relationships. Relational goals are components of life connected to the various relationships we encounter. For example, relational goals include objectives that increase our relationships at work (making us better team players), relationships within our families (strengthening marriages, improving parenting skills, getting along with siblings), relationships with neighbors (looking out and caring for each other), and community relationships (working together toward a common purpose).

Short- and Long-Term Goals

The importance of short- and long-term goals cannot be overstated. Every individual and organization (secular or religious) needs both for success. Long-term goals project a destination that may be ten, fifteen, twenty, or twenty-five years down the road, but can also include a three- to five-year range. Short-term goals keep us motivated by projecting our destination a week, a month, or a year ahead. Both are vital for motivation and a focus on the future.

There are differences between short-term and long-term goals, of which the most obvious is the time frame. In addition, short-term goals tend to be more direct. My short-term goals might look like writing a chapter a day. Another short-term goal might be to finish writing my book in the next six weeks. Long-term goals are a little more complex and can become unclear if not well written. My long-term goals might involve the number of books I write over the next five years. I might also think of a long-term goal where I will produce an updated edition of a specific book, including updated stats and facts and additional material beneficial to the reader.

Spiritual Goals

I would be remiss if I didn't take a moment to discuss the need for spiritual goals. Establishing goals for education, career, family, health, finances, and community deserves time and attention. However, establishing and achieving goals in each of these areas falls short if we forget the necessity of including spiritual goals.

Spiritual goals are designed to help us grow in relationship with God. Interestingly, spiritual goals can provide an umbrella over every type of goal we've discussed. Performance goals under the spiritual umbrella look like growth in how we serve the Lord. These include areas such as growing in the amount we give, accepting the task of teaching a Bible class, leading a prayer, sharing our faith, serving our community, etc. Learning goals under the spiritual umbrella provide growth in knowledge and new skills. This includes a Bible study plan or gaining technological skills to do live-streaming of lessons, podcasts, blogs, and more. Developmental goals under the spiritual umbrella involve areas listed above, but include how we develop as leaders, teachers, preachers, or using our gifts to benefit others. Relational goals under the spiritual umbrella directly connect to our relationship with God as our Father and each other as brothers and sisters. We establish goals to strengthen those relationships through study, prayer, love, encouragement, and edification.

Strategic Planning

The relationship between goals and planning easily works with the hand-in-glove concept. Once goals (the glove) are established, we naturally work out plans (the hand) to help us achieve those goals. We call this strategic planning. Strategic planning sessions can become long and tedious if we allow them to be. However, it doesn't have to be this way, and the end result can be fabulous.

Various tools are available to help in the process. One of those tools is known as the *planning cycle* and consists of five questions. At the heart of this cycle is the *why* discussed in the first section of this book. Each time a question in the cycle is asked, reflect on your *why* before answering the question.

Before I share these questions with you, I suggest you complete a task that will help you to answer these questions. In his book *Building Strategies*, Dr. J. Robert Clinton lays out two types of strategies for achieving goals.[7] The first is called a "closed bridging strategy." This is a strategy that moves toward a relatively fixed end as the anticipated situation. The second is called an "open bridging strategy," which refers to a strategy that allows for the final results to be changed as the plan is formulated. Both strategies have merit and provide benefits depending on the goals presented.

In order to lay the groundwork for these strategies, Clinton outlines two exercises I suggest you complete before answering the planning cycle questions. If you are working through this process in a larger group, I also suggest you divide everyone up into discussion groups of four to six people. At the end of each exercise, allow each small group to share. I'm always amazed at how one group seems to pick up on something another group missed and vice versa. A final suggestion is to have someone write the responses to each exercise down so they're available for future reference.

The first exercise requires you to write out the current situation of your organization, or the NOW. The NOW represents the present reality. Take about twenty minutes and write out specific details about your community, demographics, programs, mission work, elders, deacons, ministers, teachers in the Bible class program, youth groups, fellowship gatherings, and anything else you can think of related to your present situation.

Once you have completed this, your second exercise is to envision your desired future, or the THEN. Think about what you want your church or ministry to look like in five, ten, fifteen, or twenty years from now. The time frame is a matter of choice. If you could paint the perfect picture of what you want your organization to look like, what would you paint? Again, write specifics.

The bridging strategy is part of getting from the NOW to where you want to be THEN. Along with the information collected from these two exercises, the planning cycle will allow you to answer the following questions to guide your planning.

1) *Where do we want to go?* Follow this question with *Why do we want to go there?* Think about THEN and look at the information you gathered in the previous exercises. Once you know where you want to go, think about short- and long-term goals.

2) *How do we get there?* Remember to examine your answer to this to see if the strategy aligns with the previously established *why*. This question moves you into a discussion about the specific strategies to be developed and the plans to be implemented to achieve your goals. Each goal will have specific plans.

3) *How do we measure success?* As I previously discussed, we often think of success in terms

of numbers—but numbers are not the only way of measuring success. The key here is *measure*. You need to establish benchmarks along the way to help everyone see the progress made and how this becomes measurements of success. The common thought here is that *what gets measured, gets done.*

4) *How did we do?* If the results aren't directly related to the why, then you may not have the right results. One of the most critical components of this cycle is this question. Here you're specifically looking at the results of your efforts. Periods of evaluation are essential to growth. Was the goal achieved? If not, where did it fall short? If the goal is surpassed, how can the goal be adjusted for the future?

5) *How can we improve?* As I've stated along the way, any improvement must be considered in connection to the *why*—or it needs to be changed. After evaluating where you are at the beginning and what you've accomplished throughout the period under evaluation, brainstorm ways to improve. This step in the cycle allows for creativity to improve the amount of time spent in the work, changes desired in the lives of those involved, and the necessary resources to continue the cycle.

After the last question is answered, the cycle starts over, and you examine new goals, establish new plans, and work through the cycle again. It's vital to establish goals that can only be accomplished with God's help. If God isn't included, goals fall short. In his book *Good to Great*, Jim Collins talks about the need for "big, hairy, audacious goals (BHAG)."[8] This is why some organizations make leaps to success and others fail—audacious goals are that essential.

Goals need to be clear, challenging, and God-honoring. Goals require total community commitment. Everyone needs to be all-in.

I continue this discussion throughout the next few chapters. I outline how to achieve goals, share a tool for developing goals, and look at how to analyze the plans designed to help us reach our goals through a SWOT or SOAR analysis technique.

Chapter 6
Achieving Goals

To live a fulfilled life, we need to keep creating the "what is next" of our lives. Without dreams and goals there is no living, only merely existing, and that is not why we are here.
Mark Twain

Why do we need goals? We need goals for the same reason we need oxygen. Both breathe life into the our existence. What benefits come to an individual or congregation when goals are in place? One of my favorite learning tasks in small-group workshops is asking each group to make a list of why we need goals. Below, I share a compilation of answers I've received over the years and a few thoughts about each.

Why Have Goals?

To Use Our Time More Efficiently

How we use the time we are given each day is difficult to address. We're inundated with so many time-wasters, such as social media, television, and random internet searches, just to name a few. When we have goals, the way we use our time changes. Do you know people who have a to-do list for each day? I've learned the value of them. Each evening, my wife asks me, "So, what does your day look like tomorrow?" What I have planned helps her know how to plan her day and achieve the tasks she has scheduled. I've also learned that a to-do list helps me focus on the amount of time I dedicate to each project, thus helping me use my time efficiently. Whether you call it a to-do list or your daily goals, the practice of having short- and long-term goals will help you use your time more efficiently.

To Establish Unity, Order, and Keep Us Focused

When goals exist, it's safe to say people are more united, partly because they have something to work toward. Thus, what follows is order and focus. These three thoughts interrelate and show us why goals are so essential. Consider the alternative: without goals, people have no direction or anything to keep them focused. They end up wandering around, trying to figure out what to do, how to do it, why they should do it, and for how long. Sadly, too many people live like this each day. Goals make an amazing difference—the evidence is clear among families, churches, and businesses. You would be hard-pressed to find a major corporation that doesn't have goals. They know exactly where they're headed and how to get there. You can find the same among growing and thriving churches as well as among strong and healthy families. The power of goals to provide unity, order, and focus is immeasurable. If you don't believe me, try the following experiment: write out your goals for the next month and break down how you will achieve those goals on a weekly and daily basis. Then watch the difference it makes in your personal life.

To Unleash the Power of Potential

One of my favorite reasons for goals is the opportunity to unleash the potential of each individual. Almost twenty years ago, I worked with a congregation in Arkansas. Among other programs, events, and activities, the talent unleashed in that congregation when it came time for Vacation Bible School cannot be overstated. The men and women who came together to design, draw, paint, craft, and construct elaborate features of the program were nothing short of fantastic. My favorite year occurred when these brethren converted the entire auditorium (which comfortably seated 350 people) into a ship. There were sails hanging from the ceiling, a captain's wheel and the quarterdeck on the stage, and walls designed to look like we were in the ocean. The kids loved it—I'm pretty sure the adults did too. When we have goals, we unleash the power of people's potential to achieve great things. Try it some time and see what potential is unleashed to help you achieve your goals.

To Provide Confidence and Assurance to Followers

Another key reason for goals is the confidence and assurance it builds in the lives of followers. I believe we all want to know that our leaders are aware of where they're going and how they plan to get there. If you want to see followers' confidence and assurance destroyed, watch what happens in a congregation without goals. As I mentioned in the first section of this book, insanity is doing the same things in the same ways yet expecting different results. When your efforts are given to maintain the status quo, you set no goals and have no plans other than what you've always done, which means you'll get what you've always got. Amidst all of the other benefits, goals provide confidence and assurance to followers.

To Make It Possible to Measure Progress

When goals exist, you build into the structure the type of plans that guide you to achieve them. The means required to achieve your goals make it possible to measure your progress. Remember, what gets measured gets done. In chapter 7, I discuss three tools to assist you in the goal-setting process along with how to vet a plan to achieve goals. One of these tools is a PERT chart, which stands for "program evaluation and review technique." The PERT chart gives a visual perspective of goals and the monthly plans designed to achieve those goals. Part of this process affords us the opportunity to measure our progress.

To Give Motivation to Stay Active

According to business consultant Svetlana Whitener, there are two types of motivation: *extrinsic* and *intrinsic*. Extrinsic motivation involves avoiding something because we're afraid of the consequences. In other words, I do not steal tools from my job site, because I fear the consequences of losing my job or being sentenced with jail time. Whitener suggests that "when you are governed by extrinsic motivation, you are not fully in alignment with your goals." Intrinsic motivation is described more like a magnet that draws you toward your goal: "When you are governed by your intrinsic motivation, you are fully in alignment with your goals."[1] We are all motivated by both. However, if you want to motivate followers to stay active, you need goals that draw them toward it rather than creating fear of the consequences of failure.

To Prevent Procrastination

This is big! I used to reverse an old saying related to procrastination: I'd say, "Why do today what you can put off until tomorrow?" I said it that way so long, I almost forgot the proper way to use the saying. Procrastination threatens the whole of reaching your goals. Generally speaking, procrastination exists when you lack goals and find no real purpose in getting anything done today because you're not going anywhere. When you put off until tomorrow what you could do today, the days become weeks, weeks become months, and months become years. The next thing you know, you've accomplished nothing. This is why goals are necessary. When you have goals, you have a reason to get the work done today. You know that tomorrow will bring new work and new opportunities to further your efforts toward goal achievement.

To Hold Everyone Accountable

Building on the previous thoughts about procrastination, goals help you to hold everyone accountable for getting the work done—including yourself. When goals exist, there's work to be done if you hope to achieve your goals. Since the work involves everyone contributing their parts, you must establish ways to hold each other accountable. We've often seen accountability challenged when it comes to volunteer organizations such as churches. The result has created an atmosphere that reflects the Pareto 80/20 principle. The principle is credited to Vilfredo Federico Damaso Pareto, who was born in Italy in 1848. Through his observations on gardening, he developed a principle for investing that demonstrated that 80 percent of the results come from 20 percent of the action.[2] This principle has also been used to support the idea that 20 percent of the people do 80 percent of the work. We've allowed this principle to exist because we're not good at holding people accountable. Why? Because we lack the kind of goals and plans that produce growth. When you have a vision for the future, you establish goals and implement plans. Achievement requires everyone doing their part, and designing a system of accountability that encourages people to work in their areas of interest guides the progress.

Leaders have a great responsibility when building confidence in followers. The task becomes more difficult if they do not believe in themselves. Goals help make this possible. When leaders demonstrate the ability to set goals and establish plans to reach them, people will follow. The overall impact on leadership confidence is significant: when leaders believe in themselves, the cycle promotes greater confidence in followers. The exercises presented throughout this section will assist leaders with their goals and through the planning process.

How to Achieve Goals

The only way to succeed and win is through goals. I've learned that it's one thing to share why goals are important, but it's completely different to dig into how we can achieve them. The list I share below is a compilation of material provided through group discussions over the past ten years and gleaned from multiple authors such as Stephen Covey, Jim Collins, Robert Clinton, and others.

Begin at the End

In his book *The 7 Habits of Highly Effective People*, Stephen Covey says the second habit is to "begin with the end in mind."[3] As a runner, I enjoy watching indoor and outdoor track events. I've witnessed several races where the lead runner finished in second or third place because they took their eyes off the finish line and looked back to see who was gaining on them. The number one rule of running a race is to mentally and physically keep your eyes on the finish line. You can't go there in actuality if you cannot first go there in your mind. When you begin by thinking about what you want to achieve in the future, you work backward with a design plan to help you achieve your goals. On a personal level, think about your own eulogy. Take a few moments and consider the following: *What do you want people to say about you when you die?* Then back up and begin living that life now in order to make it happen—because it will not happen by accident. On an organizational level, think about the next generation.

Consider the following: *What kind of [church, ministry, legacy] do we want to leave to our children or grandchildren?* Again, back up, and make it happen, because it will not happen by accident.

Understand Where You Are Now

Unless you know where you are currently, you can't determine where to start in order to achieve your goals. What resources are available? Who will contribute to achieving this goal? What are your strengths and weaknesses? Without knowing personal and congregational strengths and/or weaknesses, obstacles are bound to occur—but these can be prevented. In the movie *Magnum Force,* Harry Callahan (played by Clint Eastwood) tells the mayor and his lieutenant, "A good man's gotta know his limitations." The thought expressed by Callahan indicates the self-awareness needed by every goal-setter. I'm not suggesting you dream smaller or safer or strive to achieve goals you can reach on your own—I'm saying you need a self-awareness of where you are now with resources and people: what are your personal and congregational strengths and weaknesses? An awareness of where you are now provides you with confidence to obtain what you need in order to do more.

Time-Management/Discipline

I recently read the following statement about time management:

> The fact of the matter is, you cannot control or manage time. It's simply not possible. We all have the same number of hours in a day. You can't get an extra hour no matter how good you are. And you can't re-use the minutes that you wasted the previous day. However, you can manage yourself. How? By focusing on yourself, by practicing self-discipline and by following a calculated yet flexible schedule. Self-management is not rocket science. Still, it works like a charm.[4]

The ability to manage ourselves within the time we are given is crucial to goal achievement. The concept screams priorities. Leaders must have a keen awareness of what must be done first. When work-related responsibilities, tasks, and problems mount up, I have a tendency to shut down. At times, I get so overwhelmed I struggle to see any solution—any way out. In a previous job, this scenario happened more often than I care to think about. However, on one occasion I was sitting at my desk, staring at the screen on my laptop—and had no idea what to do. A friend walked by and noticed the distant, blank look on my face and asked what was going on. After I explained, he looked at me and suggested that I decide what had to be done right now—today. In that moment, the fog lifted and the direction was clear. Determining the priority of what had to be done right then helped clarify the direction for that moment and day, the next day, and days afterward.

Minimize Distractions

It's inevitable that distractions will come. We must each establish an approach to help minimize them. The approach must be tailored for each person, depending on the nature of the distraction. However, there are a few steps that can aid everyone in this task. First, distinguish between the urgent and important. President Eisenhower once said, "What is urgent is seldom important, and what is important is seldom urgent." Knowing the difference helps in moving to the second step: identify the distraction. What's the nature and magnitude of the distraction? Why is it a distraction at this time? Third, break it down into manageable size. The old rule of elephants applies. How do you eat an elephant? One bite at a time. This step alone makes a powerful difference in handling any distraction. Fourth, know when to walk away and take a break. This step can be the most difficult to identify and practice. However, when you know the right time to walk away and take a break, you can think, evaluate, and make clearer decisions. Fifth, learn to negotiate the curve. In 2002, Arkansas Governor Mike Huckabee spoke at the Greenbrier Chamber of Commerce banquet and shared a story about a conversation he had with a former Winter Olympian in the luge event. As they discussed the speed of the sled, Huckabee asked the luger about steering decisions while in the curve, to which the Olympian responded, "You have to negotiate the curve before you get to it." If you want to minimize distractions and stay focused on the goal, you have to determine how to handle the distraction before it happens.

Write Them Down

The power and results found when we write down our goals can be challenging to measure. Research conducted by Dr. Gail Matthews demonstrated that people are 42 percent more likely to achieve their goals when they write them down. In her discussion of this statistic and why it is true, Mary Morrissey contributed this explanation: "If you just think about one of your goals or dreams, you're only using the right hemisphere of your brain, which is your imaginative center. But, if you think about something that you desire, and then write it down, you also tap into the power of your logic-based left hemisphere."[5] I have a good friend whose practice is to write down a goal and place it on his bathroom mirror, refrigerator, dashboard of his truck, and his office desk. He wants to see his goal everywhere he looks, because doing so ensures greater opportunity for success in achieving it.

Look at the Goal

Perhaps this is another way of restating the need to write down your goals, but it's vital to visually keep the goal before you. Have you ever seen or participated in a fundraising campaign where the goal was visually displayed in the form of a thermometer? Each step toward the fundraising goal is added in red to keep everyone abreast of the progress. The visual image helps us constantly see the goal, our current progress toward reaching it, and how far we need to go to achieve the goal. A thermometer is not the only way to keep an eye on a goal. Any sort of reference point by which we can see the progress as we move ahead will serve the purpose. A visual goal board is helpful. Remember, writing down your goal is only one step—next, you need to look at the goal, regularly.

Do Not Try to Do It Alone

Have you ever thought, said, or heard someone say, "If you want the job done right, you might as well do it yourself." I know

I've said this before—but it's wrong. The church is a family, and God designed this family with different personalities and talents. One of the best ways to achieve goals is by allowing everyone to get involved. Earlier in my life, I began a fitness program at a local gym. During my first week, I met a man who was forty years my senior. This man worked me under the table every time we worked out together, but what a motivator! After my wife and I decided to move to Colorado to begin theological training, I shared with him our decision. He asked me, "In all your study of the Bible, what is the one lesson you've learned?" I thought, *I have no idea. Isn't that why I'm going to school? To learn that sort of stuff?* He then said this: "Always remember: you can't make it on your own." He was right. A study of the Bible from Genesis through Revelation reveals several lessons, but one to always remember is that we can't make it on our own. God never intended for us to make it on our own—to be independent and make our own way through the world. Instead, He warns us constantly of the dangers of self-sufficiency, which can lead to arrogance. God desires that we be dependent upon and trust Him with all our hearts.

Sustain Motivation

None of these are easy, but this one takes top billing for challenging. I'm sure you've celebrated the casting of a vision or the introduction of new goals for your job, within your church, or perhaps in your family. Big, long-term goals excite everyone when they're first introduced. The challenge is sustaining motivation during the short-term. Progress requires time, work, and sustained energy. A few ideas to sustain this motivation include leaders who (1) effectively communicate progress, (2) display transparency about challenges or setbacks, (3) provide a safe environment to address likes and dislikes, (4) celebrate each small victory toward the goal, and (5) practice accountability (leaders and followers alike). In order to achieve long-term goals, we must focus on ways to sustain motivation in the short-term.

Evaluate Often

I once witnessed a congregation spend several months discovering their vision, go to great lengths to develop long-term goals, and masterfully deliver one of the best pitches I've ever heard for congregational buy-in. However, they failed to build into the structure periods of evaluation. The result? More than five years into the work, they realized no progress had been made in achieving their vision. It was time to evaluate and adjust. One way to ensure your goals are achieved is to plan specific periods of evaluation. This time to reflect on how far you've moved toward the goal is vital to sustaining motivation. People need to see progress. In the end, you can make modifications if and when necessary.

Remember the Why

Remember why you started, where you're headed, the steps to get there, and the stockholders (everyone invested in this venture). You can know every detail of *what* you do and *how* you do it, but only when you remember *why* is it possible to connect all the pieces essential to achieve your goals. Your *why* drives your focus each day and keeps you centered on the purpose for which you live.

I've covered a lot of information in a short amount of space, and more could be said. However, I believe you get the point. Please do not overlook this chapter and its significance. The reasons we need goals are substantial, and I didn't even come close to exhausting the possibilities. It's also necessary to know how to achieve your goals. Again, this list provides only a starting point. Before I conclude this chapter, I want to share a tool that helps determine if you have *SMART* goals.

SMARTER Goals

The acronym SMART has been used for years. Goals must be *specific, measurable, attainable, relevant,* and *time-bound.* Modifications exist for the A and R: *action-oriented* and *realistic.* Regardless of which you choose, the acronym provides a tool for goal-setting. Consider the following example to clarify an application of the acronym:

As our world approaches the end of one year and the beginning of a new year, we tend to talk about New Year's resolutions. These resolutions symbolize a form of goals intended to improve our lives. They may consist of healthier eating habits, weight loss, exercise, work or school achievements, spiritual growth, etc. By way of illustration, think about the following: Sam desires to lose weight, so he sets his goal to lose weight in the new year. Most people would see this as a good goal, and it is. However, based on our model, it's not a SMART goal. There's nothing specific about the goal, and measuring the goal is challenging without the specifics. It's achievable and relevant, but there's no specified time frame other than the new year. If Sam were to say his goal is to lose thirty pounds over the next twelve months, he would have a SMART goal. The goal is specific: thirty pounds. It's measurable, because six months in he can weigh himself and see if he has lost half of the weight desired. As before, it's both attainable and relevant. Plus, we know the time frame is specifically one year. With a SMART goal, Sam can now establish specific plans to help him reach that goal, such as implementation of exercise and eating habits. Each of these specific plans can be used with the same SMART acronym to ensure Sam stays on track.

The same approach can be taken toward any goal. Let's move into the arena of a congregational setting. Leadership decides to set a goal for numerical growth. As with our previous discussion, this is a good goal but not a SMART goal. Is it attainable and relevant? Absolutely. However, there are some pieces missing in the equation. (Let me be clear: I realize God causes the growth and we're not just about numbers. The point is simply to illustrate the significance of SMART goals.) If a congregation has a hundred members, then a SMART goal might look like this: *Our goal is to increase our attendance from 100 to 120 people in the next twelve months.* This goal is specific, measurable, attainable, relevant, and time-bound. It is SMART. With this goal in mind, we put plans in place to reach the goal. These plans might include more SMART goals, such as increasing our monthly Bible studies by three, reaching two families in the community that used to attend, hosting marriage and finance seminars over the next twelve months to reach out to people in the community, and connecting with at least one local community project to help improve relationships between the church and our town. Each of these are SMART goals in and of themselves, and they require some planning. These efforts may or may not produce twenty new members, but with a SMART goal, we have something to work toward.

One last thought before I introduce some tools in chapter 7 to help strengthen your strategic planning. I was first introduced to the concept of SMARTER goals during a course at Fuller Theological Seminary. One of my colleagues shared with me information from one of our professors related to the additional letters in the SMART acronym. Since then, I've seen this approach in a number of online venues. Adding an ER to SMART takes our goals to a new level: they're now SMARTER goals. The ER stands for *evaluate* and *recognize, reward,* or *revisit* if the goals were not reached. Therefore, if you want to have SMARTER goals, you'll schedule periods of evaluation (as I mentioned earlier in the chapter). This time of evaluation is to assess where you are in your trajectory toward the goal, determine where support can be provided to assist those involved in the work, and increase the motivational factors to encourage the level of involvement required to achieve your goals. When you near the end of the established time frame of your goal, recognize or reward the people involved in achieving the goal. Give honor to those to whom honor is due. If you don't achieve your goal, revisit the whole process and create new goals and plans.

Little nuances in how you create a goal and establish plans can make a major difference in your level of success. Using the SMARTER acronym will help you create goals that excite, motivate, and direct everyone toward a better future. As the air breathed into your lungs supplies and strengthens the source of life for your existence, goals will supply and strengthen the same purpose in your leadership.

As I continue the discussion about the essential nature of goals, I outline three tools to strengthen your ability to lead and succeed in achieving your goals.

Chapter 7
SWOT, SOAR, and the PERT Chart

You can never have too many tools.
James Floyd Kelly and Patrick Hood-Daniel

In the early years of our marriage, Sheryl and I used to watch the television sitcom *Home Improvement.* Tim Allen and Richard Karn provided the perfect Laurel and Hardy of the construction equipment world. One particular area of the show's dynamics was Tim the "Tool Man" Taylor's obsession with power tools. Allen played the host of a local television show called *Tool Time,* which promoted tools for the Binford Tool Company. Inevitably, in each episode, Tim caused some blunder with his inability to know his own personal limits and the limitations of the equipment he operates. Karn played Tim's sidekick assistant, Al Borland, who was capable of using all the equipment expertly and regularly rescued Tim from his crazy antics.

Behind Tim's disastrous accidents was his inability to plan properly. He had great ideas about what he wanted to accomplish, but his efforts to achieve those ideas were poorly planned, and the result was usually that Tim ended up in the doctor's office or emergency room.

Whether we're discussing electronics and technology, carpentry, or mechanics, tools are essential to do the job right. Having the right tools for the right job increases success on every level. The same is true when setting goals and establishing plans. For the next few pages, we'll look at three tools to guide the process of strategic planning.

SWOT

The first tool is a SWOT analysis. SWOT stands for *strengths, weaknesses, opportunities*, and *threats*. The origin of the SWOT analysis technique is "credited to Albert Humphrey, who led a research project at Stanford University in the 1960s and 1970s using data from many top companies. The goal was to identify why corporate planning failed."[1] Since that time, a number of approaches have been suggested for conducting SWOT analyses. As I explain my approach to this subject, I hope you find what fits best for you and your organization. Let's start with a consideration of each component.

The first component is *strengths*. Think in terms of *internal* strengths, or the attributes of the individual or organization. These consist of capabilities, processes, experience, knowledge, resources, and more. The idea represents anything that is *helpful* in achieving the objective. Depending on the goal under consideration, strengths can include the following: a strong biblical foundation, qualified and knowledgeable Bible class teachers, plenty of space, financial resources, accessible technology, a friendly atmosphere, young families, etc.

The second component is *weaknesses*. Again, think in terms of *internal* weaknesses, or the attributes of the individual or organization, such as a lack of capabilities, processes, experience, knowledge, resources, and more. While strengths are helpful to achieving the objective, weaknesses are areas that are *harmful* to achieving the objective. Depending on the goal, weaknesses can include the following: a lack of motivation, no vision or goals by leadership, poor communication, disinterest in teaching, no skills in the use of technology, tight budgets, too busy with secular activities, etc.

The third component is *opportunities*. For this component, we want to consider areas of *external* origin. These consist of attributes connected to the surrounding area, such as location, receptivity, influences, partnerships, and more. As with strengths, opportunities include areas that are *helpful* to achieving the objective. Depending on the goal, opportunities can include a good location for the building, a growing community, an excellent neighborhood school system, access to newspaper and radio advertisement, community-oriented business organizations (Lions, Optimists, Toastmasters), a poor community (a lack of material blessings often drives people to ask the church for help), and so on.

The final component is *threats*. For this component, we continue to look at areas of an *external* origin. Threats also consist of attributes in the surrounding environment, such as a lack of location, receptivity, influences, partnerships, and more. As with weaknesses, threats include areas that are *harmful* to achieving the objective. Depending on the goal, threats can include members living too far away to meet more often than Sunday and Wednesday, disinterest in spiritual discussions in the community, scheduled school activities on Wednesday nights, land-locked (the building is in a good location, but the ability to grow is limited because there's no space around it to expand), an affluent community (the abundance of material blessings seems to keep people from thinking they need God), Satan.

The information above is an illustration and not to be used per se. The idea is to get all the information about each of these four areas from members of the organization—get everyone thinking. The leader is a facilitator in this exercise and should write the brainstormed information on a whiteboard or large Post-it Notes. The leader is not to make suggestions that lead everyone to think in a specific direction. My suggestions for how to conduct a SWOT analysis with a group include the following steps:

1) I prefer to use the large Post-it Sheets, because I can place them on the walls. The size I use is 25" x 30", but any large size will work. Find something that allows you to write out everything mentioned. You may need several sheets for each area of the SWOT.

2) Start with strengths, then move through the others in order: weaknesses, opportunities, and threats.

3) Ask the group to list everything they can think of for each category before moving on through the discussion about the goal.

4) It's not uncommon for people to mention ideas that are opportunities while you're engaged in talking about strengths, or they may mention threats while the group is talking about weaknesses. This is okay. You can either ask them to hold that thought, or go ahead and write it under that section and guide everyone back to the section under discussion.

I'm confident that others have conducted SWOT analyses differently than I do. If you're aware of another way and are more comfortable with that approach, by all means, please use what works best for you. The purpose of a SWOT analysis is simply to flesh out the goal and determine if the strengths and opportunities outweigh the weaknesses and threats. If they do, then this should be a green light to move forward and work on how to establish the plans to reach the goal. But remember, if weaknesses and threats outweigh the strengths and opportunities, you might want to consider this a red light and pitch the goal out the window, or revise it and conduct another SWOT analysis. The process is time-consuming, but it makes a difference for getting the right goals in place and establishing the right plans to achieve them. The same SWOT analysis can be conducted with each new plan.

SOAR

The second tool, which closely follows the SWOT analysis diagram, is called SOAR. The acronym represents *strengths, opportunities, aspirations,* and *results.* The developers of SOAR wanted to provide an alternative to conducting a SWOT analysis. Before we look specifically at SOAR, we need to consider a little background. SOAR began with the introduction of appreciative inquiry (AI): "a vision-based approach of open dialogue that is designed to help organizations and their partners create a shared vision for the future and a mission to operate in the present."[2] Appreciative inquiry was about to give strategic planning a shot in the arm. Although SWOT analysis had been used for more than fifty years, organizations still seemed to struggle. Jacqueline Stavros, David Cooperrider, and D. Lynn Kelley believed that the inclusion of weaknesses and threats created a negative approach to the appreciative focus needed. The process was thus viewed as a 50/50 evaluation that prevented people from reaching greater success.[3] Ultimately, the design of AI is to seek "life-giving" input and reasons for past success in order to build a stronger future and focus. Examine the benefits of the appreciative approach to strategic planning. Appreciative inquiry

1)   focuses on the positive to crowd out the negative, which does not mean that negatives are ignored but are instead addressed with the hope and energy derived by seeing all that works well;

2)   builds organizational capacity beyond existing boundaries;

3)   builds relationships with partners;

4)   obtains input from all levels of the organization;

5)   obtains buy-in from all levels of the organization;

6)   allows the planning process to incorporate and connect values, vision, and mission statement to strategic goals, strategies, plans, and a positive and objective review of goals; and

7)   creates a shared set of organizational values and vision of the future organization.

David Cooperrider presented a 4-D model to describe how AI in strategic planning works. The model supplies

> a cycle of activities that guide members of an organization, group, or community through four stages: **discovery**—finding out about moments of excellence, core values and best practices; **dream**—envisioning positive possibilities; **design**—creating the structure, processes and relationships that will support the dream; and **destiny**—developing an effective inspirational plan for implementation.[4]

Including AI in the arena of strategic planning gave birth to SOAR. Therefore, by eliminating the two negative elements and presenting two positive ones—*aspirations* and *results*—SOAR provided a new evaluation process. My first look at SOAR came in a blog post from Global Learning Partners, written by Jay Ekleberry.[5]

I've included questions Ekleberry developed to conduct a SOAR analysis, and the following information illustrates what SOAR looks like in strategic planning.

Strengths: We begin with the question *What's working well?* Instead of considering internal capabilities, processes, experience, knowledge, and resources as strengths, the individual or organization examines the internal progress: What's working well? Why is it working well? How will that contribute to future growth and development? The focus is not so much on the available resources but rather to "**discover** the moments of excellence, core values, and best practices." Why these moments, core values, and best practices exist and how they can contribute to the future is the appreciative intent of this step. Knowing what works well clarifies the strengths of an individual and congregation, but you must build on those strengths as you explore opportunities.

Opportunities: Based on your strengths, ask, *What are the best opportunities for the future?* Examining the best opportunities, which build on the successful foundations laid with your strengths, takes you beyond the concept of *external* areas that are helpful to achieve the objective. This step encourages imagination: you "**dream**, envisioning positive possibilities." You explore the power behind simply asking, "What if?" and give yourself permission to really dream. This step fits well with the discussion from the first section about vision. Dream big. Consider the possibilities of what the future holds and what God can do through you if you dream gigantic dreams.

Aspirations: Based on the strengths and opportunities, ask, *What or who should we aspire to become?* Seldom do we ask this question, but when you explore what works well and give yourself permission to dream big, you'll enjoy an amazing payoff. At this point, you "**design**—creating the structure, processes and relationships that will support the dream." The purpose of this step is innovation, to project plans that incorporate the possibilities. Only when your vision is clear can you design plans that help you achieve the vision. The strategy of short-term goals provides a key component to developing the structure needed to move the individual or organization forward.

Results: The final component investigates the question *How will we measure progress toward our aspirations?* This is an inspirational step designed to evaluate progress and motivate

124

application. Cooperrider refers to this as "**destiny**—developing an effective inspirational plan for implementation." People want to be part of something bigger than themselves—something that leaves a lasting impact. However, leadership has the responsibility of guiding this process in order to develop a plan that inspires people to accomplish the work. When this happens, you will see results.

The chart below offers a contrast of these two strategic planning tools.[6]

SWOT ANALYSIS	SOAR APPROACH
Analysis Oriented	Action Oriented
Weakness & Threats Focus	Strengths & Opportunity focus
Competition Focus - Just Be Better	Possibility Focus - *Be the best!*
Incremental Improvement	Innovation & Breakthroughs
Top Down	Engagement of all Levels
Focus on Analysis ➤ Planning	Focus on Planning ➤ Implementation
Energy Depleting - *There are so many weaknesses and threats!*	Enegry Creating- *We are good and can become great!*
Attention to Gaps	Attention to Results

SOAR (strengths, opportunities, aspirations, and results) is not intended to eliminate the value and use of the SWOT analysis but, rather, provide an alternative. Both approaches to strategic planning have their own place, value, and purpose. When leaders have a vision, strategic planning guides the direction to reach it. Tools are needed to evaluate each step in the plan, and as James Floyd Kelly and Patrick Hood-Daniel suggest in the epigraph I included at the beginning of this chapter, "You can never have too many tools."[7] Let's look at one more valuable tool in the tool belt.

PERT Chart

The third tool is the PERT chart. As I mentioned in the previous chapter, PERT stands for "program evaluation and review technique." The development of the PERT chart dates back to 1958 and "a company called Booz Allen Hamilton, Inc. They were created for use by the US Navy's Special Projects unit as part of the Polaris submarine ballistic missile project." By design, the PERT chart is "a scheduling tool commonly used in project management to illustrate the dependencies and flow of project events and milestones."[8]

In its basic form, a PERT chart is a tool that provides benchmarks along a time line that allows for oversight of goals and plans. For our purposes, one side of the PERT chart describes the current situation. The information may consist of weekly membership attendance, number of elders, deacons, ministers, teachers, available resources, and any other information that describes the current status of your organization.

On the other side of the PERT chart is a list of goals to achieve during a twelve-month time period. There should be no more than five major goals. When you establish too many goals, people likely will become overwhelmed with the amount of work to be done. The result is frustration and discouragement, and—this is the worst part—they shut down. Nothing will get done. Especially in the early stages, it's better to have fewer goals that easily can be achieved. Be wise in choosing these major goals—make sure they're SMARTER.

Between these two points, you have a map. Each month of the year is listed across the top, and below are lines extending from the current status of your organization to the goals you want to accomplish by the end of the year. These lines represent different categories. You can have as many or as few as you like. From a general point of view, the following categories are fairly standard: *evangelism, advertising, activities, education, business,* and *miscellaneous.* Additional categories (*worship, youth, seniors, etc.*) can be added or swapped for any one of the six listed. Feel free to use as few as three or four. Everything depends on the nature of the goals to be accomplished.

Once the map is laid out, the next step is to place boxes along the lines under the appropriate month that describe what will be done during that month to achieve a goal. For example, under the month of

January, you may have a box on the *evangelism* line that says "revival meeting" and another box in May mentioning a mail-out of House to House, Heart to Heart. Under the month of July, on the *activities* line, you may put a box that says "July 4 Fish Fry or Cookout." The same procedure continues for each line. Note: You don't need a box under every month on every line—that would be overwhelming. Strategic planning is about knowing the goals and establishing the plans accordingly in order to aid in achievement of goals.

Once the map is completed, print it out on large paper, or have someone with artistic talent draw it on something larger. Place it somewhere visible where people can see it regularly. One possibility might be to leave several blank boxes on the map and allow everyone to write in suggestions for activities they want or areas they want to focus on. This process only strengthens leaders in better knowing their members. Ensure that everyone is familiar with the map. They need to know what the goals are for the year ahead and how the leaders plan to guide them to those goals. Organizations respond well to this knowledge.

These three major tools benefit leadership and congregation alike. They become an essential component of leadership like the life-giving source of oxygen. The ability to analyze goals and plans through a SWOT analysis, the use of the SOAR model, and mapping plans through a PERT chart all aid in building confidence for everyone involved. When people can see clearly where they're going and know the plans for getting there, a sense of stability and security exists. When this happens, people are more confident in their leaders.

Chapter 8
Legacy

Life is like a parachute jump, you've got to get it right the first time.
Eleanor Roosevelt

My dad passed away April 20, 2013, in Arkansas. He was seventy-eight years old. Throughout my entire life, I've only known his life's work as a focus on preaching the gospel. He was the best one-on-one teacher I've ever known. Untold numbers of people became Christians through his influence. His legacy was built on a vision and goals established early in his life. Let me share a little history to emphasize the significance of his legacy.

Harold Dean Turner was born March 7, 1935, in southern Missouri. He was the third of six boys born to Arch and Jewel Turner. Large families were common during those days, and because they worked on a farm, they worked hard. I remember Dad talking about my grandmother Jewel laboring over an open fire in the sweltering heat of the summer, canning food to store for the winter. He often talked about daily life on the farm: milking dairy cows, feeding chickens, and slopping hogs to slaughter for meat. In between, he worked at carrying stay-bolt railroad ties all day for about fifty cents per day. He was a physically tough man.

The Turner family wasn't religious. A few religious organizations existed close to where they lived, but the Turner boys simply observed these from the outside. As most youth do, they poked fun at some of the religious practices of the time. In high school, Dad met Mom, Mildred Louise Mallernee, and they married young. In fact, my mom was so young that she had to get signed permission from her father to get married. Not long after they were married, Dad and Mom made their way north to Iowa, where Mom's sister and brother-in-law lived.

In the early years of their marriage, both Dad and Mom investigated several religious groups, but none seemed to interest Dad much—he was looking for *something*, but at the time he wasn't sure what it was. Dad learned how to do electrical work and took a job working for a cement company as an electrician. Their move to Iowa was more providential than they could ever have imagined. While living near Davenport, Dad met a man named Travis Leopard, who invited my parents to a revival. During this meeting, Dad heard what he had been looking for—and he obeyed God's call. Mom soon followed in her baptism, and Dad was asked to start serving in the church.

Before long, my dad was asked to preach a lesson. Who would have known that with this one lesson, God began forming one of His great evangelists? From Iowa, my parents moved back to southern Missouri, where my dad began his lifelong career of preaching and teaching others about Jesus Christ. During the first fifteen years of their marriage, four children were born to them: two sons and two daughters. A legacy was in the making.

I could write an entire book on the legacy of Harold Turner and the example of Christianity he left. He wasn't perfect—as none of us are on this earth. But he was humble, and he desired nothing more than to help others know Jesus and get to heaven. His legacy involves a knowledge of Scripture few can match. He read through the entire New Testament once each month and the Old Testament twice each year. He knew the Bible. His legacy includes a love of family. He fiercely loved his wife, children, and grandchildren. I'll always remember how he would say of Mom, "She's a mighty good woman." And she was. Whatever he had, he was willing to give. His legacy involves more friends than I can count. But above all, his legacy is eternal. He shared his love for God and Jesus with everyone who would listen. I cannot remember a time when he wasn't studying with someone each week. He helped more people come to know Jesus throughout the years than I can remember. He had a gift.

Legacy! What legacy will you and I leave for our families, friends, and the church? An endless supply of books have been written about legacy—what it means, what type of legacy to leave, who we leave a legacy to, examples of legacies, and more. I begin by defining the word. Legacy has three definitions:

1) A gift by will, especially of money or other personal property;

2)   Something transmitted by or received from an ancestor
        or predecessor or from the past;

3)   A candidate for membership in an organization (such
        as a school or fraternal order) who is given special
        status because of a familial relationship to a member.[1]

   While the most common understanding of legacy relates to a
monetary gift left for an individual or organization, for the purposes
of this book, I'm not talking about a physical gift. A legacy received
from an ancestor or predecessor—or one that we leave for the future—
speaks to something of greater substance.
   From a leadership perspective, John Maxwell says,
"Achievement comes when someone does big things **by** themselves.
Success comes when they entrust others to do things **for** them.
Significance comes when they develop leaders to do great things **with**
them. **Legacy comes when we put leaders in a position to do great
things without us**" (emphasis mine).[2] Leaders in the church today
need to give serious consideration to the legacy they leave the church.
Over the past few years, I've studied, investigated, asked, and talked
with leaders across the country.
   I've visited, worked with, and heard about numerous
congregations and leaders, and I find it terribly frightening that of
these, only two churches had active plans for preparing the next
generation to lead. We're living in a time when congregations suffer
from the poor legacies of previous generations that did not adequately
equip others to lead. If something isn't done now about this situation,
the future will continue down the same path.
   Biblically speaking, we see a number of legacies with God's
leaders. We could easily pick apart the flaws of imperfect men God
used to lead His people, but think about the legacy Moses left for
Joshua. Moses had many great qualities: we read that God would raise
up a prophet "like" him (Deuteronomy 18:15–22), which we later
learn is Christ (Acts 3:22). Moses's failure to treat God as holy by
striking the rock instead of speaking to it kept him from entering the
promised land (Numbers 20:8–12). Overall, Moses left Joshua with a
commission and a legacy that allowed God to work through Joshua

to lead his people into the land He had promised Abraham (Genesis 13:15).

We can also see this in the life of David and the legacy he left to Solomon. Again, David had more than a few flaws. His adultery with Bathsheba and murder of her husband Uriah come to mind (2 Samuel 11). However, we also need to remember his greatest characteristic: he was a man after God's own heart (Acts 13:22). The book of Psalms helps us to see the heart of David and his passion for God—the best descriptions of God and His nature come to us from the writings of David. His plans to build the temple demonstrate the desire he had to honor God in a physical and elaborate way. Although he was ultimately not allowed to build it, he passed on the plans to his son Solomon. The temple constructed by Solomon indicates the legacy David left to him.

When we read the Gospel accounts of Matthew, Mark, Luke, and John, we find the greatest legacy ever: the one left by our Savior, Jesus. The fact that Jesus lived a perfect life goes without saying. We can easily point to the compassion of Jesus and how He healed the sick, fed the hungry, gave sight to the blind and strength to the lame, and raised the dead . . . and with these we're only at the tip of the proverbial iceberg. In perhaps a slight exaggeration, John indicated that if Jesus's works "were written in detail, I suppose that even the world itself would not contain the books that would be written" (John 21:25). In Scripture, we read the amazing way that Jesus led people to see Him differently—especially those who were not of Jewish descent. The account of Jesus with the Samaritan woman at the well led her and her people to see Jesus not just as an ordinary Jew but as the Savior of the world (John 4:42). The secondary purpose of this was to help the disciples recognize that Jesus came for more than just one nation of people—He also came for the Samaritans, with whom the Jews would not associate (John 4:9). Consider the legacy Jesus left for how to deal with people who are caught in sin. Do you remember the woman caught in adultery (John 8)? Through this, we learn a powerful lesson about how to deal with accusers and the accused. Finally, there is the legacy of what we call the Great Commission (Matthew 28:18–20; Mark 16:15–16; Luke 24:46–49): Jesus instructed the apostles to go into all the world, and He promised He would be with them. Suffice it to say that the legacy of Jesus is one that continues nearly two thousand years later.

The last legacy is one the apostles left to the church. Building on the legacy left by Christ, the apostles carried the baton forward. At one point, the gospel had been "proclaimed in all creation under heaven" (Colossians 1:23). How fulfilling to know they had accomplished the task. The legacy left by the apostles involves more than the proclamation of the gospel—although this task remains the anthem of Christianity today. The apostles passed the same baton to us they received from Jesus. We begin with a legacy of relationships. At least twenty-four times throughout the New Testament, as Christians we're reminded of our relationship to "one another." We're taught to love one another (John 13:34–35), be devoted to and give preference to one another (Romans 12:10), comfort one another (1 Thessalonians 4:18), serve one another (Galatians 5:13), encourage one another (Hebrews 3:13; 10:25), pray for one another (James 5:16) . . . and these are just a few. We also find a legacy of praise. God is worthy to receive all glory, honor, and power (Revelation 4:11). He deserves our adoration and praise because of His grace, mercy, and love (Ephesians 2:4–10). Not only did the apostles write about the need for us to praise our God, we also find their example in the most difficult of circumstances. Paul and Barnabas had been arrested, beaten, and thrown into prison for preaching Jesus. The text tells us that at about midnight, they were "praying and singing hymns of praise to God, and the prisoners were listening to them" (Acts 16:25). Are you listening to them and carrying on the legacy today?

Legacy Preparation

How you approach the legacy you want to leave is a personal decision. However, if you want to know how to prepare for this legacy, let me share a few steps presented by John Maxwell in *21 Irrefutable Laws of Leadership.*

Vision

Lead today with tomorrow in view. I refer you back to section 1, in which I discussed vision. When you know where you're headed tomorrow, you know how to live today. It's vital to recognize that your actions today influence the outcome of tomorrow's leaders and that the concept of leadership changes with each generation. Generation Z views leadership differently than their parents do. In a recent interview with a college sophomore, Dr. Tim Elmore asked how Gen Z saw leadership differently. The response might surprise you:

> I think my parents' and grandparents' generations see leadership as a position to fill and a responsibility to fulfill. I see it as activism. Even Millennials colored within the lines when they were students on campus. We feel leadership is about making changes to corruption, waste, misspending, and the mistreatment of marginalized people.[3]

With this major paradigm shift in thinking about leadership, we have to consider how we will lead with tomorrow in view. What is your vision for leadership and how to grow leaders?

Learn to Multiply

Maxwell says, "To grow, lead followers. To multiply, lead leaders." In Mac Lake's book *The Multiplication Effect*, Lake focuses on developing a plan for training future leaders. His reasoning is based on the following explanation:

> *The greater reason for developing leaders is to cultivate the God-given leadership gifts in others. . . .* When we're driven by others' potential rather than our pain, leadership development takes on a whole different feel. It is then that our efforts at leadership development become a natural way of thinking. It becomes a part of our regular routine. We don't start with the position that needs to be filled; we start with the person that can be developed.[4]

Lake's approach to leadership development is based on the model of Jesus walking alongside others to "transform their spirit and skills." Leading today is not only about ensuring that people know how to follow and where to go—leading today must include a focus

134

on preparing the next generation to lead. The task before us requires a great deal of time and energy, but the benefits of investing in future leaders pays dividends that exceed our lifetime. This is our legacy, and it comes with a price.

Sacrifice

Pay the price today to ensure success for tomorrow. I've never met anyone unwilling to sacrifice whatever is necessary when they know the benefit of the sacrifice. One of the most powerful examples is a mother and her children. Have you ever watched a mother go without in order that her children have what they need or want? I've seen mothers go hungry in order to feed their children. I've watched mothers go without nice clothes so their children could have the basketball shoes they want. I've witnessed mothers go without sleep to ensure their children were safe and healthy. I was the beneficiary of my mother's sacrifice, and I've observed this sacrifice in my wife as a mother, as well as in my daughter and daughters-in-law with my grandchildren. There's something in a mother that naturally compels her to makes these sacrifices. When leaders understand that their legacy is about preparing future leaders, they must develop a natural ability to make necessary sacrifices for the leaders of tomorrow.

Group Leadership above Individual Leadership

No one can do it alone. The larger the group, the more important this concept is. In the book I mentioned earlier, Mac Lake discusses the difference between mentoring and creating a culture of discipleship. He claims, "We will never create movement unless we develop a culture in which leadership development is normative. . . . And if we don't build a culture of leadership development today, we will have a deficiency of leaders in our pipeline tomorrow."[5]

Lake doesn't favor the one-on-one mentoring approach or groups larger than six. The larger the number, the more difficult to maintain a relational connection. Lake favors an approach of group leadership development that focuses on three to five people. The idea is to teach people who desire to learn leadership skills, using whatever time is needed to prepare them to work with three to five of their own, and so on. The web effect of this approach quickly multiplies those who continue to create a pipeline of leaders for the future.

Walk Away with Integrity

Learn how to walk away and allow your successors to do their own thing. Lincoln Young is a paraplegic; he spoke at my work one wintry day in Denver. His story is amazing, and his motivational ability is nothing less than incredible. He shared several thoughts with us that day, but one that stood out to me was about "walking away." He talked about the number of people in the Bible who walked away from God or Christ and the impact on their lives. In *21 Irrefutable Laws of Leadership*, Maxwell emphasizes the need to walk away with integrity. I've seen many professional athletes retire, only to return to their sport with another team or in a different position. Before long people witness the lack of the speed and ability that had made them the legends they were. On many occasions, I've thought they should have walked away while they were on top—go out as winners. I appreciate that they desire to continue doing what they're passionate about—something their whole life has been focused on. But there comes a time when the next generation must carry the baton. The same is true for leaders. We need to know how to walk away and allow the next generation to lead. Our task—should we choose to accept it—is to prepare them. We're to train the next generation so that when we walk away, we can do so with the integrity of knowing we left a legacy of leadership worthy of following.

Building Your Legacy

Before you finish reading this chapter, stop and take a few moments to list ways you can build a legacy for the future of your family and church. If you're working through this material with a group of people, give each person a 3" x 5" card and ask them write down two or three ways to build a leadership legacy for your organization. Compile the answers and share them with the group. The following are a few suggestions to add to your list.

You Must Know the Legacy You Intend to Leave

You cannot decide this for anyone but yourself. Each person must know the type of legacy they desire to leave. Martin Luther King, Jr. was a great civil rights leader who left a legacy and vision we have only begun to see fulfilled. His famous "I Have a Dream" speech continues to echo through my mind. It was my second birthday, August 28, 1963, when King stood before a crowd of more than 250,000 people in Washington, DC. In this, he left a legacy of hope for a better future in America. King knew the legacy he wanted to leave for this country—he wanted America to be a place where people were not judged by the color of their skin but by the content of their character. Leaders today need to know the legacy they desire to leave—but it takes more than simply knowing it.

You Must Live It Now

Consider the speech King gave on that hot summer day; his dream for unity, equality, freedom, and fellowship among blacks and whites will only happen when people live those ideas today. The legacy we intend to leave for tomorrow means little as long as it remains a mere concept. We have to live it each day. King did, and it cost him his life just four years and seven months later. The heart of leadership rests in the task of living now the legacy we want to leave for tomorrow. In chapter 6, I asked you to think about your eulogy. What do you want people to say at your funeral? Whatever you want them to say must be lived now. Character is the result of intentionality—it doesn't happen by accident. And your legacy must not end with you.

You Must Determine Your Successors

Who will carry the torch of your leadership? As a father, I want my sons and son-in-law to be leaders in their families. More than that, I want them to help the church as future leaders. Additionally, I work with leaders across this country with the intent of helping them see the value of preparing leaders for tomorrow. How about you? Who will carry on your legacy? Maybe you are planning for your sons, sons-in-law, daughters, or daughters-in-law. Perhaps you're planning for someone in your circle of influence. I pray that you're looking to the next generation in the church and implementing ways to prepare them to lead. With the numbers of Christians declining across this country, young people leaving the church, and members abandoning the faith, we have a serious crisis on our hands. We can't sit on the sidelines and hope someone else will come along to change it. It's up to us to make a difference.

You Must Train Them

I realize this can be the most challenging part of the discussion. Maybe you realize the need—but you don't know how to go about it. Developing a plan for training others to lead requires focus and conviction. The task will not be easy. However, it's worth the effort. I encourage you to set aside a specific time each week to work through material on leadership with your successor(s). There are lessons or books that will assist in filling this gap. You might start with online lessons at the Sunset Academy of Leadership Training (salt.sibi.cc/category/saltlessons/). Another resource is the book by Mac Lake I mentioned earlier: *The Multiplication Effect*. Lake provides information on starting a plan for training leaders. But most importantly, begin! Sometimes the most difficult step is the first one. Once that step is taken, the rest will seem easier.

One of the most important topics leaders can discuss is legacy. When you or I are no longer here on this earth, how will we be remembered? We must ensure that we do not make the same mistakes today that others have made in the past. The legacies we leave must be ones that ensure the future of leadership for the church—not only for the next generation but for the one after that. The words of Batterson sum up the thought well: "Your greatest legacy isn't your dream; it's the dreams you inspire in others! You aren't just a dreamer; you are a dreamcatcher."[6] It begins with you and me . . . *now!*

A section on goal planning is not the most exciting to read. However, the steps I've identified will help you and your ministry as you think about why you need goals, how to create and achieve goals, and implementing plans to move you forward. The SWOT, SOAR, and PERT chart tools will aid you in the journey. Goals are essential to the success of your leadership like the essential nature of the air we breathe for life. You've endured, and if you've come this far, I encourage you to keep reading. There are two more life-and-leadership essentials to discuss: next is your character as a leader.

Building Block 3
Character: The Influence of Life and Leadership

The Lead-In: Where There Is Water There Is Life
Thousands have lived without love, not one without water.
W. H. Auden

Rachel Beckwith was a little girl with a desire to provide clean water to people with little or no access to it. As her ninth birthday drew near, she did not request any gifts but instead tried to raise $300 to support an organization called charity:water, a nonprofit that provides access to clean drinking water. They have now funded 51,438 water projects in twenty-eight countries around the world. More than eleven million people have access to clean drinking water as a result of their efforts.[1]

After learning about charity:water, Rachel wanted to help. Her mom shared online how strongly her daughter felt about the situation:

On June 12th 2011, I'm turning 9. I found out that millions of people don't live to see their 5th birthday. And why? Because they didn't have access to clean, safe water so I'm celebrating my birthday like never before. I'm asking from everyone I know to donate to my campaign instead of gifts for my birthday. Every penny of the money raised will go directly to fund freshwater projects in developing nations.[2]

Despite her efforts, she didn't reach her goal: she only raised $220. Her mom assured her it was enough and that she could raise more the next year. But Rachel died in a car accident just a month later. News outlets picked up on Rachel's story and shared her selfless vision of helping others obtain access to clean drinking water. The result was a campaign that has raised more than a million dollars to bring clean drinking water to countries around the world.

Devastated at the loss of her daughter, yet overwhelmed by the outpouring of support, Rachel's mother posted, "I am in awe of the overwhelming love to take my daughter's dream and make it a reality. In the face of unexplainable pain you have provided undeniable

hope. Thank you for your generosity! I know Rachel is smiling!"
Ryan Meeks served as pastor of the Eastlake Community Church,
where Rachel's family attended. The following is his description of
Rachel and the result of her vision for clean drinking water: "There's
nothing natural about losing a 9-year-old girl. It's horrible. *But there's
something that we're attracted to when life comes out of death*"
(emphasis mine). Rachel's dream has been realized thousands of
times over, and charity:water continues to provide life through clean
drinking water to millions of people every day.

Nearly one out of every ten people globally (785 million) live
without clean water, which is double the population in the United
States. Where there is water, there is life. The validity of this thought
is demonstrated every day. According to Scott Harrison, founder and
CEO of charity:water, the number of people who die from a lack of
access to clean water is more than any form of violence, including war.

A major shift in my life took place in 1992. I used to drink
a twenty-four ounce glass of milk every morning for breakfast (and
anytime there were cookies to eat) and at least two liters of soda each
day. You could safely say I was a hefty young man. During this period
of life, my hair began thinning, and I lived in denial for several years
before eventually shaving it all off. Since I didn't have any control
over the receding nature of my hair, I felt compelled to do something
about my weight. My first step was to cut out soda. Within thirty days,
I lost about ten pounds. It was the boost I needed. For the next thirty
days, I cut out milk. Another ten pounds came off. I was motivated!
I witnessed visible results with a few small changes. Exercise came
next, and I enjoyed the lifestyle change that continued to move me
toward my goal weight.

I had cut out soda and milk, but I had to drink something.
Water was my go-to drink. Like many people, I did not much care
for water. After all, it has no flavor. Isn't flavor the reason to drink
anything? I pressed on, and after several months, I began acquiring
more of a workable relationship with water consumption. I discovered
that water does in fact have flavor. If you've ever experienced the
differences between well water, municipal water, filtered water, and
spring water, you know exactly what I mean. There's a difference.

My exercise routine increased, and I drank more water and
began actually to enjoy the flavor. Fast-forward to 2000. I decided to

learn more about the health benefits of food and water, and in doing so, I came across a wealth of information about the essential nature of water.

The chemical breakdown of water is H2O: two hydrogen atoms bonded with one oxygen atom. Read that again. How amazing is it that oxygen—which is essential for life—also comprises the third essential! As a foundation, consider the following: "Water is the only natural substance that is found in all three physical states—liquid, solid, and gas—at the temperatures normally found on Earth. Water freezes at 32° Fahrenheit (F) and boils at 212°F (at sea level, but 186.4° at 14,000 feet). Water is unusual in that the solid form, ice, is less dense than the liquid form, which is why ice floats."[3] Children learn these basic facts early in their educational journey. However, there is even more to this incredible life-giving substance.

Molly Sargen's research at Harvard University led to significant findings about the essential nature of water. She writes, "Water makes up 60–75% of human body weight. A loss of just 4% of total body water leads to dehydration, and a loss of 15% can be fatal. Likewise, a person could survive a month without food but wouldn't survive 3 days without water."[4] Sargen goes on to say, "Water is directly involved in many chemical reactions to build and break down important components of the cell. Photosynthesis, the process in plants that creates sugars for all life forms, requires water." The food and oxygen provided by plants also requires the essential nature of water for life.

Of the earth's surface, 71 percent is covered in water. Not only does most of the earth consist of water, so do our physical bodies. The majority of resources claim that approximately 70 percent of the body is water: 73 percent of the brain and heart, 83 percent of the lungs, 64 percent of our skin, 79 percent of our muscles and kidneys, 31 percent of our bones, and 83 percent of cells. According to the Unites States Geological Survey organization, water is essential to keep our bodies going for the following eleven reasons:

1)   Forms saliva (digestion)

2)   Keeps mucosal membranes moist

3)   Allows body's cells to grow, reproduce, and survive

4)   Flushes body waste, mainly in urine

5)   Lubricates joints

6)   The major component of most body parts

7)   Needed by the brain to manufacture hormones and neurotransmitters

8)   Regulates body temperature (sweating and respiration)

9)   Acts as a shock-absorber for brain and spinal cord

10)   Converts food to components needed for survival-digestion

11)   Helps deliver oxygen all over the body[5]

Matt Weber says, "There are organisms on Earth that do not need oxygen to live. They metabolize hydrogen or methane or a number of other compounds. But all life on Earth shares one thing in common: we all need water to live. Without exception."[6] In humans, water "acts as both a solvent and a delivery mechanism, dissolving essential vitamins and nutrients from food and delivering them to cells."[7]

The adage "Where there is water, there is life" provides a powerful truth to the essential properties previously discussed. In fact, the National Aeronautics and Space Administration (NASA) begins their efforts to find life on other planets by searching for water. Scientists believe that if they find water, there's potential for some form of life. While there may not be the potential for human life, the association of water to life is evident.

As I come to the end of this discussion, think about the essential nature of water and why water is such a life-giving substance. Live Science assistant managing editor, Tia Ghose, writes, "Water is found everywhere on Earth, from the polar ice caps to steamy geysers.

And wherever water flows on this planet, you can be sure to find life."[8] She further explains, "Water is essential simply because it's a liquid at Earth-like temperatures. Because it flows, water provides an efficient way to transfer substances from a cell to the cell's environment." The result points us to the essential nature of water.

Science indicates how water makes up the largest part of our body and shows water to be the foundational building block to and substance of life. Just as water is the very substance of life, character is the substance of leadership. Character is the building block of leadership success. Without character, there is no leadership. This section focuses on this substance of character. The character of the individual determines the strength of their influence and leadership ability. I begin with a look at the biblical precedent of character and leadership.

Chapter 9
Godly Character—Psalm 15

*It is the way one treats his inferiors more than
the way he treats his equals which reveals one's real character.*
Charles Bayard Mitchell

More than four billion fortune cookies are made in the United States each year. The fortune cookie was initially intended to be a dessert and later came to symbolize—among other things—good fortune, fate, wisdom, and the mysteries of the unknown.[1] When you understand the essential nature of enzymes (food), these facts are important. However, I'll be the first to tell you that I don't put much stock in fortune cookies. After all, they really don't tell us about the future. They are more like proverbial statements that apply to everyone.

However, I've received a few fortune cookies that were somewhat . . . well . . . *amazingly* accurate. In the spring of 2009, I was preparing for my first trip out of the United States as director of extension schools for the Bear Valley Bible Institute International. At the time I accepted the position, I did not have a passport. The first order of business was to expedite the process. A few weeks later, I received my passport and prepared for my first of many trips. The first stop was Nigeria.

The week before I was scheduled to leave, my wife and I visited a little Chinese restaurant close to our home. The fortune cookies arrived alongside the bill, and when I opened mine, I read, "Your feet shall step on the soils of many lands." I still have this slip of paper to remind me of that phase in my life. In addition to Nigeria, I've visited numerous countries all over West and East Africa. I've been to Europe, Nepal, India, Korea, and Cambodia as well as countries in Central and South America. My feet have stepped on the soils of many lands.

A few years later, my wife and I were back at this same Chinese restaurant. After the meal, I opened my fortune cookie. This time, the message said, "God has given you one face. You make for yourself another." I saved this one as well. This message is about character—God has given us the face that everyone sees, but the one we make for ourselves is about our character.

Earlier this year, I was asked to speak at a leadership retreat for a church in Fredericksburg, Texas. I enjoyed meeting the leaders in the congregation and discussing various facets of leadership, along with the needs for the congregation. I also shared the story about my fortune cookie experience. While driving home later that afternoon, I received a text from one of the ministers who had lunch at a—you guessed it—Chinese restaurant in town. When he opened his fortune cookie, this is what it said: "Character matters; leadership descends from character." You can't make this stuff up. As I said, I do not put stock in fortune cookies, but I've certainly seen some interesting thoughts surface from them.

I've collected several interesting quotes about character, but two rise to the surface. The first is from General Norman Schwarzkopf, who said, "Leadership is the potent combination of strategy and character. If you must be without one, be without strategy." The other statement is from J. R. Miller. His thoughts were, "The only thing that walks back from the tomb with the mourners and refuses to be buried is the character of the man. What a man is survives him. It can never be buried." Both thoughts highlight the significance of what I believe to be one of the most essential components of leadership: character. The challenge is determining the nature of our character.

Over the past ten years, I've reflected on character many times. God truly gives us one face, but we make for ourselves another. John Maxwell wrote, "Talent is a gift, but character is a choice." The choices we make in life determine our character, and our character determines the choices we make. The people we choose to most often associate with says a lot about our character. The activities we choose to participate in speaks about our character. The words we choose to use when around others communicates much about our character. Our choice of priorities indicates the nature of our character.

Character is vital to our relationships with others, including our relationship with God. First, think about the people in your life that you admire. Is it not their character that causes you to admire them most? Think about the way the world views high-profile people. We're all familiar with professional athletes, entertainers (actors and actresses), musicians, politicians, and more. These are people who have unbelievable talent— talent that most people would give anything to possess. But sadly, talent alone does not reveal their character. There are many times in moments of weakness or vulnerability that these talented individuals make decisions that damage their character. When that happens, it changes the way we see them. The same is true for all of us. Because we're Christians, people watch everything we do and listen to everything we say. They measure our choices with what we profess to believe. When we face those moments of weakness or vulnerability, we can make choices that damage our character at best and destroy it at worst. The same is especially true for leaders. Just as water is the substance of life, character is the substance of leadership, because both provide the building blocks for survival and success.

Secondly, we also find that character is critical in our relationships with God. Biblically speaking, we could turn to numerous passages to explore the subject of character. I've chosen a passage from the book of Psalms. Psalm 15 is a powerful description of the type of character that God seeks from those who desire a relationship with Him. In writing this Psalm, David did not exhaust all the possibilities of what it means to have character, but what he did say drives home the point we need to consider as it relates to our character.

The psalm begins by asking two questions in verse 1. I initially approached this verse thinking it was a Hebrew parallelism. In the Hebrew language we often find parallelisms; that is, saying the same thing but in two different ways. However, upon digging a little more deeply, I discovered something relevant to the discussion. David asked, "O Lord, who may abide in Your tent? Who may dwell on Your holy hill?" Both questions deal with being in the presence of God. When we examine the two words associated with the individual in God's presence, we find two different thoughts expressed. First, he asked, "Who may abide?" The word *abide* is a word that means to "dwell for a time as a newcomer."[2] The concept involves entering into the presence of God. Second, he asked, "Who may dwell?" The word *dwell* means to "settle down to abide."[3] The idea expressed by this word is permanence. It would appear David was asking what type of character can enter into and stay in God's presence. The answer to the question comes in verse 2 with a threefold response: "He who walks with integrity, and works righteousness, and speaks truth in his heart." Let's look at each.

First, "He who walks with integrity." The word *integrity* carries a range of implications. For a number of years I've asked a variety of people the following question: "How do you define integrity?" Responses usually include ideas such as honesty, goodness, truthfulness, trustworthiness, etc., but the most common response I hear is "Integrity is who you are when no one else is watching." In a similar way, from a spiritual perspective, I've heard it said, "Being a Christian is who you are in the dark." The thought speaks to practicing the presence of God.

Years ago, I was preaching in Arkansas, and I prepared a series of lessons that focused on practicing the presence of God. I really thought I had come up with something unique— something no one else had thought of before. Two days later, I received a book in the mail: *The Practice of the Presence of God* by Brother Lawrence.[4] There really is nothing new under the sun. Think about the application for just a moment. If there are places you would go, things you would say, activities you would participate in that you would not if your spiritual leaders were sitting next to you, then you give more respect to a person than you do to God. God sees it all anyway. Simply because we cannot see Him with the naked eye does not mean He isn't there or that He cannot see us. Practice the presence of God.

Integrity is a powerful thought. When we look at the original word, we find an interesting definition: the Hebrew word, *tamim*, has to do with being "complete, whole, entire, healthful, sound, wholesome, unimpaired, having integrity."[5] The word is used most often in the book of Leviticus in reference to the sacrifices offered to God. These sacrifices had to be without blemish—complete, entire, unimpaired, having integrity. The equivalent Greek word is used in the New Testament in connection to Jesus. As Peter writes about the price of redemption that Jesus paid, he describes it as "precious blood, as of a lamb unblemished and *spotless*, the blood of Christ" (1 Peter 1:19; emphasis mine).

We could look at several locations in Scripture where this concept is found, but the point is the same: integrity is vital to one's character. When we examine the character of an individual who can walk into and stay in the presence of God, the first quality listed is one who walks with integrity.

Second, David wrote, "and works righteousness." As with integrity, when I ask people to define righteousness, I get several responses. Generally, the thought is doing what is right—or doing what is right in the sight of God. While this is correct, there is a bit more to this word. Closely associated with the word translated as "integrity," righteousness speaks to a moral and ethical standard of what is right, specifically relating to weights and measures.[6]

What I find most significant about this word is that it's also translated as "just" or "justice." Throughout the Old and New Testaments, we find the word *righteous* or *righteousness* and *just* or *justice* used interchangeably. We most often find *justice* translated in association with God's relationship to His people, specifically His actions toward them. God also instructed His people, "You shall do no injustice in judgment; you shall not be partial to the poor nor defer to the great, but you are to judge your neighbor fairly" (Leviticus 19:15). Moses later wrote, "Justice, and *only justice,* you shall pursue, that you may live and possess the land which the Lord your God is giving you" (Deuteronomy 16:20). After describing how Israel's iniquities and sin had separated them from God, Isaiah pointed out that Israel did not "plead honestly. They trust in confusion and speak lies" (Isaiah 59:1–4). Later, Micah asked the question, "O man, what is good; and what does the Lord require of you but to do justice, to love kindness, and to walk humbly with your God" (Micah 6:8)? The message was clear: God intends His people to demonstrate justice.

Each of these passages directly relates to the practice of justice for the poor, orphan, widow, and stranger in the land. In the law, God required Israel to leave the corners of the harvested fields and fallen fruit from the vineyard for the needy and the stranger (Leviticus 19:9–10). God held Israel responsible for carrying out these acts of justice for those who were less fortunate. When they failed to fulfill this instruction, God brought justice upon Israel. He punished them, and they were sent into captivity. Amos reminded Israel of this truth and urged them to "Hate evil, love good, and establish justice in the gate! Perhaps the LORD God of hosts may be gracious to the remnant of Joseph" (Amos 5:15).

I mention this because of how it fits with the words of Jesus. The greatest sermon ever recorded is found in Matthew 5–7—what we call the "Sermon on the Mount." Consider the audience: Israel. Think about their understanding of the word translated "righteousness" or "justice." Even though our English translations use the term *righteousness*, read through these passages again and think about them in light of what we now understand regarding justice. Jesus said, "Blessed are those who hunger and thirst for [justice], for they shall be satisfied" (Matthew 5:6). Near the end of chapter 6, he said, "Seek first His kingdom and His [justice], and all these things will be added to you" (Matthew 6:33). Have you ever considered why Jesus said to seek first God's kingdom *and* His justice? One might assume that if we're first seeking God's kingdom, this would include his justice. Jesus, however, emphasized both. Perhaps the answer is that Jesus questioned why we are anxious about what we eat, drink, or wear; He said that the Gentiles seek after these things and our Father knows we need them. Then, He told us to seek first God's kingdom and His justice. When we do all these things, what we need will be added to us. In between these two passages, we find Jesus saying, "Beware of practicing your [justice] before men to be noticed by them; otherwise you have no reward with your Father who is in heaven" (Matthew 6:1). Immediately following this thought, He spoke about giving to the poor.

The religious leaders of the day were focused more on being seen than they were on fulfilling what God desired of them. As a result, we find Jesus saying, "Unless your [justice] surpasses that of the scribes and Pharisees, you will not enter the kingdom of heaven" (Matthew 5:20). Jesus knew and taught this necessity to His disciples to ensure that those who were less fortunate received what they needed. This is God's justice. Jesus's brother later wrote, "Pure and undefiled religion in the sight of *our* God and Father is this: to visit the orphans *and* widows in their distress, and to keep oneself unstained by the world" (James 1:27). Christians, we need to wake up to the calling of our God when it comes to how we use our wealth in the world today. It has not been given to us for ourselves but as a tool to help those in the world who do not have the same benefits. In this, I'm speaking to myself as much as I am to you.

Returning to the text of Psalm 15, we reflect on the character of the individual who can walk into and stay in the presence of God. David said this is the one who walks with integrity and works justice. When we think about character, how does it get any clearer than God's desire for those who carry out His justice by providing for those less fortunate?

Finally, David revealed that the one who goes into and stays in the presence of God "speaks truth in his heart." There are two parts to examine here: truth and heart. When you think about truth, you may have thoughts related to honesty, i.e. what is true. Or you may think about God's Word. Jesus said, "Sanctify them in the truth; Your word is truth" (John 17:17). By definition, the Hebrew word *met* means "firmness, faithfulness, truth, reliability, sureness, sure reward."[7] The definition fits with how we might associate someone speaking truth in their heart.

When David uses the word heart, we tend to think about the seat of one's emotions. As I mentioned in chapter 4, Simon Sinek identifies two parts of the brain: all emotions flow through the limbic, or inner, part of the brain. Certainly the value of processing truth through the heart is essential to the character that enters and stays in the presence of God. Also, consider the fact that David said, "He speaks truth *in* his heart" (emphasis mine). Initially, we might associate this thought with the following statement of Jesus: "But the things that proceed out of the mouth come from the heart" (Matthew 15:18). The remainder of the psalm shares thoughts related to how this individual speaks: "He does not slander with his tongue" (Psalm 15:3a) and "he swears to his own hurt and does not change" (15:4b). However, in verse 2, David was not addressing what comes out of our mouths but what is spoken *in* the heart. The difference is key to knowing the character of one who enters into—and remains in—the presence of God.

For the majority of my life I've heard lessons that focused on Psalm 15, especially on the three words I've discussed for the last few pages. After digging a little more deeply, I learned something significant about this text and its relationship to the discussion of character. While the three words—*integrity, righteousness, and truth*—are key words to understand, they're not the three most important words in this passage. The three most important words to which I refer are *walks, works,* and *speaks*. In the original language, these words are known as noun-verb participles. What that means is that they function as both noun and verb at the same time. The psalmist wanted the reader to know that character is not just about what someone does but about who they are on the inside. As we understand character, it all fits. As I'm sure you've experienced, people can do the right things on the outside with a corrupt heart. My dad used to say, "You can fool some of the people some of the time. You might even fool most of the people most of the time. But, even if it were possible to fool all the people all of the time, you still can't fool God."

When it comes to character, David identified the type of character that can enter into and stay in the presence of God. The individual who *walks* with integrity, *works* justice, and *speaks* truth in their heart. Again, this idea involves more than just what someone does—it's about who they are on the inside. If I were to sum up the whole of these three words and the context of David's question, the word that comes to mind is *trustworthy*. This is where true character resides. Like springs of water supply life to our bodies, a trustworthy character becomes the spring of life to our leadership. In the next chapter, I turn our attention to trust.

Chapter 10
Trust

The best way to find out if you can trust somebody is to trust them.
Ernest Hemingway

In 2006, my wife and I attended the Chamber of Commerce banquet in Greenbrier, Arkansas. The guest speaker that night was Houston Nutt, former head coach of the Arkansas Razorback football team. He began with an explanation about how every incoming freshman in the Arkansas Razorback football program was approached by the coaching staff. They impressed upon the young player what an incredible privilege it was to be part of the Razorbacks. Then, they asked each one of them three questions:

1)   Can I trust you? *Can I trust you to go to class? Can I trust you to do your assignments? Can I trust you to be at practice on time?*

2)   Are you committed? *Are you committed to being an Arkansas Razorback? Are you committed to giving 100 percent of your effort both on and off the field?*

3)   Do you care?

I don't remember anything said after the third question. All I could remember was thinking, if you take an individual—or a group of people—you can trust, who are committed to the cause, and who care, you can change the world. In fact, it's the only thing that ever has.

While exploring all three questions would be time well spent, I want to focus on the first one: *Can I trust you?* For as long as I can remember, I've heard Bible lessons about the need for us to put our complete and total trust in God. I remember the first time I ever preached before a large congregation. I had not yet begun my theological studies, but my dad thought it would be good for me to get a little experience. I reluctantly agreed. To me, it seemed I should get a little education before on-the-job training, but he saw things differently

. . . so there I was. About ten minutes before services were to start, I sat down in the front row of seats in the church. Dad came and sat down beside me. I guess he could see I was a little jittery, so he asked, "Son, are you nervous?" All I could say was, "Yep!" My dad responded by opening his Bible to Proverbs 3:5–6: "Trust in the LORD with all your heart and do not lean on your own understanding. In all your ways acknowledge Him, and He will make your paths straight." I get it—we need to trust in the Lord with all our hearts. But that's not the question we need to be asking here. That question is *Can God trust us?* Can He trust you and me?

When the apostle Paul wrote to the church in Corinth, he said, "Let a man regard us in this manner, as servants of Christ and stewards of the mysteries of God. In this case, moreover, it is required of stewards that one be found trustworthy" (1 Corinthians 4:1–2). The word for *trustworthy* is also translated as "faithful," and isn't trustworthy how we describe people who are faithful? Consider the impact of this thought: *We are to be worthy of God's trust in us.* If there was ever something we need to pray daily, it would be that God help us to always live in ways worthy of His trust. It moves me to ask several questions.

Can God Trust Us to Be Good Students of His Word?

Don't misunderstand what I'm about to say, but I'm not a big fan of reading the Bible through in a year. It's not that I dislike the thought or plan, but for me it becomes more of an exercise in making sure I've completed the reading assignment rather than understanding what I read. I find myself rushing through the text to check the box. I appreciate the pat on the back and mention from the pulpit or in the bulletin that I read the Bible through in a year, but did I really learn it? I realize there are hundreds of plans for studying the Bible and each person has to decide what works best for them. My preference is what I refer to as *intentional study.* The idea is to read a book or letter through several times, usually nine or ten times. I've been known to read a book through thirty times, once every day for a month. Each time I read through the book, I intentionally look for something specific. I may look for a word or a phrase that's repeated several times. I then highlight that word or phrase in a unique way so that when I look at the text, it stands out. I also ask several questions related to the text:

1) Who is speaking or writing?

2) To whom was it written or said?

3) When was it written or said? Old or New Testament?

4) Why did the author say this at this time? What is going on with this individual or people to cause the author to write or say this?

5) How does it apply to me?

There are other questions I could ask, but these get the ball rolling for me to think about the purpose of the book or letter. The design of any Bible study is to dig beyond the surface of what is written and learn the original intent and meaning.

Another technique is the *inductive study* method. The concept is threefold:

1) *Observation:* This involves a thorough examination of the paragraph, chapter, or book. What do you observe? Repeated words? Interesting phrases?

2) *Interpretation*: What does this mean? What did it mean to the original recipient(s)? Does it mean the same thing today?

3) *Application*: How do I apply this today in my context?

Again, it comes down to the question you must ask yourself: *Can God trust me to be a good student of His Word?*

Can God Trust Us to Reach Out to Those Who Do Not Know Jesus?

I struggle to wrap my mind around the number of people who live on planet Earth. The World Population Clock on the United State Census Bureau website reflects the growth rate of our world. Watch it some time—it's astonishing. As I write these words, there are 7,646,435,501+ who live on this third planet from the sun. I used the plus sign because the clock just keeps rolling. I cannot fathom this number of people.

I also learned on the Census Bureau website that 1.8 people die every second. What that means is that in the time it takes us to listen to a thirty-minute sermon on Sunday morning, 3,240 people will die. In the time it takes us to watch a two-hour movie, 12,960 people will die. Most of these people—if not all of them—are unprepared to stand before the Creator of the universe. God has only one plan, and that plan is for us—human vessels—to influence the people in the world with the message of God's grace. When Jesus instructed the apostles to "go therefore and make disciples of all the nations" (Matthew 28:19), He meant, *as you are going into the world.* How can you make disciples as you go to the grocery store, bank, post office, department store, or anywhere else you find yourself? The driving force in our lives must be to help others know our Savior. Therefore, ask yourself the question: *Can God trust me to reach out to those who do not know Jesus?*

Can God Trust Us to Love His Church?

This is a big one! As I approach this question, I want to be careful not to leave the wrong impression. I think we would all adamantly say we love the church. However, there are times when our actions do not reflect our words. As a whole, we tend to disagree over matters of doctrine and opinion. I do not intend to attempt to settle this matter in this small space. My point is simply this: if we cannot agree on these matters and they drive a wedge of division among God's people, then can we really say we love His church? I can already hear people saying, "If you love something, you have to protect it and keep the doctrine pure—even if that means dividing." I understand.

Again, I'm not here to argue the matter but to ask that we consider our actions and how we've gone about our methods of protecting. I easily admit that I have a hard time looking at myself in the mirror and asking the difficult questions about how I handle every situation. But I know it begins there first. I've lived long enough and experienced enough to know that we're all the same when it comes to the way we see ourselves versus the way others see us. We judge ourselves by our intentions—others judge us by our actions. There are few, if any, exceptions. But remember that Jesus died for the church, and since we know love by this example, we're instructed to "lay down our lives for the brethren" (1 John 3:16). Also remember that Jesus wants us to treat others the way we want to be treated (Matthew 7:12). We call this the Golden Rule. Contrary to the way one particular friend of mine jokes about it, Jesus was not teaching us that the one who has the gold, rules. The point Jesus made here was that we need to treat others how we want to be treated—and we're to treat them that way first. The world tells us to do this backward: to treat others the way we have been treated—a vengeance and get-even mentality. The world also tells us to treat others poorly before they have a chance to do it to us—a get-ahead mentality. This is not what Jesus taught. Ask yourself, *How do I want others to treat me?* Do you want them to be kind, compassionate, caring, loving, forgiving, tolerant, understanding, patient, serving, friendly, helpful, etc.? If that's how we want others to treat us, Jesus says we must demonstrate that treatment of others first. Where this begins is in His church. What do we tell the world by the way we treat one another? Ask yourself, *Can God trust me to love His church?*

Can God Trust Us to Lead His People?

God has always required leadership for His people. We find great leaders identified throughout the Bible, some I've already discussed. When we look at the design of the church, nothing has changed. God designed the church to have leadership. While we tend to focus on only a few people with leadership qualities, leadership extends to everyone. If we understand leadership to mean influence—moving people from one point to another—then we must not limit this to a few. God assigned specific roles to people within the structure of His church: apostles, prophets, evangelists, pastors, and teachers (Ephesians 4:11). We read about elders, deacons, and ministers throughout the text. All of these individuals have roles to play within the body of Christ. Despite this, we see a lack of leadership across the board. I've heard people say, "Well, I don't have the desire" as justification for not taking up a leadership role. Maybe that's true—maybe they don't have the desire. Honestly, I get a little concerned when people *desire* a position of leadership—at least in the way we understand desire. When someone is vying for a position of leadership, they tend to campaign and recruit people to support them. I don't believe this is what God intended. I may be wrong, but consider my thoughts here: When it came to leading God's people, not even Moses wanted—*desired*—the responsibility. However, he did desire to do what God wanted of him. The same should exist for us. Instead of making a checklist of "qualifications" and gracefully bowing out because we don't have the desire, how about we grow in our desire to do what God calls us to as leaders? When we have the desire to do what God wants, we then fulfill these responsibilities with the purpose of keeping God's church alive and growing. One final thought: As the church, we have a responsibility to build up those who fill these positions. The leadership roles in the church have been scrutinized for so long that no one wants to give any consideration to the responsibility. When leaders are seen only as people who deal with conflict, criticism, and controversial members, then no one will voluntarily step up and take on another job—they already have one of those. I asked a group of elders what they had learned since becoming elders that they wished they'd known beforehand so they could have been more prepared. I received several good responses, but one really stood out. One gentleman said, "I wish I would have known how many lives I would change." This is what we need to promote about leadership. We are in the life-changing business. *Can God trust you to lead His people?*

There are many more questions we could ask but it always comes back to asking, "Can God trust you and me?" Can God trust us to be good students of His Word? Can God trust us to reach out to those who do not know Jesus? Can God trust us to love His church? Can God trust us to lead His people?

Trust is the most precious commodity any leader possesses. People will not follow leaders they do not trust, except under compulsion. Of course, that's not what we're talking about or what God expects.

Trust Lost

Before exploring how to develop and improve our level of trust, let's consider how someone loses trust. The old adage "It is easier to maintain than regain" is certainly true when talking about trust. The list below will not be exhaustive.

Lying

Nothing breaks down a relationship of trust more quickly than a lie. Honesty is vital to trust. When we keep secrets or lie about where we've been, what we've done, or what we said, we destroy trust. Remember the story about the boy who cried wolf? He lied about there being a wolf so he could laugh at people when they ran out to help him. Then, when people no longer trusted him and the wolf was actually there, he cried out for help, but no one came.

Hypocrisy

Closely associated with lying, hypocrisy represents individuals who claim to be one thing when, in reality, they're someone else. From a Christian perspective, when we profess to be Christians but our lives reflect anything but Christianity, people cannot trust us. Instead, they see us as hypocritical. This was the problem Jesus addressed in Matthew 23. He pointed out that what the religious leaders *taught* was good and should be followed, but He also told his disciples not to *do* what these leaders did, because they were hypocrites. The religious leaders said one thing but did something else. They held everyone else to one standard, but they were unwilling to live it themselves. When leaders expect others to do things they're unwilling to do, the inconsistency is seen as hypocrisy. The result is a lack of trust.

Selfishness

It can be hard to admit, but we live in a narcissistic culture. We're a society that's more and more consumed with "me." If there's not some benefit for me, then I see no purpose in getting involved. Sadly, we approach relationships in much the same way. If we feel a relationship will benefit us at some point down the road, we work to cultivate and nurture that relationship. However, if there's no benefit, we neglect, ignore, or reject it. When people recognize that a leader's conversations and actions are all focused on themselves and not on others, they lose trust and develop a sense of instability and hopelessness. They become frustrated with the leader and seek someone else to follow.

Indecisiveness

Leaders make decisions. When they become indecisive, those who follow lose trust. I'm not referring to those who take time to carefully gather all the possible information in order to make wise decisions—I'm talking about those leaders who can't seem to pull the trigger. They have the information, but fear prevents them from making a decision—fear that someone might get upset and leave.

From my perspective, one of the most challenging professions is sports officiating. I've experienced this in a small way by officiating kids' sports—and it's not fun. When our children began playing sports at a high school level, I bowed out and took the position of announcer. I sat next to an older gentleman and friend who has since passed away. He kept the statistics for the officials. I will never forget one night as we watched the game and were both frustrated by the officiating. He leaned over to me and said, "Every call, at its best, is only 50 percent right." It took me a second, but he was right. When officials make a call, if it's in favor of the home team, the home crowd loves it and visitors hate it. The same is true in reverse. Officials know that regardless of the decision, they will only be 50 percent right. Leaders may face the same situation, but like officials, they still have to make the call. Indecisiveness will cause them to lose trust.

Unsafe Environment

Not all leaders value the feedback of followers, especially if the feedback is negative or controversial. When leaders are more agenda-driven and someone calls them on it, the response is not always favorable. Once followers feel that it's no longer safe to talk to leaders, they will talk to others, which is not always a good situation. I remember hearing a leader say one time, "If you like what's going on, tell others. If you don't, then tell us." In theory, it sounded great. In reality, no one talked to them because they were unapproachable. They couldn't see it, but everyone else did. As a result, they did not provide people a safe environment to share feedback, express their opinions, voice their likes and dislikes, or anything else. Trust was lost.

Lack of Adequate Communication

Followers need to be informed. When leaders fail to communicate—or if they withhold information—they lose trust. Tim Elmore, founder and CEO of Growing Leaders, describes three topics leaders need to discuss with their team. One of these is "Communication Frequency." He says, "During times of change, it is imperative that leaders communicate more clearly and frequently. Negativity can prevail because 'people are down on what they're not up on.'"[1] The last part of this statement is critical. When people sense a lack of communication or are uninformed about a current situation, they become negative toward leaders. Transparency and open communication are vital to leadership trust. The more transparent and open leaders are, the stronger the bond of trust becomes.

Distrust in Others

The micromanaging leader is one who doesn't believe anyone else can do the job as good as they can. They have to know every detail and approve every decision, no matter how large or small. Their hands-on approach to oversight creates a distrustful environment. I realize they may have the best of intentions—they want the work done well, efficiently, and cost-effectively. However, leaders often fail to realize this approach communicates a lack of trust in the people who do the work. Several years ago, a friend of mine told me, "If you give someone the responsibility, then give them the authority to carry it out." Wise words! Far too often, leaders give people the responsibility but no authority to make any decision to fulfill the work. When this happens, leaders lose trust.

When people no longer trust their leaders, they follow another leader they trust, or they simply follow their own self-guided direction. Either way, the damage created by the breach of trust is nearly impossible to repair. For example, when a husband has an affair, trust is broken. Even though his wife may be willing to work through the problem and attempt to make the marriage work, the road ahead presents difficult challenges to overcome. Every time her husband doesn't arrive home at the scheduled time, she will question where he is and who he's with. Every time the phone rings and her husband leaves the room, she will wonder who has called. Is it his mistress? Every time her husband looks at another woman, she will wonder what he's thinking. Trust is hard to rebuild once it has been broken. The same is true for all leaders.

Building Trust

As we near the end of our journey, we need to explore ways to build trust—or perhaps regain trust once it has been lost. If we work to do the opposite of those behaviors that cause a leader to lose trust, we can gain, maintain, or regain trust. While I won't go back and look at each of these areas, there will be some overlap in the discussion ahead. Consider with me a few ideas to develop a relationship of trust as leaders.

Effective Communication

I could devote an entire chapter to the discussion of communication. Perhaps that's a book for another time. I cannot overstate the necessity of effective communication. Leaders need to be transparent, open, and honest in their communication with followers. Of course, there are confidential elements that aren't always appropriate to be shared with everyone, but that's not what I'm talking about here. The first step in effective communication is listening—

often referred to as *empathetic listening.* When followers feel as if they're heard rather than dismissed, scoffed at, or belittled, they feel valued and they trust. Leaders have to listen with more than just their ears—they have to listen with their eyes and hearts. They have to be more patient and understanding, learning to ask questions to help them empathize with the individual who has come to them. Additionally, leaders must recognize that it's not about *if* they think they understand, but *does* the individual leave knowing they were heard and understood. This requires much effort.

Most relationships today are extremely shallow. We rarely, if ever, get below the surface. And when we do, we don't always like what we see, which is why we tend to avoid communication. If you want to communicate effectively, do not just get up and read a speech to the group and then sit down. Invite people to ask questions or comments. If you're uncertain of what to communicate, let people know you want to answer their questions and address their concerns, but ask everyone to write down what they want to ask. Once they submit their questions or concerns, take a little time to formulate a response and communicate to the group. People will value and appreciate your openness, honesty, and transparency.

Demonstrate Competence

Our competency level grows with increased knowledge, skill capability, and decision-making ability. We develop competence over time. It's not a one-time, one-and-done kind of decision. People observe how we lead over time. I remember a true story about a couple who came to visit the local preacher to discuss a specific area in their life. They told him they'd been listening to and observing him for five years and finally felt comfortable enough to share what was on their hearts, believing he would be honest with them. Did you catch that? Five years! This is how competence works. If we believe that people think we're competent because we made one good decision or demonstrate good judgment in one situation, we're fooling ourselves. People observe over time, and then it's like a lightbulb turns on. All of a sudden, they feel comfortable talking to you about the deepest areas of their life. When leaders demonstrate competence, it may take one, two, or even five years, but people develop a strong level of trust when it connects.

Eliminate Inconsistencies

As I mentioned earlier, nothing is more destructive than hypocrisy. Jesus condemned it and people also do so today. The intent here is to encourage the practice of eliminating inconsistencies in our lives. As we all know, this is much easier to say than practice. We must not deny or neglect those areas in our life but work on changing them. Therefore, the design of this practice is to become more consistent. I have more to say about this in the final chapter of this section, but for now, suffice it to say, consistency breeds trust. No one expects you to be perfect, but how you handle those imperfections communicates volumes about the consistency level in your life.

Cultivate Integrity

In order to cultivate integrity, I suggest going back to look at chapter 9 and the discussion on Psalm 15. The point here overlaps with that point about integrity. When the life that people do not see is reflected in the life people do see, integrity has a foundation—at least if that private life is godly. It's important to be the same person whether you're in front of people or in private. The cultivation of integrity involves time and practice. In fact, it's a culmination of everything I've discussed up to this point. When you avoid areas that break trust, practice effective communication, demonstrate competence, and eliminate inconsistencies, you're well on your way to cultivating integrity. Your work ethic, moral standard, others-centered mindset, honesty, and transparency establish the integrity that builds trust. And when you're trustworthy, people will follow.

Seek and Follow Wise Counsel

Over the course of fifty-eight years, I've sought counsel from others, and others have sought counsel from me. What I'm about to say is true both ways. There were times I went for counsel only to reject the advice I was given. To be perfectly honest, I had my mind made up before I sought this counsel. I knew what they were going to say. I didn't want to hear it, so I rejected the counsel before I even heard it. The same has been true when others came and asked for my advice. They left my office never intending to apply my suggestions. I'm sure others probably felt about me the same way I did in those moments: "Why ask for advice if you don't intend to follow it?" It's quite possible my counsel was not wise, and it's possible they never intended to follow it regardless. My point is this: If you want to build trust, then you need to surround yourself with people you consider wise. When you go to them and seek counsel, your intent must be to follow that counsel. If not, then don't go. If you already know the decision you plan to make, then don't go. However, if you want others to trust in your decisions, you must be humble. Seek and follow wise counsel.

Life and water. Character and leadership. One depends on the other and both go hand-in-hand. As water is an essential building block to life, character is an essential foundation stone to leadership, and character is built on trust. I cannot say enough about trust. Stephen Covey's book *The Speed of Trust* is worth taking the time to read. One area of his focus is the "principle of credibility" and how credibility factors into trust.[2] I discuss this further in the next chapter. Authors James Kouzes and Barry Posner also write about the vital nature of trust in leadership. One chapter is dedicated to the fact that you cannot take trust for granted.[3] These are only two of many resources available that highlight the necessity of this invaluable commodity we call trust—but trust does not function alone. It must be coupled with respect and credibility.

Chapter 11
Respect and Credibility

As all human beings are, in my view, creatures of
God's design, we must respect all other human beings.
That does not mean I have to agree with their choices or agree with
their opinions, but indeed I respect them as human beings.
Stockwell Day

I met Ryan Poe for the first time while attending a master's level course in Colorado Springs in 2012. Ryan, four others, and I were part of a small group that worked together during the two-week intensive. The six members of our group knew little about each other: our backgrounds, levels of comfort, personal likes and dislikes, or what really made us tick. However, we worked together on various activities throughout the time together and grew closer, developing a bond of friendship. Each group was assigned to conduct a specific activity on a particular morning the first week. As my group discussed what we would like to do, I became very uncomfortable with the suggestions for worship which I was unaccustomed to practicing. Because I didn't know everyone well, I was uncertain about what to do. I didn't say anything, but all day I pondered what to say and who to talk to about the way I felt. At the end of the day, Ryan must have noticed my quietness, because he came over and asked, "Are you okay?" I responded with the typical "Sure, I'm doing okay." He was a bit more perceptive than I gave him credit for, because he said, "No— are you *really* okay?" I asked him to sit down, and I explained the whole situation.

After we talked at length, Ryan thanked me for sharing how I felt, and we both left for the evening to our respective rooms. The next morning, Ryan led the activity as planned. Each person had a specific role and part to play during the activity. At one point, he "called an audible"—that is, he changed the plan in order to make me comfortable. No one was aware of what he had done except the two of us. His decision allowed me to participate without feeling uncomfortable and without calling attention to me on a personal level. In that moment, I gained more respect for Ryan than I can describe.

He exercised good judgment, which pointed to his credibility and elevated my respect for him. The lesson I learned that day is one I wish I'd learned much earlier in life. What I learned was this: *You do not have to agree with someone in order to show respect.* This one lesson has helped me more than any other when it comes to building stronger relationships.

Like two sides of the same coin, respect and credibility go hand in hand. When people conduct themselves in ways that gain respect, we find credibility. And when we witness the actions of people who are credible, we find respect. A strong bond exists between respect and credibility as they contribute to trust. All three are pillars of our character. Let's look at each of these pillars and how to gain both respect and credibility.

Respect

I'm sure you've heard people say, "Respect is earned." I recognize the need to possess a respect for positions of authority, but it doesn't always mean we respect the person in that position of authority. In the first class on leadership I taught in Denver, a young man sat in the front row and listened intently. As we discussed the critical nature of respect as leaders, he said, "My dad always told me that respect is never commanded, but demanded by our actions." Nothing could be more true. Our conduct is what earns respect. I realize I'm not the first to say it, but people do not follow leaders by accident—they follow leaders they respect.

Take a few moments and consider the challenges within the political framework of our country and the lack of respect shown toward government officials at all levels. Think about the corruption in the corporate world and how employees possess such disgust for leaders whose hypocrisy and capitalistic greed make them more tyrannical. Look at the home and the hypocrisy witnessed by children when parents appear like Dr. Jekyll and Mr. Hyde because they act one way around people outside the home and another way inside the home.

Respect is an essential pillar in our character, and character is essential for long-lasting leadership. Since this is the case, we need to take steps to ensure we gain the respect of others. Remember: the time is now. You can't change the past, but you can do whatever it takes now to change the direction of the future and the respect you either lose or gain in your life.

Losing Respect

When conducting workshops on leadership, I commonly ask small groups to discuss how we lose something before we talk about how we gain it. The same is true when examining the subject of respect. How do we lose something so critical to the nature of our character and leadership? Over the years, I've collected quite a list from these workshops. Below, I share the top ten answers I've received.

Hypocrisy

I introduced this subject in the previous chapter. When people claim to be one thing, but act another way, they're hypocritical. The word originates around the idea of acting in a play—someone pretending to be someone they're not. Sadly, people can see this in every area of life and leadership. Spiritually, when we only pretend to be Christians one day a week and live like the world the rest of the week, we're hypocrites. Almost twenty-five years ago, I had someone explain to me they had one type of language they used in their home, another type they used on the job, and a completely different language around Christians. In his mind, certain abusive language was appropriate on the job, but not around family or Christians. My immediate thought was, *Did he really just admit to such hypocrisy?* Needless to say, I lost respect for him. We lose the respect of others when our lives display these tendencies.

Poor Decisions

The inability, laziness, or lack of effort to gain necessary information often leads to poor decisions. Poor decisions impact others in our homes, on the job, and in our communities. These decisions often impact the physical, emotional, and financial well-being of the person who makes the decision as well as others involved. When someone consistently demonstrates poor decision-making, people lose respect.

Inappropriate Behavior

Naturally, what one person considers inappropriate will be different from what another person considers inappropriate. There's a level of subjectivity when defining something as inappropriate. However, everyone recognizes certain types of behaviors as inappropriate, and when these are demonstrated, people lose respect. In every setting, we're well served to discuss with all parties involved what is and what is not appropriate behavior.

Lack of Respect for Others

A failure to show respect for others is the quickest way I know to lose respect—not only from the one who is disrespected but also from those who observe such conduct. You might be surprised to learn how many domestic problems, how many gang fights, and how many national and international wars were all started because of a lack of respect for others. Cultural differences also play a major factor in this discussion. How one culture shows respect differs from how other cultures show this. This is why it's so critical to learn all we can about cultural nuances that exist and practice those customs that demonstrate respect.

Arrogance and Inappropriate Pride

I grew up hearing "Pride goes before the fall." I'm sure this is true on numerous levels. However, the type of inappropriate pride or arrogance I'm referring to here is something people usually do not see in themselves, but others recognize it. Arrogance evidences itself when we put down others as less knowledgeable on specific matters, when we think we're a little better than others, when we believe no one can do the job as well as we can, or when we demonstrate narcissistic tendencies. The list goes on, but we all recognize it. The challenge is be self-aware and understand how pride can cost us respect.

Blaming Others for One's Own Actions

No one enjoys being held responsible and accountable. Children learn this at a young age. If they feel they'll receive punishment for something they did, they quickly respond in denial and blame. We shouldn't be surprised—this has been around since the garden. Adam blamed Eve. Eve blamed the serpent. If accepting responsibility for our actions will cost us financially or socially, in the heat of the moment, we deny or blame someone else. Either way, we lose respect quickly.

Talking about Others behind Their Backs (Truth or Lies)

Obviously, here I'm not referring to praising someone behind their back. The old adage "If you don't have something nice to say, then don't say anything at all" provides the kind of sage wisdom we all need to learn. We lose respect when we go to others with a story about someone rather than to the person most affected by it. If we have information about someone that casts that person in a negative light, we need to talk to that person and resolve the situation. When we talk to someone else, we lose respect both from the person we talk about and in the eyes of those who listen. This practice can destroy a leader's influence.

Abusive Language

Our world has grown to accept abusive language. I remember talking with someone years ago about the language in a movie they recommended. When I pointed out what I knew, their response was, "I don't even hear it anymore." How sad. Have we become so calloused to our surroundings that we don't hear inappropriate language? An older gentleman once told me that when someone curses, that person has a pretty limited vocabulary. I've read research related to the subject that disagrees, and I'm not here to argue with anyone one way or the other. I will say that how we use our words—regardless of the type of words we use—costs us respect. I may never use a curse word in a moment of anger, but how I speak in my anger can be destructive to my character so that I lose respect.

Lying

Few things frustrate me more than a liar. When someone lies to me, I lose all respect for that individual. Sadly, I may not know every time someone lies to me. There are people who have become too good at it. I also know there are people who have lied so much they begin to believe what they say is true. Talk about self-deception. The moment I learn that someone has lied to me, I struggle to trust them again. Based on conversations with people from all walks of life, the response is the same. Lying damages respect.

Inconsistency

We have almost come full circle. There are many similarities between inconsistency and hypocrisy, depending on how we define them. However, there is a difference in my way of thinking. Hypocrisy is more intentional—it's pretending to be something we're not. Inconsistency exists when we make certain decisions one way one time, but we make them differently the next time we face the same situation. This type of inconsistency creates doubt on the part of followers and often causes us to lose respect.

Gaining Respect

These ten areas we've described represent ways to lose respect, but how can one gain respect? I could simply tell you to do the opposite of the list above—and that would be true. However, I want to focus on seven ways to gain respect and how these provide the support structure to increase this vital component of your character.

Preparation

Be prepared for every situation. When leaders demonstrate knowledge of the subject or task at hand, they gain respect. When you do this, it means you have to put forth time, effort, and energy to learn. The more prepared you are, the more respect you receive. Preparation shows the desire and intent to know and do the right things. It shows you care.

Follow-Through

I see this especially in the home, but it's true across the board. When parents tell children certain activities receive specific punishment and then fail to follow through, children eventually lose respect for the parents. Have you ever heard a parent say, "If I have to tell you one more time . . ."? It doesn't take long before children learn not to believe the parent and subsequently lose respect for them. We discover this also in our commitments. For example, you agree to attend a certain function or have dinner at someone's home, and later you're offered something you perceive as better. How do you respond? It's important to follow through with your commitments and do what you said you would do. Follow-through on commitments produces respect.

Admit Mistakes

Take responsibility for your actions. Never blame someone else. I know I've made my share of mistakes in parenting. Nothing is more difficult as a parent than to sit down with your children and admit you made a mistake. However, nothing is more powerful in gaining respect. Not only is this true in parenting but also in every level of leadership, especially in the church. Every person I've met knows that leaders are not perfect. We tend to treat them as though they are perfect, even though we know they're not. How leaders respond when they make mistakes makes all the difference. When a leader genuinely admits a mistake and seeks restitution, respect is gained.

Demonstrate Good Manners

"Please" and "thank you" are two of the most signifiant ways to gain respect. Maybe you're thinking, *How simple!* True—it is quite simple, yet so missing in the vocabulary of many. As with other areas, it all begins in the home. Children must learn early on in life how to make requests and express gratitude. How much more so as adults! In 1992, the school I attended was hosting an activity in the fellowship room. I walked into the chapel area and informed everyone that they must head downstairs to participate in the activity. Later, one student talked with me privately about my need to *ask*, instead of *tell*. The point was well made, and I learned how saying "please" makes all the difference. Even more so is the need to express gratitude. No one has to do anything for anyone else. When they do, doesn't it make sense that two words—"thank you"—can generate their willingness to do more? More importantly, respect is gained for those who express such gratitude.

Put Others First

Our culture is so self-driven that the concept of putting others first is rarely seen, but when it is, the results are beautiful. The COVID-19 pandemic of 2020 provided us with numerous examples of selfless conduct, as nurses and doctors worked tirelessly on the front lines, were exposed to the virus, and chose to quarantine from their own families—all in an effort to care for patients. Additionally, we read about and watch stories of Good Samaritans across the country who provided aid to people at risk during this pandemic. They gained our respect because they put others first. Leaders gain respect when they demonstrate this same quality.

Show Respect to Others

Back to the story of Ryan Poe I shared at the beginning of this chapter. Because Ryan showed me respect, he gained my respect. He didn't have to make the decision he did, and in that moment my respect for him grew immensely. That's the power of showing respect to others. We're all made in the image of God. For this reason alone, we need to show respect to others. We need to realize that no one is better than anyone else, we all share the same problem with sin, and we all need the same solution of forgiveness. Maybe through this we can put into perspective how a little respect shown toward others can open doors to share the message of Jesus. Even if we do not have the opportunity, showing respect gains respect from those to whom it is shown.

Our personal appearances, attitudes, and types of language we use all speak volumes about how we see and respect ourselves. The level of respect we have for ourselves often determines the level of respect we show to others.

Respect is so easy to lose and so hard to gain. It's vital to work daily at establishing the kind of character that people respect. When people respect an individual, they will follow. I cannot emphasize enough how crucial this is in the church today. The church needs leaders who are respected and demonstrate the kind of character that people will follow.

Credibility

Credibility is the sister companion and fellow worker to respect. John Maxwell says, "Every message people receive is filtered through the messenger who delivers it. If the messenger is credible, then so is the message." He goes on to say, "We tend to try and get people to believe in the dream, idea or program without establishing credibility in the leader first."[1] Both statements reflect the need for and power of credibility in life and leadership.

Four Cores of Credibility

In *The Speed of Trust*, Stephen Covey describes "Four Cores of Credibility."[2] The first and second (*integrity* and *intent*) deal with character. The third and fourth (*capability* and *results*) involve competence. I discuss each of these briefly to show their significance, and I then discuss how to develop greater credibility.

Integrity

In chapter 9, I discussed in detail the subject of integrity as described in Psalm 15. Covey adds that integrity is "integratedness. It's walking your talk. It's being congruent, inside and out. It's having the courage to act in accordance with your values and beliefs.

179

Interestingly, most massive violations of trust are violations of integrity." When leaders possess integrity, they're seen as credible.

Intent

Leaders who have hidden agendas lack the credibility followers seek. Leaders who don't have the best interests of others in mind raise suspicion and lose credibility. Covey says intent "has to do with our motives, our agendas, and our resulting behavior. Trust grows when our motives are straightforward and based on mutual benefit—in other words, when we genuinely care not only for ourselves, but also for the people we interact with, lead, or serve."

Capability

Capability involves "the abilities we have that inspire confidence—our talents, attitudes, skills, knowledge, and style. They are the means we use to produce results." I remember when my dad required open heart surgery. The surgeon had performed more than ten thousand bypasses. His education and experience demonstrated his capability and provided us with comfort that Dad was in good hands for this procedure. The same is true for leaders who demonstrate their capabilities not only for education but also experience.

Results

Leaders who have not produced any results lack credibility. Covey writes, "This refers to our track record, our performance, our getting the right things done. If you don't accomplish what you're expected to do, it diminishes your credibility." You increase a level of credibility by producing the right results. Although activity and achievement are often confused, there's a significant difference: Simply because someone is active does not mean they achieve results. If leaders desire credibility, one of the core elements points to productivity.

Building Credibility

Covey develops a separate chapter on each of these "four core" elements to credibility. The connection of credibility to trust and, of course, character is essential to life and leadership. I could spend more time discussing areas related to defining credibility and looking at examples of men and women throughout the Bible and history who point us in the right direction to understand this topic. However, I want to move in the direction of examining eight ways you can build credibility as a leader.

Develop Good Relationships with People

John Maxwell describes this as the "Law of Connectivity." Leading is about relationships. Are you connected to the people you lead? You build credibility when others have an opportunity to know you. Your transparency and openness in those relationships help people see your character more than on-the-job observation. It's important to connect with people individually and personally. Truth be told, church members more widely accept ministers who lack speaking ability when they're more pastoral and connect with people. These ministers sit with families at the hospital while their loved ones have surgery. They look after families when they lose loved ones. Meet people where they are. Show them who you are inside and out. Love on people. Connect with them. The result builds credibility.

Be Honest, Authentic, and Develop Trust

These three components have a strong interconnected relationship. Honesty is a given, and I spent an entire chapter on trust. Think about the importance of authenticity. People appreciate and value authenticity. The ability to be genuine in your relationships leads to credibility. No one likes a fake or phony. We desire to be around people who are genuine and authentic. Demonstrating these qualities will push your credibility meter up in the eyes of those who see and know you.

Hold Yourself to a Standard of Excellence, Set the Example

One of my favorite words is *excellence*. Businesses often claim to provide excellence as the standard for the service they offer to their customers. When you set an example of excellence in your leadership, you become a magnum force. From a biblical perspective, Christians were urged to "excel still more" (1 Thessalonians 4:1, 10). They were involved in love and the encouragement of others, but Paul encouraged them to do more. We find *excellence* referenced in 1 Peter 2:12, as Christians were told, "Keep your behavior excellent among the Gentiles." The background of this word is powerful, because excellence involves the type of conduct that contributes to the salvation of others.[3] If you desire to build credibility, your conduct needs to contribute to others' salvation. They will then see that you have their best interests at heart.

Provide Tools and Resources for Others to Do Their Jobs Better

How well do you equip others to improve in their work? Certainly, it's clear that you must do this in the work place, but how about in your home? Parents, we have a responsibility to provide the tools and resources to help our children do better. Leaders in the church, there's a level of responsibility required that equips everyone involved with the tools and resources to do their work better. Paul said leaders must equip "the saints for the work of service, to the building up of the body of Christ" (Ephesians 4:11–12). Are you providing others with the right tools and preparing them in the right ways to do their jobs? Or do you hire a preacher and expect everyone to attend Bible class or worship service and figure it out on their own? Credibility increases when you provide the tools and resources others need in order to improve.

Help Others Achieve Their Personal Goals

Imagine the difference that would occur in the home, church, and world if everyone went about helping others achieve their personal goals. It would be an amazing place, would it not? Take time to integrate your life into the lives of church members. Get to know individuals' personal goals and assist each person toward their goals. Push yourself to lead in ways that help others in those areas of life that are most important to them. Leaders who do so are recognized as credible and worthy of people's trust.

Develop Others into Leaders

The impact on someone's life when a leader takes the time to customize a strategy for them to become a leader is immeasurable. Mac Lake's book *The Multiplication Effect*[4] deals with an approach to help leaders accomplish this task. My prayer for each congregation I work with is to help them establish a plan that prepares others to lead. The "pipeline" that Lake refers to dries up if leaders are not diligent to work with others and train them to lead. They may not all become leaders of hundreds or thousands, but they can lead small groups. Who knows, from those you train, you may raise up a Goliath killer, like David.

Add Value to People's Lives

What adds value and how we add value are the two main areas to consider. People are different, so what adds value to each person's life will vary. Spend time with people and learn what adds value for them, and then find ways to incorporate those activities into your leadership. How they add value is determined by the level of support they provide in the moment of need. Lift up the hands of those who labor to hold up the vision, and champion the cause. Strengthen the legs of those who labor toward goal achievement. Inspire the hearts of those who seek to honor God. When leaders accomplish all three, they gain credibility.

Be Patient

It goes without saying, but credibility is earned over time, just like respect. I wish I could say that patience is one of my virtues, but I struggle with it. I'm like the guy in the story who prayed for God to give him patience and give it to him *now*. I once heard a missionary talk about how he quit praying for patience because he didn't want the trials that went along with developing patience. While both thoughts possess an element of humor, they're also true. Learning to be patient with others instead of creating unrealistic expectations will strengthen your credibility.

As with respect, you can lose or gain credibility. Maxwell adds this thought about credibility: "Without credibility it is impossible to develop sustained leadership. People may walk into the room with you, but if you do not have credibility, they will not stay in the room with you." I could spend much more space exploring several areas related to respect and credibility. If you would like to pursue this further, I encourage you to read more from leaders such as Stephen Covey, John Maxwell, and James Kouzes and Barry Posner. But do not leave this chapter without knowing how essential trust, respect, and credibility are to your leadership. When these three pillars exist, people will follow wherever you lead. Character is essential to leadership. The water we drink fills our bodies with a life-giving building block and character that consists of trust, respect, and credibility provides a life-giving essential for leaders.

Pressing ahead, I enter the final chapter of this section and a focus on application. How can you improve your character? What steps will guide you to greater influence and stronger leadership? The answers to these questions and more unfold in the next chapter.

Chapter 12
Improving Character

To learn and not to do is really not to learn.
To know and not to do is really not to know.
Stephen Covey

The final chapter of this section focuses specifically on application. Water is an essential life-giving source, but only if you and I drink it. We must take water into our bodies to enjoy its benefits. Character is no different. Until we develop this essential and grow our leadership, others cannot benefit. I've talked about character, and the journey led us through discussions about trust, respect, and credibility. Character is a choice, and choosing to develop trust, respect, and credibility strengthens our character and its influence. All of these discussions fall short if we fail to focus on how we can improve our overall character. Since character is a choice, what choices should you make to guide your character development? In this chapter, I focus on three steps to improve character. While the list is far broader than this discussion, these three steps provide substance to the choices you make to improve your character.

The Choice Diagram

The question I'm most frequently asked is, "What are the top three to five books you recommend regarding the subject of leadership?" I cannot describe how difficult it is to select only a few to recommend, because there are dozens of books that are beneficial for all leaders to read and apply in their leadership. However, without exception, there's one series of books I recommend every time: *Leadership and Self-Deception*,[1] *The Anatomy of Peace*,[2] and *The Outward Mindset*.[3] These books produced by the Arbinger Institute are powerful for leadership development, especially as it relates to character.

Each book is built around a concept known as "the box." The box of self-deception—or betrayal—represents a struggle each one of us must face and deal with daily. To understand the direction of this concept, let's back up and look at what the Arbinger Institute describes as "the choice diagram." Here's how it works: An individual faces a situation where they must make a choice. There are two possibilities: choose to do what the person senses or believes to be the right thing, or choose not to honor that sense or belief. In that moment, if the choice is to do the right thing, then everything moves ahead normally. However, if the person chooses not to honor that sense of what is right, they betray themselves and get into what is called "the box" of self-deception. When that happens, everything changes. The person begins to think differently. The way they feel changes. They become angry, depressed, bitter, or justified. The way they view themselves changes. They view themselves as better than others, a victim (owed), made to be bad, or to be seen well. The way they view others changes. They view others as having no rights, instrumental in robbing them of peace, as threats, or as bigots. Even their worldview changes—they see the world as unfair, unjust, burdensome, or against them. The result is a situation where they begin to inflate their own virtues, inflate the faults of others, blame others, and inflate the value of things that justify their actions. When they're in the box, they see people as objects rather than as people with feelings and rights. Basically, people are a means to accomplish what is best for them. The only value they place upon others is the benefit to their own lives—not the other way around.

In the first book, *Leadership and Self-Deception*, an illustration from the book helps clarify the development of the material above: Bud and his wife, Nancy, have a four-month-old son. At 1:00 in the morning, the child began to cry. In that moment, Bud had a sense—a feeling—about what he should do, which was to get up and take care of their son. However, he decided not to honor that sense and, as a result, got into the box of self-betrayal or self-deception. When this happened, he began to think differently. First, he began to see his wife as lazy, inconsiderate of his feelings, unappreciative, insensitive, a lousy mom, and a lousy wife. In fact, she probably wasn't really asleep—she was faking it just to get at Bud. Second, while this was unfolding, Bud began to view himself differently. He saw himself as a victim. After all, he worked hard to provide for his family, making it possible for Nancy to stay home and take care of their child. He saw himself as important, adding value to the family. He was fair, sensitive, a good dad, and a good husband.

Now before I go further, consider the situation. When did Bud begin to see his wife and himself in these ways? Before or after the baby cried? These changes occurred after the baby cried. The point here is this: Before the baby awakened Bud, Nancy was nothing like what he had envisioned in his mind. It was after he betrayed the sense of what he should do and got into the box of self-deception that he began to perceive her that way. Right then, Bud's feelings changed—the way he viewed himself and the way he viewed his wife all changed.

In *The Anatomy of Peace*, Lou, the owner of the company for which Bud worked, describes the science behind the concept of the box. Lou talks about four types of boxes an individual can get into at any time of the day or moment.

The first box is the "better-than" box. In this box, an individual feels impatient and indifferent toward others. They view themselves as superior, important, and always right. They view others as inferior, incapable, and wrong. As a result, they view the world as competitive, troubled, and in need of them. From a Christian perspective, this is the "holier-than-thou" box. Anytime we find ourselves feeling superior to others because they don't know the Bible as well as we do or they're not as spiritually mature as we are, then we're in this box. When we characterize others as ignorant of Scripture or think, *How could anyone believe something so incorrect?* we're in this box. It's a dangerous box for Christians, because it lacks the humility needed to see others as people and souls searching for the Lord.

The second box is the "I-deserve" box. In this box, an individual feels entitled and deprived of the better things in life. They view themselves as meritorious, mistreated, and unappreciated. They view others as mistaken, mistreating, and ungrateful. As a result, they view the world as unfair and unjust, and they think the world owes them something. I'm not sure anyone can pinpoint the exact time or generation when people began to feel they deserved anything. Each generation I've witnessed has had the desire to make life better for those who follow after them. But it leads toward this box. Once a generation begins to feel like the world owes them something, we face a difficult situation. Sadly, even though we intellectually know it isn't true, we can begin to think that somehow God owes us. After all, we were good enough to choose his team. This box has done more harm to the understanding of grace than any other I discuss.

The third box is the "must-be-seen-as" box. In this box, an individual feels anxious, stressed, afraid, and overwhelmed. They view themselves as someone who needs to be well thought of, and they feel fake. They view others as judgmental and threatening, and the world seems to be their own personal audience. As a result, they view the world as dangerous, always watching and judging them. I often think of this box as the "Christian" box. How many times do we find ourselves in conflict with our families on the way to church on Sunday mornings? Once we arrive, we suck it up, put smiles on our faces, and walk into the building, telling everyone that everything is great: praise God—it's great to be a Christian! Immediately after services, we're back in the car and in the midst of the conflict again. Why? Because we feel we "must-be-seen-as" a specific image of what we believe Christianity is all about. We can't allow others to see us with problems.

The fourth box is the "less-than" box. In this box, an individual feels helpless, jealous, bitter, and depressed. They view themselves as not as good as others, broken, deficient, and fated. They view others as advantaged, privileged, and blessed. As a result, they view the world as hard and against them, and they feel that the world ignores them. I think of this as the "poor, poor, pitiful me" box. Low self-esteem is a reality for far too many people. Parents who ridicule their children or make them feel less than anyone else damage the emotional stability and social acceptability of their children. Children grow up thinking they can do nothing right, they're a hindrance to society as a whole, and the world would be better off without them.

These four boxes explain much about the world we live in today, both from a secular and spiritual perspective. We can get in any one of these boxes at any time during the day. It's even possible to be in more than one box at a time! When you understand how the choice diagram works, you can recognize how the four types of boxes relate and apply to various settings on a daily basis.

The concept presented in the third book, *The Outward Mindset*, is one of the most biblical principles I've seen in any secular book. Considering others above self was the whole of how Jesus lived, what He taught, and what He passed on for every generation that followed. Even though the book does not address biblical teaching, the connection is there.

190

The Outward Mindset speaks to the need for leaders to think about the impact of their words, attitudes, actions, and decisions on the other person—but with a little twist. *Will what I'm about to say or do make life better for the people who are affected by it?* We all face thousands of situations on a daily, weekly, monthly, and yearly basis. When these situations occur, we need to consider how our response to them effects change in the lives of those who are recipients of those decisions.

Biblically speaking, this is how Jesus lived His life—from leaving heaven to live as a bond-servant (Philippians 2:6–8) to teaching the necessity of denying self (Luke 9:23) to washing the disciples' feet (John 13) to His death on the cross (Matthew 27). We find this principle throughout the apostles' writings, specifically in the letter Paul wrote to the church in Philippi: "Do nothing from selfishness or empty conceit, but with humility of mind regard one another as more important than yourselves; do not merely look out for your own personal interests, but also for the interests of others" (Philippians 2:3–4).

What does this have to do with improving your character? When you understand the choice diagram, you realize that your choices determine your character. Making decisions that honor the sense of what you believe to be right strengthens the development of your character. If you can focus on how your decisions affect others, you strengthen the way others view your character.

10–10–10 Principle

About ten years ago, I purchased the book the *10-10-10 Principle* by Suzy Welch.[4] In order to understand the significance of the principle described in the book, let me illustrate how it worked in a certain scenario. At the time I received a phone call from a woman and her husband who were having marital problems, I sort of knew the CliffsNotes version of the book. Since I knew this woman and her husband well, I agreed to do what I could to help.

I arranged a time to meet with both of them. As I listened, it was apparent that he was unhappy that she had contacted me to help. There was no infidelity—they were just fighting about everything and could not get along. They were headed for divorce. I finally asked if

I could talk with just the husband. I figured now was as good a time as any to see if the 10-10-10 principle worked. I asked, "Can you live with this decision ten minutes from now? Can you live with it ten months from now? And can you live with ten years from now?"

I told this young man that I knew him well enough to understand that he was mad—really mad. He was mad enough that I was sure he would have no problem ten minutes from now living with the decision to divorce. I also expressed that I figured he was mad enough that he would have no problem living with it ten months from now. But, "Can you really live with it ten years from now?" He broke down and began to cry. He told me I was correct. He was mad enough that he had no problem living with the decision ten minutes from now and he was mad enough it would be no problem living with it ten months from now. Then he said, "But I don't want to be alone ten years from now."

I'm happy to report that this man and woman are happily married and faithful Christians to this day—in part because of what started with my CliffsNotes version of the 10-10-10 principle. I never dreamed the power those three questions could have, but the evidence was there before me.

Although these questions are powerful and critical, there's much more to the book and this principle than simply asking three questions. *First*, the principle starts with a question: "What is the issue surrounding the need for a decision?" You can follow this with another question: "What about the situation makes this a pressing issue for all parties involved?" Ultimately, it comes down to a consideration of how this decision will impact the lives of those connected to the issue.

Second, the principle moves to data collection. As you approach a situation, make sure to collect as much information as possible before making any decision that involves other people and your character. Consider the pros and cons of the decision as it relates to the people most closely associated with the situation.

Third, the principle involves analysis. Once you have all the data before you, compare the information with your core values. After the comparison is made, if the outcome of the decision does not align with your values, you may need to make a different decision. You may also need to go back to the beginning and start the process over.

These three steps provide a foundation to asking yourself the relevant question: "Can I live with this decision ten minutes from now, ten months from now, and ten years from now?" Ultimately, the discussion is personal. The components contribute to a self-examination more than asking questions of someone else. However, these questions are beneficial for those who are facing difficult decisions in their lives.

As you think about the impact decisions have on your character, imagine the power behind stopping to ask yourself these three questions. The next time you face a moment of weakness or a situation where you are vulnerable, before making a decision that has strong implications to your character, you need to ask yourself if you can live with the decision in the short-term, mid-range, and long-term. You might be surprised by the difference it makes in your choice of decisions and the way it shapes your character.

Character Audit

As with other times in my life, just when I thought I had come up with something unique, a short time later I read where someone else already had the idea. Such is the case with my concept of the character audit. I know the thoughts I share with you are not new, but hopefully revisiting them will renew a sense of purpose for molding your character in the right direction.

A character audit is exactly what you might imagine: the idea is simply to sit down and list your core values. What are core values? Core values make up a person's foundational belief structure. They are the "guiding principles that dictate behavior and help people understand the difference between right and wrong."[5] Both positive and negative core values make up different people's belief structures. As a way of example, here are a few positive core values to consider: kindness, integrity, diligence, discipline, respect, service, love, loyalty, fairness, authenticity, balance, compassion, and hundreds more.

While you consider your own personal core values, take time to write them down, regardless of how many you list. Once you have all your core values listed, look back over the previous week or even the past thirty days. Are there areas in your life where you can see that you have not lived up to your core values? If there are, do not deny it, neglect it, ignore it, or in some way try to sweep it under the rug, hoping it will go away. An approach of this nature will not work. In the short-term it may appear to be working, but it won't last for the long-term. Ultimately, this will eat away at the core of your being, because you cannot continue to live against the core values in your life and mentally survive. When you see those inconsistencies in your life, the only solution is to fix them.

Each morning you draw air into our lungs, you're blessed with the opportunity to approach the day with a renewed focus on correcting inconsistencies in your life. When you focus on improving your character, you cannot rest as long as these inconsistencies exist. I previously talked about consistency, but now it's time to make application. How does one develop greater consistency? Here are a few suggestions.

1) *Pray*: Start and end each day seeking help from God. The one who knows you best desires that you improve your consistency, because when you do, it strengthens your character. "Pray without ceasing" (1 Thessalonians 5:17).

2) *Determine your core values*: I provided a list of several core values above. Look through and select from that list, or add your own. You know those core values of your life that will not change. Write them down and look at them daily.

3) *Conduct a character audit daily*: At the end of each day, take time to look back over the day and see where you did not live according to those core values. Pray about it and ask for help. Start the next day with an emphasis on changing that area.

4) *Resolve to focus on one at a time*: Don't get overwhelmed with trying to focus on multiple areas. Focus your attention on one, and work on it until you succeed with consistency. Then focus on the next area. If you need to start over, then do so.

5) *Keep emotions in check*: Emotions can be deceptive. Above all, emotions change. A person can struggle to become consistent if emotions take over. Work to prevent emotions from justifying an area inconsistent with your core values.

6) *Seek an accountability partner*: This step will help immensely. You can select a spouse, parent, friend, or coworker. Find someone you're comfortable sharing the inadequacies of your life with, and ask that person to help you develop consistency. Talk regularly about it and how to improve.

Life and leadership. Just as water is essential to life, character is essential to our leadership. Both provide the foundational building blocks that make up the very substance of our existence. Throughout this section, I examined biblical teaching in relationship to the type of character that can enter into and dwell in the presence of God. Character is far more than what you do—it's who you are on the inside. This was David's point in Psalm 15. If I were to sum up the thoughts expressed in this psalm, I could do so with one word: trustworthy. Each of us needs to live a life worthy of God's trust in us, and the question that demands our consideration is "Can God trust me?" The companions of trust are respect and credibility; they're two sides of the same coin, and all three contribute to the development of our character. However, all the information about character won't help if you don't figure out how best to apply what you've learned. *The Choice Diagram, 10-10-10 Principle,* and *Character Audit* challenge you to consider the decisions you make and how those decisions determine your character. Remember, choices determine your character, and your character determines the choices you make. Imagine the power of character when it's accompanied with passion, which I examine in the next section.

Building Block 4
Passion: The Intentionality of Life and Leadership

The Lead-In: Living to Eat, or Eating to Live?
Our food should be our medicine and our medicine should be our food.
Hippocrates

I have a confession to make: I love to eat—and I love to eat all the time. The idea of eating to live is a foreign concept to me. Do you remember in *The Avengers* when Captain America tells Bruce Banner, "Dr. Banner, now might be a good time to get angry"? The Hulk's response is classic: "That's my secret, Captain: I'm always angry." Before mealtime each day, my wife often asks me if I'll be hungry. Well, I usually say something like "That's my secret: I'm always hungry." My favorite thing to do is snack. I would snack all day if it were possible. Let me back up and explain a bit of my journey.

In 2000, I became friends with a man in Arkansas who was a raw foodist. Before you start asking, "Did he eat raw meat?" "Where did he get his protein?" and a dozen other questions, let me say that a raw foodist eats fruit, nuts, and vegetables in the food's natural state. Nothing is cooked or processed, and—just for the sake of clarification—they don't eat raw meat. As our friendship grew, I felt it might be interesting to try this raw-food diet and see what happened. Before I dove into what I considered to be the craziest thing I'd ever heard (I know you were thinking the same thing, so I thought I'd go ahead and say it), I did a little research.

My research took me down several interesting paths. I read books such as *Nature's First Law: The Raw Food Diet* and *12 Steps to Raw Foods: How to End your Dependency on Cooked Foods.* Among other materials, I looked at several websites and read numerous articles. I even received an interesting DVD from a company that discussed the value of enzymes. I continue to be amazed by the fact that all food in its natural state has enzymes. These enzymes serve a distinct purpose: to aid in the digestive process of the foods we eat. Additionally, when we consume food in this natural state, we benefit from the full nutritional value of the vitamins contained in that food. There's something about the cooking process that robs food of the majority—if not all—of its nutritional value. (Note: I don't intend this to be a discussion about what you eat or how much you eat—I'm simply explaining my journey and what I learned.)

When I learned that eating a raw food diet would not hurt me in the short- or long-term, I decided to try it. Initially, I experienced a few physical changes as I lost weight rather rapidly. I discovered that my body went through a purging process, which took about sixty days. There were times when I felt physically drained (partly because I continued to exercise at nearly the same level as before), but I stuck with it. After about two months, big changes began to happen. I slept better at night, and I had more energy during the day. My weight balanced out, and I felt physically better than I've ever felt in my life. I also experienced a few challenges, mainly from a social perspective, as people did not know what to prepare for me to eat and, as a result, they no longer invited my wife and me over for meals. When we did meet in social gatherings, there were tons of questions about why anyone would eat this way. Also, when we went out to restaurants, the challenges continued—few restaurants cater to the raw food diet, with the exception of salads, which few do well.

While I have not continued to follow the raw food diet, I learned many lessons and am thankful that it made me more aware of what I eat. Later, as I studied more about the parallels between life and leadership, I came across an interesting article about enzymes. University of Missouri professor Olen Brown suggests enzymes possess what he considers to be "near-miraculous abilities." He goes on to explain why in his article about the essential nature of enzymes to life:

> They are catalysts that greatly accelerate reactions by providing an alternate reaction pathway with a much lower energy barrier. Thus, although they do not create new reactions, they greatly enhance the rate at which a particular substrate is changed into a particular product. *Every chemical reaction in the cell that is essential to life is made possible by an enzyme*[1] (emphasis mine).

Enzymes contribute to the whole of life, and they're essential because they work as a digestive agent in all natural foods. According to Kara Rogers, editor of Encyclopedia Brittanica, enzymes provide a catalyst in the digestive process:

> The biological processes that occur within all living organisms are chemical reactions, and most are regulated by enzymes. Without enzymes, many of these reactions would not take place at a perceptible rate. Enzymes catalyze all aspects of cell metabolism. This includes the digestion of food, in which large nutrient molecules (such as proteins, carbohydrates, and fats) are broken down into smaller molecules; the conservation and transformation of chemical energy; and the construction of cellular macromolecules from smaller precursors.[2]

Digestive enzymes are essential to processing the food we consume. Amylase, protease, and lipase are enzymes involved in the digestive process. Each provides a specific function in the breakdown and process of digesting foods within the intestinal track. Sadly, when heat, disease, and harsh chemical conditions exist, the effectiveness of enzymes is altered and damaged and they no longer work. According to Ryan Raman for Healthline, "If the body is unable to make enough digestive enzymes, food molecules cannot be digested properly. This can lead to digestive disorders such as lactose intolerance. Thus, eating foods that are high in natural digestive enzymes can help improve digestion."[3] Ultimately, the inability to properly digest foods leads to disease and death.

The study of food enzymes and their value is impressive. Food enzymes supply essential nutrients to strengthen our physical lives. Dr. Howard Loomis points out, "Plant enzymes can enhance the digestion of food and the delivery of nutrients to the blood even if you have a compromised digestive system. The same cannot be said of animal enzymes such as pancreatin."[4] Three broad classifications of enzymes include the following:

1) *Food enzymes*—occur in raw food and, when present in the diet, begin the process of digestion.

2) *Digestive enzymes*—produced by the body to break food into particles small enough to be carried across the gut wall.

3) *Metabolic enzymes*—produced by the body to perform various complex biochemical reactions.

Let that sink in for a moment. Imagine the powerful life-giving nature of the food we eat. The result leads me back to the concept of living to eat or eating to live. Usually, the approach of living to eat leads down a path of consuming foods that are typically not the most healthy. When our approach is eating to live, we tend to think about what we eat and the long-term effects on our physical health and well-being. I've heard others talk about how the foods that taste good aren't good for you—and I've been guilty of this as well. Speaking these words should be an indicator that I'm more concerned with living to eat as opposed to eating to live.

We have to stop and consider the scope of the foods available and the measure of health value they possess. I remember telling my students, "When we break for lunch and you end up at a fast food restaurant, do not ask God to bless that burger and fries to nourish your body—it would take a miracle to make that happen." I don't intend to get into a discussion about what you eat and why you choose the food you eat. I'm guilty of knowing far better than I practice. Writing the introduction to this section reminds me of how much I need to work on this area in my life. I'm a stress eater and a bored eater. What that means is that I tend to eat for comfort when I'm stressed or bored. When I feel anxious, I think about food. If I don't stay active, my first thought is to eat something, anything. Herein lies the battle for me, and I know others share the struggle.

I grew up hearing people say things like "You are what you eat." It took many years before I understood the truth behind that sentiment. If what we eat does not give us life, then the alternative must take life away. When the food we choose to eat provides us with energy and life, doesn't it make sense we would focus on eating healthier? Again, that may not be your choice, and that's okay. I have my battles, and you have yours. I hope we both remember that God gave us food for a reason, and it wasn't to destroy us but to give us life—to provide energy. We need to be moderate, cautious, and thoughtful to steward our health in the way God intended.

While they aid the digestive process, these enzymes also work to build and stabilize our immune systems. I appreciate the words of Pam Omidyar, founder of HopeLab: "Enzymes are the catalysts that make possible biochemical reactions. Enzymes increase the rate of a reaction, but are not themselves consumed by the reaction. . . . In short, enzymes are nature's activists." Thus, we should all *be* enzymes. As nature's activists, enzymes are essential to life, and the nature of enzymes describes another essential to leadership: passion. Passion is the activist for leading. As I move through the following chapters, I discuss passion and the impact of a passionate leader. Join me in these final steps to understanding the essentials of life and leadership.

Chapter 13
Defining Passion

Having a passionate interest in something burns our heart and ignites the fire and makes us concentrate on what we love, curiously learn more about it and persistently follow our desires and create a productive impression out of it.
Pantea Kalhor

I love the work I do. I don't know how to express adequately the level of my passion about working with leaders, learning from and sharing what I've learned with them. Like enzymes, you could say that my passion is the spark, activist, or life-giving energy behind my work. For me, it doesn't get any better. However, it has not always been this way. I started college directly out of high school. While I did well in high school, college really wasn't for me. I went one year, earned about thirty credit hours, and took the next year off to work. A year later, I found myself married and starting a family. Over the course of about ten years, I tried just about everything. I packed ice cream into trucks at the local Yarnell's Ice Cream plant, worked in quality control at Travenol Laboratories, stuffed flyers into a local newspaper, performed clerical work for United Way, served as a disc jockey at a roller skating rink, sang in a country/rock-n-roll band, reported news and weather for a radio station, installed car stereos and sold instruments at a music store, and managed a construction equipment company. My work experience is vast. As I neared the age of thirty, I developed a desire to learn the Bible and teach. Almost sixteen years after I graduated, I worked in the mission field and served a local congregation. It was not until a few years later, while teaching for my alma mater, that I discovered what I was most passionate about: leadership.

The seeds were planted in those first few years of education, but the fire was ignited almost ten years ago, and I've poured everything I know into reading about leadership, talking with leaders, and speaking at every opportunity. My future became clearer and my heart burned with the desire to help change the course of the future by developing leaders.

Jonathan Byrnes defines leaders as "people who leave their footprints in their areas of passion." Passion is the fuel for leadership vision. Passion is the activist behind the achievement of goals. Passion changes lives. In reality, how can a leader change the lives of others if their own life has not first been changed? Here is where their passion begins.

Ask yourself, "What am I passionate about in life and work?" There should be something exciting about waking up each day. When was the last time you could not sleep because of something you were excited about? John Maxwell reminds us, "A leader with great passion and few skills always outperforms a leader with great skills and no passion."[1] Passion is the driving motivation within leaders. Passion gets them up and moves them forward like enzymes activate the chemical reactions in our body.

Apathy and indifference destroy passionate leadership. The Bible reminds us of the dangers and consequences of both. Jesus addressed this in Revelation 3:14–22 with the church of Laodicea. The result of the apathetic Laodicean attitude was self-reliance and blindness to their true needs. Because the Laodiceans were so lukewarm, Jesus said, "I will vomit you out of My mouth" (3:16 NKJV). Passion will not allow us to remain lukewarm.

John Wesley is credited with saying, "When you set yourself on fire, people will come to watch you burn." Give this some thought. If you and I are going to be activists as leaders, passion is a must. Mark Batterson wrote, "We die when our hearts stop skipping a beat in pursuit of our passions, when our hearts stop breaking for the things that break the heart of God."[2] How can you and I have the kind of passion to bring success to leadership? In this chapter, I explore several areas related to the power of passion—the key to being an activist, a spark-plug in the world surrounding us.

Passion is defined in three major ways: (1) emotion—intense, driving, or overmastering feeling or conviction, an outbreak of anger; (2) love—a strong liking or desire for or devotion to some activity, object, or concept, sexual desire, an object of desire or deep interest; and (3) suffering—the sufferings of Christ, the state or capacity of being acted on by external agents or forces.[3] As humans, we experience all three definitions of passion. I will focus more on the third definition in the next chapter.

Over the past ten years, I've asked numerous people in different workshops and classes to define passion. A few of the ideas shared include the following: (1) a strong emotion, barely controllable; (2) a feeling of enthusiasm or excitement about what we do; and (3) an extravagant desire for any activity, sport, study, etc. As odd as it may sound, apart from these definitions, we most often associate passion with excitement and enthusiasm. People can get excited about work, family, faith, friends, recreation, hobbies, sports, and more. When we see their exuding enthusiasm, we tend to identify them as passionate.

Before I dig more deeply into the topic, I need to distinguish the difference between intensity and passion. Based on the definition of passion, it would seem that one feeds into the other; after all, from an emotional perspective, passion is intense. There's some truth to this connection. Intensity is defined as "the quality or state of being intense (marked by or expressive of great zeal, energy, determination, or concentration), an extreme degree of strength, force, energy, or feeling."[4] However, Steve Moore explains the difference between intensity and passion by contrasting the characteristics associated with both concepts in the list below.

Intensity	**Passion**
I want *you* to believe	*I* really believe this
Marked by *emotion*	Marked by *conviction*
Packaged by *hype*	Comes with *authenticity*
Appears *superficial*	Appears *natural*
Talks *loudly*	Talks *plainly*[5]

The first time I read through these distinctions, I began to reflect on periods of my life where I had tried to convey passion but instead expressed intensity. I was attempting to convince others to act when I had not acted myself. Somehow, I believed that enough hype and elevated volume made the message more believable. The truth in these distinctive marks of intensity and passion were helpful. I hope they will benefit you as you examine what you're passionate about and how you express that passion to others.

Why is passion so important to leadership? I could spend an entire chapter discussing this question and never reach the depths of the answer. Leaders without passion will not lead. They lose interest, they cannot inspire others, and they lack the drive to achieve their vision. In an article for Growing Leaders, Steve Moore said,

> Passion is important for leaders for at least two reasons. First, your passion as a leader is one piece of the self-awareness puzzle that will enable you to focus your energies on the causes that resonate with the core of who you are. In addition to your personality, natural talents and gifts, you need to understand and tap into your passions. Second, as a leader you will need to help others understand their passions so you can place members of your team in areas of responsibility that contain what I call "passionators," intrinsic motivational forces that flow from inner passion.[6]

Crucial to this discussion is understanding that when passion exists in the life of a leader, they surround themselves with people who light their fire and keep them motivated to lead. The infectious nature of this cycle changes the whole organization.

In his book *The Entrepreneur Roller Coaster: Why Now is the Time To #Join the Ride*, Darren Hardy identifies what he calls "four passion switches."[7] Each of these passion switches connects to a biblical thought expressed by Paul. Let's take a look at each one and how they relate to Christianity today.

Passionate about What We Do

This is the area most people think about in relationship to passion. People believe that a person must be passionate about what they do for work and in daily tasks for home and business, most of which go unnoticed and receive no glory. Most think that when someone is passionate about what they do, we see it in their actions. In reality, even if people are passionate about what they do, they're not always passionate about the hard work they have to do in order to achieve success. Observers tend to see only the thirty minutes to an hour of a performance from an entertainer, athlete, actor, or actress. We miss the thousands—if not tens of thousands—of agonizing hours they spent preparing for that short time period. However, the reason they struggle through those preparatory hours is because they are passionate about what they do. There will always be specific parts of what you do that require greater effort, even when it comes to your passion.

The Driving Power Principle: In Paul's letter to the church at Corinth, we see his passion for what he did. The evidence is clear in all of his writings. Paul was passionate about the main thing—and the main thing was preaching the gospel. His passion was so strong that he wrote, "If I preach the gospel, I have nothing to boast of, for I am under compulsion; for woe is me if I do not preach the gospel" (1 Corinthians 9:16). He reiterated this thought throughout this chapter and all of his letters. Paul was passionate about what he did.

Passionate about Why We Do It

This passion switch ignites greater passion about what we do. Understanding the *why* behind what we do often makes the difference moving forward. *Why* becomes the proverbial "game-changer" for passion. Hardy explains that even though someone may not always be passionate about what they do, they may be passionate about why they do it. He says,

> For me, the why is being able to impact people, being able to serve you guys, being able to help awaken people's potential, help change people's mindsets or level of thinking. Help them grow and improve themselves in their lives. Helping people make changes. Helping people explore different choices, and options, and opportunities that could help impact people's lives. For me, that why is exciting. The fact that I get to do that is pretty powerful.[8]

It's vital to consider why you do what you do and why you're passionate about it. When the why factor exists, your passion levels soar.

The "So That" Principle: As Paul continued to express his passion in his letter to the Corinthians, he used the phrase "so that" seven times between verses 19–23. Each time Paul used these two words, he followed them with an explanation of why he was passionate about preaching the gospel: "So that I may win." His idea of winning was not like winning a sports event. For Paul, it was about winning souls to Jesus. In fact, not only was Paul passionate about why he preached, he also urged these Christians to live for the same purpose. He concluded the chapter with a final reference to his *why*: "I discipline my body and make it my slave so that after I have preached to others, I myself will not be disqualified" (1 Corinthians 9:27). Paul was passionate about why he preached the gospel.

Passionate about How We Do It

The third passion switch is one that involves the effort given to ensure a greater quality of outcome. When people do their jobs with a smile, when they go above and beyond what is required, and when they do so naturally, they're passionate about how they do their jobs. They're never satisfied with doing just enough to get by, to maintain the status quo. This concept involves excellence above and beyond the minimum. Too often we see people that do as little as possible to get by and still get a paycheck. Students often do the bare minimum in order to pass the test or class. Children only do what they're specifically told to do and nothing more. A number of factors contribute to this behavior, but the lack of passion for how they do these tasks is clear. When someone is passionate about how they do what they do, it's easily and quickly recognized. There's an added component here: not only is it about the effort to ensure quality, but it's about the mindset that accompanies it—finding joy in doing the extra because it provides quality. I told our children growing up to choose a career they loved. If they discovered they didn't love what they were doing, they should quit and do something else. Life is too short not to love what you do and do what you love. When you love *what* you do, you become passionate about how you do it.

Principle of Flexibility: Paul was also passionate about how he preached the gospel. We see this in the description of what I call the *principle of flexibility*. Notice in the text how Paul was willing to adapt to the situation in order to help others come to know Jesus. He began by saying, "Though I am free from all men, I have made myself a slave to all, so that I may win the more" (1 Corinthians 9:19). Consider

208

the depth of this thought. Paul was free; he owed no one anything. However, he made himself a slave for the purpose of winning souls to Christ. He followed this thought by saying, "To the Jews I became as a Jew . . . to those who are under the Law, as under the law . . . to those who are without law, as without law . . . To the weak I became weak . . . I have become all things to all men so that I may by all means save some" (9:20–22). Note that Paul never compromised truth, practiced sin, or condoned sinful behavior. He was, however, flexible. The work was not about him—it was about others and helping them come to know Jesus. If that meant adapting, Paul adapted. We could learn much from this principle today. Paul was passionate about how he went about the work.

Passionate about Who We Do It For

The final passion switch is the most significant of the four. Hardy identifies the outward focus of this passion switch. When you're passionate about who you do this for, you turn your attention away from yourself and put it on others. Who you do this for may be the company, your boss, coworkers, direct reports, etc. It may be your family, spouse, children, parents, siblings, etc. You may turn your attention toward friends in an effort to help them reach their potential. You can also focus on the people in your community to help improve the growth and development of where they live. While passion exists for *who*—family, friends, work, community—there's something far greater at work here, as we see in the life of Paul. Being passionate about who you do this for becomes a strong force in the direction of your life.

Ultimate Principle: Paul was definitely passionate about who he did this for, as the text indicates. We might start with acknowledging the people Paul wrote to in the Corinthian letter. He was passionate about these Christians. We might also point to the people he wanted to reach with the gospel: the Jews, those under the Law, those who were without law, the weak, and anyone else. Ultimately, we know that who Paul did this work for was Christ. The Lord directed him, as he identifies in 1 Corinthians 9:14. Paul knew that it was only by God's grace that he had hope for the future resurrection. This factor was the driving force behind Paul's passion, and it continued throughout his ministry, whether he was in prison, beaten, shipwrecked, or anything else. He kept his focus on the Lord and wanted everyone to know about the saving power of the message entrusted to him.

These four passion switches relate and apply to our lives today. From a spiritual perspective, we have the evidence of Paul's letters to guide us in all four areas. We cannot read about Paul's life and study the letters he wrote to individuals and the church without walking away impressed with his passion.

Passion is contagious. The infectious nature of passion draws people to leaders. When passion fuels the heart of a leader, people follow. Like the enzymes in food ignite a life-giving source to our bodies, passion lights the direction and ignites the activities that achieve success. Tim Elmore presents "three fundamental issues" that he highlighted in the form of three questions:

1) What do we really want? (This is about your **desires**),

2) Why do we want it? (This is about your **motives**), and

3) How badly do we want it? (This is about your **passion**).[9]

Knowing our desires, motives, and passion will provide a foundation to better understand the application of the four passion switches (*what* we do, *why* we do it, *how* we do it, and *who* we do it for).

By now, you should have an awareness of passion and how passion impacts the direction of life and leadership. Angela Duckworth's book GRIT addresses the power of passion and perseverance.[10] I cover more from her book in chapters 15 and 16, but her concepts help illuminate the significance and power of passion. Let me explain with an illustration.

Passion develops as we discover what we most enjoy doing. How many times are young people urged to pursue their passions, yet they don't know what they're passionate about? High school seniors parade through one university after another, wooed by a university representative who tells them all the reasons why their educational establishment is better than the rest. A common question asked of these spry young people is "What are your interests?" I realize not every high school senior was like me—and we should be thankful for this. However, my experience has shown that a large majority of young people have no idea what they want to do when they select a university to attend where they will spend the next four years of their life and thousands of dollars each year. Is it possible that these young people enter college believing that in the first two years of college, they'll learn the basics and that by the end of that time, they'll figure out what they really want to do? At some point, they have to select a major, or the years and financial debt mount quickly.

In large part, the problem stems from the socioeconomic status forced on high school seniors. From birth, we parents tell our children they need to plan to attend college, get a degree that will help them find a job, and make enough money to support themselves and a family. The list goes on and on. We inform them that if they want a car, they have to pay for it. If they plan to put gas in it, they need a job. Of course, there's insurance. Just to have transportation, young people are shoved down a massive hole of debt. Additionally, there are student loan debts, eating out, cellphone bills, clothes, and extracurricular activities. By the way, I haven't yet touched on the idea of passion. We want our young people to be socially connected and financially stable. Yet how many parents or high schools actually equip young people with the skills to manage money—especially when they leave university with an on-average debt of more than $100,000? I'm not stating an absolute, because I realize it isn't the same for every young person entering or exiting college, but it applies to many.

Imagine the difference if young people were encouraged to take the necessary time to explore different areas that might interest them. When they find something they love to do, maybe we could say "passionate about," *then* focus on the educational needs to prepare them for that specific field of work.

How long will it take you to find your passion? I don't have the answer. I only know how long it took me. But when it happens, you'll know it, and all of your life will change. There will be ups and downs, highs and lows, challenges, obstacles, and roadblocks. At times, it will seem like everyone and everything is trying to stop you. However, when that passion burns inside you, it will be like Jeremiah when he tried to stop speaking God's word: "Then in my heart it becomes like a burning fire shut up in my bones; and I am weary of holding it in and I cannot endure it" (Jeremiah 20:9). Enzymes are essential to life, as they activitate and energize our bodies to move and function. Passion in leadership is essential for the same reasons. Passion sparks the driving force to conquer and achieve. I pray you discover your passion and pursue it with all your strength. When you do, you will begin to understand the direction of the next chapter.

Chapter 14
Passion—Sacrifice

He who would accomplish little must sacrifice little;
he who would achieve much must sacrifice much;
he who would attain highly must sacrifice greatly.
James Allen

Three years ago I had the privilege of visiting with Steve Moore, current president of Growing Leaders and author of *Who Is My Neighbor: Being a Good Samaritan in a Connected World.* Our visit was the result of my efforts to learn about passion. A few months prior to my discussion with Steve, I was researching the subject of passion. I read everything I could find on the subject—books, articles, blog posts—and I listened to podcasts. I was convinced that if it was possible to determine what someone was passionate about, you could direct that passion in a spiritual way to the glory of God and the benefit of His church.

During my research, I came across a blog post at growingleaders.com. The article featured (at the time) guest writer Steve Moore. In the article, Moore mentioned a passion profile he had developed. Through a series of emails and phone calls, I was able to connect with him and we talked about the passion profile, how it worked, and the material as it related to his book. You can see a sample of the profile at whoismyneighborbook.com. I am excited to share some of the ideas from Moore's book in this chapter about passion.

In chapter 13, I referenced Moore's distinction between intensity and passion. In *Who Is My Neighbor*, as he develops the concept of passion, he discusses three types of passion.[1] The first is an "interest-based" passion. An interest-based passion is characterized by areas we find enjoyable, do leisurely, have fun participating in, or have some natural abilities or giftedness in (e.g., golf, basketball, football, baseball, knitting, tennis, hunting, etc.). The second is an "issues-based" passion. An issues-based passion involves areas that bring fulfillment, purpose, and legacy. These are causes that often emerge from experience (e.g., homelessness; children's homes; physical, mental, emotional and sexual abuse; environmental causes; social justice, etc.). Everyone has both interest- and issues-based passions. Moore says, "We tend to like things we are 'good at' and are good at things 'we like.'"

The third type of passion provides a different perspective and leads to an important part of the focus in this chapter; it is an "incarnational passion." Moore describes how threads that blend our interest-based passions with issues-based passions come together to form incarnational passion. By way of example, he describes "a person who has musical interests, plays the guitar and sings. If this person had a corresponding issues-based passion for social justice, they could weave these threads together in a band, like Bono and U2. This is what I call an incarnational passion, and is lived out in real life situations or roles."

After he explains these three types of passion, Moore describes what he calls "the passion pyramid." The passion pyramid has four levels. These levels of passion guide our understanding of how the types of passion play out in our lives. I encourage you to pick up a copy of Moore's book to see a visual of what I will explain below.

- Level 1: *Learn more about it.* This connects to both interest- and issues-based passion. When we're passionate about specific areas, we begin to look for information. We want to learn more about particular interests or issues. We read articles online, find books with more information, and talk to people who have expertise in those areas. We put forth a great deal of effort to learn as much as we can before we decide to take the next step and move to the second level.

- Level 2: *Engage in activities.* Once we've done our research and read the information as it relates to the areas we're passionate about, we get involved in activities. This may take us down the path of helping at a homeless shelter, serving in a children's home, etc. We may also pick up sports (golf or tennis), get involved in recreational activities (boating, camping, etc.). After we've learned information that satisfies our interests or issues, we become motivated to engage in a variety of related activities. We want to learn if this is something we'll like. If we do, we go to the next level.

- Level 3: *Influence others*. At this level, we begin talking to others about what we've learned and experienced. We want others to see the enjoyment, value, benefit, or need that might attract them to also get involved. We find great satisfaction in seeing others follow the same path we've taken. We take advantage of every means available to influence others: text messages, emails, phone calls, and face-to-face discussions. We become so passionate we cannot confine the information to ourselves. We want others to know and participate. Regardless of how people respond to our influence, we have moved to a decision connected to the next level.

- Level 4: *Even when sacrifice is required*. The final level identified by Moore is one that takes passion to the highest level. In this level, one is ready to make whatever sacrifice is required to participate in their area of passion. What sacrifices are required at this level depend on the specific areas of interest or the issues we're passionate about. However, when we reach this level, nothing stands in the way. We're willing to make any sacrifice, because we see the value of what we have committed our lives to fulfill.

The ideas expressed by Steve Moore in the passion pyramid have a broad range of application to every area of life. Although he illustrates these in the form of a pyramid, with level 4 being the pinnacle of passion, I see the pattern as more cyclical in nature. Here's why: Once someone spends the time to learn about a specific area, they get engaged in activities related to it and realize how much they love it. They then influence others and start making the sacrifices necessary to continue. When they reach this point, it's a matter of starting over. At this stage, I find that I want to learn even more about this area. I read more books, articles, and blog posts, and I talk to more people who are experts in the area. I also get more engaged. I spend more time meeting the needs of the issue. Of course, I broaden my scope of influence and work to get more people involved than before. The step to making more and greater sacrifice seems natural. From there, it starts over again and grows and grows. This is how passion works.

I also visualize the pyramid at work from a Christian perspective. People naturally find themselves at all different levels spiritually. Biblically, leaders are tasked with the responsibility of helping others move up the pyramid, encouraging brethren to move from level 2 on up the pyramid. If we're not careful, it's easy to stay in the area of learning and learning and learning. In fact, we tend to enjoy this mode of learning in church weekly, which isn't bad, but we can't stay there. For the most part, we've moved into the activity level. We get engaged in activities such as worship, fellowship meals, game nights, ladies' days, leadership retreats, Vacation Bible School, etc. We enjoy being with like-minded people.

The challenge arises when we move to level 3. Now it's time to influence others. We need to tell others about what we've learned and the activities we participate in each week. Developing relationships with others in order to influence them for Christ is tough. We can make all kinds of excuses, but the bottom line is we need to move to this level. Only when we move to this level do we recognize the importance of making sacrifices. We have to stop and ask ourselves what level of passion we have in our Christian walks. We might also ask what level we would use to describe our congregations. Are we dabbling in learning, half-heartedly engaging in worship but nothing else? Are we afraid to speak to anyone about Jesus? We grow in passion when we're willing to make sacrifices to serve the Lord, grow in fellowship with His people, strive to achieve greater unity and maturity, and help others come to know Him.

An examination of the early church reveals that when the apostles were persecuted and put to death, the church thrived. On one occasion, after some apostles were imprisoned, beaten, and then released, they returned to their companions and reported what happened. They prayed together and immediately "the place where they had gathered together was shaken, and they were all filled with the Holy Spirit and began to speak the word of God with boldness"

(Acts 4:31). Their passion grew, and the church grew proportionately in every way. This is the power of passion when connected to sacrifice.

Ultimately, when we talk about passion, we're talking about sacrifice. It's the focus of this chapter and what is most important to understand about the subject. You're probably familiar with Mel Gibson's movie *The Passion of Christ. Passion* is a word that comes to us from the Latin word *passio*, which means "to suffer."[2] Thus, *The Passion of Christ* was really about the suffering of the Christ. One only needs to watch the movie to understand the direct correlation between the two words.

We recognize a number of individuals throughout history who, because of their passion, suffered immensely—some to the point of death. Martin Luther King, Jr. once again comes to mind. He said, "If a man has not discovered something he will die for, he isn't fit to live." Take a few moments and let that resonate. How would you relate this thought to your own faith? Are you passionate enough about your relationship with God that you're willing to die for it?

Knowing about Sacrifice

In his book *The 21 Irrefutable Laws of Leadership,* John Maxwell talks about the "law of sacrifice."[3] He shares what leaders need to know about sacrifice.

There Is No Success Without Sacrifice

Anyone who experiences success in business, in the home, or any area of life (academic, social, physical) knows there are sacrifices to be made. Leaders sacrifice much in order to achieve success. I often ask groups at workshops to make a list of what leaders must sacrifice in order to lead. Here are a few of the responses I've collected: time, family, influence (popularity), money, privacy, personal needs, power/ authority, relationships, ambition, benefits . . . and the list goes on. Think about your own successes. Did any of them come without any level of sacrifice?

To Lead Means to Sacrifice

When leaders are passionate, they know sacrifice is a part of the package. Although Maxwell did not specifically list this in his book, the thought is implied. When someone takes on the responsibility of leading, it means sacrifice. There are a couple of reasons this is true. First, their focus is no longer on themselves but on others—they seek to meet the needs of those who follow in order to help them reach their greatest potential. Second, every leader knows they're responsible, and with that responsibility comes accountability. Leaders must give an account for those they lead, and the mental stress of that contributes to the sacrifice involved.

Leaders Are Asked to Give Up More Than Others

Leaders give up the right to think about themselves. The reason behind this connects to the other four statements in this list. Leaders are asked to give up more than others because they have greater responsibility and accountability. If everything rises and falls on leadership, then success or failure is part of the equation, thus the validity of the thought expressed here. Leaders give up more because they must constantly work at improving who they are as leaders and because they're required to make greater sacrifices. More could be said, but the truth remains: leaders will always be asked to give up more than others. Both the consequences and rewards are greater, and the responsibility of leading requires one to bear the burden.

You Must Keep Giving Up to Stay Up

Maxwell terms it this way: "Leadership success requires continual change, constant improvement, and on-going sacrifice." Change is the one constant in life. Everything and everyone changes. Leadership is no different. The changes that exist require a leader who knows the changes to make and when to make them. In order for leaders to keep up with the challenges before them, they must constantly work on ways to improve. This means learning from others, trial and error, and a willingness to admit wrong, learn from it, and move forward. Leaders willingly make these sacrifices because they know the outcome is the improvement of the overall individual, team, organization, or church.

The Higher the Level of Leadership, the Greater the Sacrifice

I cannot imagine the sacrifice required for someone to serve as the president of the United States. The constant scrutiny they face from the press, opposite party, and disgruntled Americans is beyond my capabilities. This is not the only level of leadership that establishes this point. When a husband and wife become parents, their level of leadership goes up and requires greater sacrifice. When an employee accepts a promotion, their level of leadership goes up and requires greater sacrifice. The higher we continue to go, the more this is true. Regardless of the location—home, world, or the church—as people ascend to a higher level of leadership, they will be required to make greater sacrifices. This is part of leadership.

Developing the Mind of Sacrifice

Anyone who has served or currently serves as a leader acutely understands the point of this chapter. Sacrifice factors into every decision leaders make. The journey has never been nor will ever be easy. However, it's vital to consider what it takes to develop a mind of sacrifice. A leader who willingly makes necessary sacrifices must examine four key areas, which I examine below.

See the Need

The need for leaders in the church has reached crisis level. I believe that unless churches develop plans for training the next generation to lead, there will not be a church left. Research supports this: In a recent report from the Barna Research group,[4] more than fifteen thousand eighteen- to thirty-five-year-old adults were surveyed regarding the leadership crisis. Approximately 82 percent of those surveyed stated we face a leadership crisis today. When asked about the greatest challenges facing leaders today, 50 percent claimed people are too busy to deal with the problem, and 38 percent referenced the problem of the older generation not allowing the younger generation to lead. David Kinnaman, president of Barna Research, says, "If we're not making room for younger leaders today, they won't be around tomorrow." I don't have all the answers, but the need seems pretty clear. The test will be our willingness to see the need and act upon it in ways that change the direction of the future. Perhaps we need to literally and metaphorically apply the words Jesus spoke to the apostles: "Lift up your eyes and look on the fields, that they are white for harvest" (John 4:35). We face greater needs when we look at the physical, emotional, and spiritual needs in the world surrounding us. Jesus looked on the multitudes of people and described them as "sheep without a shepherd" and instructed the disciples to plead with God, the Lord of the harvest, to send forth workers into His harvest (Matthew 9:36–38). The workers are you and me. It's time we see the need, roll up our sleeves, and get to work.

Know the Value of the Gift

Do you really understand the value of the gift you have to offer? Until you do, you'll never see the need to offer it. I'm saddened when I think about the older generation's wealth of wisdom that has been pushed aside for newer, faster, and shinier. By this, we're missing out on one of the greatest resources. Imagine the power of older men mentoring younger men to be leaders. The intergenerational relationships created from this approach would change both sides of the spectrum, but it will take both sides demonstrating humility to learn from the other. The older generation needs a willingness to learn new technology, even if they think it's difficult and don't like it. The younger generation needs to listen and be patient, learning from the past and determining how it can impact the direction of the future. Think about what Jesus offered people: he didn't give them clothes, vehicles, money, houses to live in, etc. What Jesus gave people was of such a nature that the recipient could not exchange or return the value. He offered freedom, forgiveness, opportunity, compassion, and love. He gave them *hope*! Jesus gave people hope of a better future. You have the same gift. Again, do you know the value of the gift you have to offer others? When you do, it will change the direction of how you interact with others and the decisions you make toward life and leadership.

Consider the Greater Good

The greater good involves consideration of what's best for the good of the many, not of the one or few. In *Star Trek: The Wrath of Khan*, Spock left the bridge for the engine room, which had been flooded with radiation. After the ship was out of danger, Captain Kirk was called to the engine room, where his friend was dying. When asked why he sacrificed himself, Spock responded, "The needs of the many outweigh the needs of the few, or the one." This point speaks to the whole of humanity, which should be considered. However, we need to begin with thinking about the greater good of the kingdom— God's people. The greater good of the kingdom presently includes the need for leadership development. The survival of the church depends on leaders. God has always required leadership of His people—this is as true in the twenty-first century as it was in the first century. Serious consideration must be given to the greater good of God's people and, naturally, the greater good of the world. I'm confident you're familiar with the statement "People do not care how much you know until they know how much you care." You may have an encyclopedic knowledge or all the wisdom of Solomon, but if you don't show people that you care about them physically and emotionally, they'll never listen to what you have to say about what will help them spiritually. They won't care if they feel that you don't care. I once heard a man express how he had been to several churches seeking help. The consistent response he received was, "I will pray for you." To which he responded, "That's great. I appreciate the prayers, but my stomach is empty." May we consider the greater good and act to make a difference.

Ask the Question

Ultimately, it all comes down to this point. I've talked about the sacrifices required of leaders. You know what they must give up in order to lead. I've looked at the need, the value of the gift, and the greater good surrounding us, yet you have a question to ask. It's not complicated—although it is blunt. You must answer for yourself the most crucial question of this chapter: *Will I make the sacrifice?* I cannot answer the question for you. I can only answer for me, and I know I will be held accountable for how I answer. The road ahead is long and arduous. It's the road less traveled, yet it's one that cries out—screams—that someone take this road. How will you respond?

The enzyme value of food moves us into action, every action that is essential to life. Passion is essential to leadership—and passion leads us to sacrifice. We have seen it over and over throughout this chapter. Passion and sacrifice are terms that naturally go together. As I said, the word passion means "to suffer." Leaders who are passionate will make whatever sacrifice necessary to achieve the vision before them. A late friend from Colorado once gave me a pin for the lapel of my sports coat. The three words on that pin represent a motto to reflect on in terms of life and leadership and their relationship to passion and sacrifice: *Whatever it takes.* I encourage you to take a moment and write that down. Commit it to memory. *Whatever it takes.* Life and leadership require us to give whatever it takes, which is why, next, I introduce conviction and perseverance.

Chapter 15
Conviction, Passion, and Perseverance

You cannot build a dream on a foundation of sand.
To weather the test of storms, it must be cemented in the heart with
uncompromising conviction.
T. F. Hodge

Sir Winston Leonard Spencer-Churchill entered the realm of politics when Great Britain needed someone with conviction. He served as the prime minister of the United Kingdom from 1940 to 1945, and was instrumental in Great Britain's victory over Nazi Germany during World War II. Whether we agree or disagree with or like or dislike his personal life, political ideology, or the controversy surrounding his position on race and human rights, Winston Churchill is one of the most signifiant figures in history. He was a man who embodied conviction.

After serving in the military and fighting numerous battles in the late 1800s, Churchill entered the political arena at the age of twenty-five. His initial political career was cut short as World War I knocked on the door. Entering into military service again, Churchill fought for his country. When the war ended, he continued his involvement with politics. The early rise of Nazi military dominance in Germany during the 1930s concerned Churchill. He battled to reinforce the military infrastructure of Great Britain.

As Germany made its march on the world in 1940, Great Britain would need Churchill's conviction, passion, and perseverance. In late 1940, Ralph Ingersoll reported,

> Everywhere I went in London people admired [Churchill's] energy, his courage, his singleness of purpose. People said they didn't know what Britain would do without him. He was obviously respected. But no one felt he would be Prime Minister after the war. He was simply the right man in the right job at the right time. The time being the time of a desperate war with Britain's enemies.[1]

Churchill's conviction can be demonstrated in his willingness to fight against Germany's terrorism rather than seek terms of peace, which he believed would not yield any different results than fighting. In a speech to the House of Commons on May 13, 1940, he said,

> You ask, what is our aim? I can answer in one word: It is victory, victory at all costs, victory in spite of all terror, victory, however long and hard the road may be; for without victory, there is no survival. Let that be realized; no survival for the British Empire, no survival for all that the British Empire has stood for, no survival for the urge and impulse of the ages, that mankind will move forward toward its goal. But I take up my task with buoyancy and hope. I feel sure that our cause will not be suffered to fail among men.[2]

Although he experienced times of discouragement and even pessimism regarding the outcome of the war, he held firm to his convictions. Churchill is credited with saying, "You have enemies? Good. That means you've stood up for something, sometime in your life." Standing for something is exactly what he did, and his conviction for it is why he represents one of the great leaders in history.

I first heard Angela Duckworth speak at the Global Leadership Summit in August 2017. The message she shared that day was based on material from her book *GRIT: The Power of Passion and Perseverance*.[3] Duckworth's book contains a wealth of information—and I highly recommend reading it—but as I reflected on the material and its application, I felt something was missing. Perhaps this is a matter of semantics, but it didn't seem that passion and perseverance were enough. After thinking through it and discussing the material with others, I came to the conclusion that grit also has to be based on conviction.

Why does conviction belong to the equation? I believe that conviction is the foundation upon which passion and perseverance are built. Here's why. Take a moment and look up the definition of *conviction*. Among the variety of definitions provided, notice the following way in which conviction is described: "A strong persuasion or belief, the state of being convinced, the act of convincing a person of error or of compelling the admission of a truth, the state of being convinced of error or compelled to admit the truth."[4]

Without conviction—i.e. a strong persuasion or belief and being convinced—passion and perseverance do not exist. The convictions we have flow into our passion and are the reason why we persevere. Think for a moment about the characteristics of people you know who have conviction. They won't change, despite circumstances. They're inflexible. They have confidence. They're bold and live out their beliefs and possess strong determination. There's more I could list, but I believe you understand the point I'm trying to make. Conviction is a critical piece of this equation, because conviction fuels our passion and perseverance like the enzyme value of food that fuels our life. Therefore, I first look at conviction.

Conviction

In the discussion about vision in chapter 2, I mentioned the importance of conviction, and I examined the life of Caleb. His conviction is what fueled his passion and drove him to eradicate giants from the mountains, even at age eighty-five. I refer you back to that section, because Caleb is a great biblical example of the power and positive nature of conviction. But I also want to consider another scenario: What happens when someone does not remain focused on or loses sight of their conviction? Such is the case with the apostle Peter.

In some ways, I feel I can relate more to Peter than to any other apostle. Peter made decisions quickly, whether right or wrong. He spoke his mind, only to realize he should have kept his mouth shut. He was impetuous—but bold. How can someone express a willingness to die for Jesus in one breath and in the next deny Him three times? Peter was all in—and then not in at all. He was a man who possessed conviction but struggled in his faith. Perhaps you can also relate to many of these characteristics.

Peter was a fisherman by trade. He knew the challenges of working all night and returning home empty-handed. Based on what we learn from Scripture, he was married, which brought with it responsibility. We don't know if he had children. But we do know that Peter said that he and the other disciples left everything to follow Jesus (Mark 10:28). The commitment to make such a decision doesn't exist without conviction.

As I've mentioned, Peter was far from perfect, but he became one of the first to follow Jesus. Andrew, Peter's brother, introduced Peter to Jesus, and the bond was quickly formed between them. His name was Cephas, but Jesus changed it to Peter because of the close relationship between the name Peter and the Greek word for "rock": *petra*. Jesus said, "I also say to you that you are Peter [*petros*], and upon this rock [*petra*] I will build My church; and the gates of Hades will not overpower it" (Matthew 16:18). He certainly saw something in Peter that even Peter did not see in himself. The work ahead would require someone who understood the rock-solid foundation of Peter's divine acknowledgement of Jesus: "You are the Christ, the Son of the living God" (Matthew 16:16). Conviction of this truth would be the foundation upon which Jesus built His church.

Peter's life as a disciple of Jesus teaches us many lessons, both good and bad. Later, we find Peter as the mouthpiece of the gospel, which was instrumental in the establishment of the early church (Acts 2). Not only is Peter represented here, but we also find his role in the inclusion of the Gentile nation. The first convert, Cornelius, and his household were taught the hope of the gospel by Peter. From the beginning, and throughout the church's early growth, Peter's role is evidenced as the fulfillment of the promise made by Jesus: "I will give you the keys of the kingdom" (Matthew 16:19).

Not until some time later do we see a question mark regarding Peter's conviction. Paul referenced his confrontation of Peter in Galatians 2. Paul condemned Peter for his inconsistent and hypocritical approach to fellowship among Christians, which even influenced Barnabas. The problem was simple: before certain (Jewish-background) leaders in the early church came to visit, Peter ate with and enjoyed fellowship with the Gentiles. However, when these leaders arrived, Peter became distant and removed himself from the fellowship. The text tells us he was afraid, which is not how we understand conviction. Paul addressed this situation directly; he told Peter, "If you, being a Jew, live like the Gentiles and not like the Jews, how is that you compel the Gentiles to live like Jews? (Galatians 2:14). You can read the remainder of the chapter to get the full details of Paul's thoughts. The point is simply that Peter's lack of conviction when facing fear indicates the opposite of how leaders must conduct themselves.

When your foundation consists of conviction, passion and perseverance will follow. As I proceed in this discussion about perseverance, I again mention the incredible conviction and perseverance of Winston Churchill. His conviction moved an entire nation of people and convinced an army to fight with perseverance in the face of insurmountable odds. The result led Great Britain to rise up victorious. Since this is the case, I have to ask, "What prevents people from persevering or being resilient?"

Perseverance

Resilience is a beautiful byproduct and bedfellow to perseverance, because resilience involves bouncing back after adversity. The idea is to rise up in the face of failure. Leaders all experience failure at different times in life. How failure impacts leaders and their response to it determines their resilience. Confucius is credited with many powerful sayings. I'm uncertain as to the validity of all of them, but it's recorded that Confucius claimed, "Our greatest glory is not in never failing, but in rising up every time we fail." Perhaps you heard the same phrase as I did growing up: "If at first you don't succeed, try, try, again." This is resilience. When we rise up in times of failure, we find strength to use failure as a stepping-stone to greater success.

Jake Olson was blind by his twelfth birthday. At eight months of age he was diagnosed with cancer in his eyes. Even though he went through numerous treatments and surgeries, the end result was the loss of his sight, one eye at a time. Left completely blind, many would have abandoned their dreams and visions for the future, but not Jake. His desire to play football was undeterred. With the help of coaches, faculty, and friends, Jake not only played high school football but also went on to play for a Division 1 Top 10 team in the NCAA. How was this possible? What makes Jake so resilient? In Tim Elmore's article about Jake,[5] he shares three lessons about this incredible story.

1) *Relationships*: Elmore points out, "Resilience almost always requires a person to surround themselves with a circle of support. People who are 'fountains' not 'drains' in your life, who replenish your energy and

perspective when you want to give up." Jake's family, friends, and coaching faculty knew how to guide and support him to achieve his dreams.

2)   *Resourcefulness*: Jake knew the task ahead was not easy. Elmore states that Jake "knew he'd have to be resourceful to play on a Division 1 team, so he gained weight (going from 180 to 235 lbs.) and practiced countless hours, holding onto a teammate each time he ran onto the field. With his vision gone, he learned to rely on his other four senses heavily."

3)   *Responsiveness*: Perhaps the most significant part of Jake's resilience is identified by Elmore's description of resilience: "Resilient people by nature are not brittle or stuck in their ways, but they're flexible. They adapt to setbacks and make them set-ups for their goal. I learned a long time ago that people meet changes in one of two ways: they either react or respond. The more responsive people are to setbacks, the more resilient they tend to be." Jake's vision of playing football in the NCAA was not defeated by his setback. Instead, he responded with an attitude and passion that drove him to persevere.

Resilience and perseverance work together, and the result is life-changing, but let's get back to the original question: "What prevents people from persevering or being resilient?" Based on discussions with numerous leaders throughout the country, I've concluded there are three major reasons. This is not an exhaustive list, but as you will see, nearly everything else falls under these headings.

Discouragement

Discouragement is one of the most powerful and destructive tools in our enemy's arsenal. Leaders become discouraged for a number of reasons. The first involves people. When people lack commitment and confidence (insecure) and they constantly complain (never satisfied), leaders struggle. I've heard it said before that leading would be easy if it weren't for the people. There's truth in that thought, but without people, there's no leadership. Second, leaders get tired. It's not uncommon to hear of leaders experiencing what's often called *burnout*. Perhaps a better way to refer to this would be *worn out*. The demands of time, energy, and sacrifice wear on leaders. They require space to refresh, renew, and revitalize their focus and strength. Third, leaders become frustrated. We've all heard the phrase the "best-laid plans of mice and men . . ." When plans aren't correctly implemented, a lack of resources exists and there's a constant drain on a leader's emotions, resulting in frustration. At times, they're simply frustrated with themselves and the situation. They also can become frustrated with the people they lead. Fourth, failure is imminent, and any time leaders experience failure, discouragement soon follows. Success is built on the steps of failure, but when failure stares them in the face, it's hard for leaders to recognize anything ahead. Fifth, unrealistic expectations contribute to discouragement. When goals are set too high, the supply of adequate resources is exhausted and pride sets in, and our expectations can become unrealistic. A healthy amount of confidence benefits leaders throughout any project. However, they must be careful about the twists and turns that move them toward an unhealthy course of action. Finally, leaders get discouraged when they experience fear. People react differently to fear. Some do things as a result of fear that they would not normally do. Others fail to do the things they would normally do. Fear is real and it is powerful, and leaders must learn how to act rather than react when facing fear. These are a few of the various kinds of reactions, and certainly there are more. The worst part occurs when discouragement becomes strong enough that leaders quit. Leaders must rise up in the face of discouragement and press on.

Unwilling to Pay the Price

I've heard people say, "Everyone has their price." Of course, this usually refers to what someone is willing to accept to sell out their convictions, which is not the point I'm trying to make. What prevents people from persevering or being resilient? They're unwilling to pay the price for success. During high school, I wanted to play in a rock-n-roll band more than anything else—or so I thought. I didn't know how to play an instrument, so I took up drums. I laugh as I think about the situation in hindsight. Several guys from school decided to start a band, and we all showed up for practice. We had two drummers (myself included), two six-string guitar players, and one bass-guitar player. The problem was that no one could sing, and not one of the three guitar players knew how to play their instrument. I decided that if I wanted to play in a band, I would have to learn to play the guitar. The challenge came when I told my dad of my dream. I should add here that my dad was one of the finest guitar players I knew. His ability was amazing. I asked for lessons. However, Dad wanted me to learn the basics, and I only wanted to learn the songs. I thought I would be set up if he would teach me how to play "Stairway to Heaven" or "Sweet Home Alabama" or "Smoke on the Water." This was not his plan, so we clashed, and I quit in an attempt to find someone who would let me learn my way. Looking back, I can only imagine what could have happened if I'd been willing to pay the price. I was discouraged. You should know that I eventually found someone who taught me one song, and I went on to learn how to play the guitar and participated in several bands. But this journey would have been far better and easier had I paid the price early on and not become discouraged. Success in life and leadership comes with a price. The price required will be different for each person. When leaders are unwilling to pay that price, they're also unwilling to persevere. The result can be devastating.

Lose Sight of the Goal

A good friend of mine also works in the area of leadership development. When he meets with a group of church leaders, he begins by asking them three questions:

1)   Where are you now?

2)   Where are you headed?

3)   How do you plan to get there?

Each of these questions reveals a great deal of information about the congregation and her leaders. You would be surprised at the number of leaders who don't know how to answer the second and third questions. *Where are you headed?* This seems simple enough, but reality indicates that few individuals know how to answer it. Imagine the result in the church when leaders don't know where they're going. Maintaining the status quo is priority one. The thought of perseverance and resilience does not exist. What is there to persevere in? Why do they need resilience? The entire second section of this book is dedicated to goals and plans. Short- and long-term goals provide great motivation to keep us focused on the road ahead. However, when leaders lose sight of the goal, they tend to revert back to what's familiar and comfortable. I admit there are congregations that seem to function—at least in the short-term—without any idea of where they will be in ten years. Sadly, too many leaders don't care. It's almost as if they took a play out of Hezekiah's handbook of leadership. When representatives from Babylon came to visit Jerusalem, Hezekiah showed them the treasuries of the kingdom. Later, Isaiah rebuked Hezekiah for his carelessness. Hezekiah learned that "'days are coming when all that is in your house, and all that your fathers have laid up in store to this day will be carried to Babylon; nothing shall be left,' says the LORD" (2 Kings 20:17). Because it would not happen in Hezekiah's reign as king, he responded with little concern: "For he thought, 'Is it not so, if there will be peace and truth in my days?'" (2 Kings 20:19). He lost sight of the goal. When leaders today lose sight of the goal, they fail to consider what will happen to the next generation. They only want to ensure it will not happen in their lifetimes.

Throughout the Bible we find examples of people who demonstrated both perseverance and resilience. Job is one of the best examples from the Old Testament. In the first two chapters of Job, we learn about a discussion between God and Satan. Job became the object of that encounter. Satan couldn't see what God saw about the character of Job, so he challenged God and was given permission to hurt Job by doing anything except take Job's life. This happened on two occasions, and each time Job suffered greater loss. Satan wasted no time in the first attack: Job lost all his children and then all his material wealth. His response is classic: "Naked I came from my mother's womb and naked I shall return there. The LORD gave and the LORD has taken away. Blessed be the name of the Lord" (Job 1:21). Job had great faith in God, and despite his hardships, he didn't sin or blame God.

Round two was no less intense. This time, Satan attacked Job's health. The description of the sores, or boils, Job experienced over his entire body is hard—if not impossible—to imagine. The pain must have been indescribable as he sat in an ash heap and scraped the sores with broken pottery (Job 2:7–9). After witnessing her husband suffer so greatly, Job's wife asked Job to curse God and die. I'm confident it hurt her deeply to see her husband suffer. (And remember, she had also lost her children.) Again, Job's integrity remained intact. Job's perseverance and resilience became an example used in the book of James. The Christians to whom James was writing had heard of Job's perseverance and were encouraged to practice the same (James 5:11).

Volumes could be written about the perseverance of Jesus. The Gospels provide an amazing picture of all Jesus encountered through the rejection of religious leaders, false accusations, an unfair trial, brutality beyond comprehension, and His ultimate death on the cross. I don't feel it is necessary to reiterate what you already know and can read throughout Matthew, Mark, Luke, and John. I do want to point to the instruction given by the writer of Hebrews. Here we read,

> Therefore, since we have so great a cloud of witnesses surrounding us, let us also lay aside every encumbrance and the sin which so easily entangles us, and let us run with endurance the race that is set before us, fixing our eyes on Jesus, the author and perfecter of faith, who for the joy set before Him persevered the cross, despising the shame, and has sat down at the right hand of the throne of God. (Hebrews 12:1–2)

The imagery presented in the Gospels comes into full view with the description provided in this passage. We also need to recognize the significance of the instruction to us as Christians. We must run the race before us with endurance, or perseverance. Jesus persevered through far more than Christians encounter today, and when we focus on Him, the difficulties we face take on a whole new perspective.

We find Scriptures throughout the New Testament that instruct Christians to demonstrate perseverance in their walk with God (e.g. 1 Peter 2:19–20 and 2 Peter 1:5–7). However, I want to look at one last thought. The letters written to the church at Corinth teach us many great truths. In the midst of the divisive spirit that Paul addressed in the first letter, he turned their attention to love: Love "bears all things, believes all things, hopes all things, endures all things. Love never fails" (1 Corinthians 13:7–8a). Love endures—or perseveres through—all things. The love Jesus had for all of us is why He persevered. We must keep our eyes on Him. And because of love, we also persevere.

Conviction and perseverance are two key pieces of the power passion has in our lives and leadership. From this point, we need to consider a path for increasing our conviction, passion, and perseverance. A look into history and biblical teaching helps us understand the benefits of these components in our lives and leadership. They are essential to both. As enzymes (food) kindle the energy within our bodies, conviction and perseverance set aflame the passion that drives our leadership. In the next—and final—chapter, I focus on the application needed to develop these characteristics and strengthen us in our walks through life.

Chapter 16
Biblical Implication and Application

There is no passion to be found playing small—in settling for a life that is less than the one you are capable of living.
Nelson Mandela

We need *grit*! Angela Duckworth would concur. Her book with that title presents evidence through the successful training of cadets at West Point, spelling bee champions, and more. In the second part of *Grit*, Duckworth explores four areas that contribute to the application of developing grit. As we focus on how to grow conviction, passion, and perseverance, let's examine the information she shares.

Interest

Unfortunately, most people—especially our youth—don't know where their passions lie. Research shows a couple of areas that need to be considered at this point.

Duckworth writes, "People are enormously more satisfied with their jobs when they do something that fits their personal interests."[1] I would agree. As I discussed earlier, we need to take time to determine those interests. I conduct an exercise when working with groups. I warn them in advance that I intend to ask three questions, and I give them approximately three seconds to write down their answers. I don't want participants to sit and ponder—I want them to write down the first thing that comes to mind. I ask the following:

1) If you could do anything and make a living at it, what would it be?

2) What's your favorite hobby?

3) What's one thing you love most about the church?

It is not a challenging test. And as you would imagine, the most common response for the first and the second questions is the same. If people could do anything and make a living, it would usually be their favorite hobby. Not always, but I've found this to be generally true. I ask the third question because it gives me an opportunity to encourage people to use the areas in life that interest them most as opportunities to share Jesus. It really is that simple. If we can focus on developing relationships with others who share the same interests and incorporate Jesus into the conversations we have with them, imagine the impact it will have on the lives of those we know.

Duckworth adds a second thought: "People perform better at work when what they do interests them." These two thoughts go hand-in-hand. It makes sense. The challenge before us is in reaching this point. As I stated in the exercises above, when you find ways to incorporate the hobbies you love with how you make a living, life changes. Sadly, our careers are laden with the task of simply making enough money to pay the bills and eventually retire, with the hope we live long enough to enjoy the years we have left. Life becomes miserable for many, and retirement the only focus of their vision. To take this a step further, consider how life-changing it would be for young people to discover areas of interest early on, take time to develop their giftedness in those specific areas, and pursue them with all the passion they can muster. Not only would life be more enjoyable, they would have something to look forward to every day.

It's also important for people to spend more time exploring several different interests. I can already hear the naysayers: "Bob, it's just not realistic." I have no intention of arguing the point, but I encourage you to go back and read the information I shared near the end of chapter 13. When it comes to exploring interests, eventually something tends to occupy our thoughts, and this often becomes areas we're passionate about. I don't know why certain people have interests in one area and others have no interest in that area at all. The possibility exists that our interests are developed around each phase and activity of life from childhood through adulthood. I know my interests have changed over the years, but there's one constant I cannot seem to shake: my passion for leadership. Duckworth suggests, "Passion for your work is a little bit of *discovery*, followed by a lot of *development*, and then a lifetime of *deepening*."

Children are too young to know what they want to do when they grow up. However, we continue to ask them and chuckle at what we hear. As children grow and interact with people, events/circumstances, and the education process, they explore different interests. However, it requires more than this. Duckworth says, "Interests thrive when there is a crew of encouraging supporters, including parents, teachers, coaches, and peers. . . . who provide the ongoing stimulation and information that is essential to actually liking something more and more." The best way to help a young person discover their passion is to encourage them in numerous areas and allow them the opportunity to develop their abilities to determine if the interest is there or not.

When our daughter was younger, she had numerous interests. My wife and I always encouraged our children to participate in everything school offered—at least, whatever they wanted that was offered. I remember attending basketball games, soccer games, badminton games, volleyball games, softball games, track and field, band concerts, and choir concerts. Whatever they did, we were there. Our daughter decided to try figure skating when she was eight. Initially, she loved it and couldn't get enough. On one occasion we drove to a location in the tundra of Canada, Fort Saint John, in the middle of February. We were told to take two sets of keys for the car. One set was left in the car to keep it running while we were inside the rink facility. The other set we kept with us to unlock the car when we returned to the car. I know there are colder temperatures, but I've never experienced it. The actual temperature was forty-four degrees below zero. I heard the comedian Jeff Alan once say, "That means it could warm up forty-four degrees and still be zero." Let that sink in for a moment.

By this point, we were thinking long-term. Will she want to train to be an Olympian? What kind of arrangements will we need to make for her to compete at that level? How much money will all this cost? You know: all the questions that eager parents ask of their eight-year-old children. The questions were unending and—as we later discovered—premature. Once the coach started forcing more difficult drills and skills, our daughter lost interest. When it stopped being fun and became hard work, she was ready to try something new. We went from the ice rink to the swimming pool. I will say the temperature was much better in the pool area. Those were the days. My point is this: not everything young people try out will become their passions, but it's sure better for them to learn that at a young age than to regret never having tried at all. Eventually, they will discover their passions.

Practice

Duckworth emphasized that the key to success is *deliberate* practice. She was not talking about spending "more time on task." Duckworth talks about the quality of time, i.e. "better time on task." Research indicates that experts practice differently. A few of the findings from her research include those I examine below.

Stretch Goals

Duckworth learned that experts focus on a specific area—usually not one of strength but weakness—and they intentionally find someone or something to challenge them in that area. The deliberate nature of this practice makes it possible to improve, turning weakness into strength. Back to our daughter and ice-skating. At first, the learning was fun. She loved being on the ice and skating around. She enjoyed participating in something she had seen on television, and she had friends who were also skaters. The combination seemed like a win-win. As with children, the things that come fairly easily or naturally are fun to do over and over, because we're good at them. However, when her practices began to focus more time on specific routines, jumps, and spins that stretched her beyond her natural abilities, the luster of professional ice-skating was no longer the same. The design of stretch goals is to direct our attention and practice in areas we don't do well in order to improve and perfect them.

Feedback

Experts crave and seek feedback. From 2008 to 2016, I taught a course on sermon preparation and presentation. During that time, it was common to have students ask for feedback, only to hear a bit of grumbling when the feedback was not as they expected. I learned that many of those who asked didn't really want feedback, they wanted praise. In their minds, the papers they submitted or sermons they preached were A+ quality. Only a few valued genuine feedback, taking the information and improving in the areas I suggested. People can be very sensitive when receiving feedback, especially if the feedback is negative in nature. The one thing about experts is they want to know what they did wrong in order to fix it. They find more value in the areas that need work than in simply hearing what they did right.

Repetition

Note that Duckworth is not talking about just doing something over and over. Her research indicated that experts use repetition with reflection and refinement. One of the assignments in my class on sermon preparation and presentation was for students to videotape themselves preaching a sermon and then watch it. As they watched the video, they had criteria to look for and were to make comments based on what they'd learned from class. If you're like me (and I think most people are like this), I would rather hear someone rake their fingernails across a chalkboard than listen to or watch myself. I'm not sure what it is about hearing the sound of our own voices that makes this difficult. They also had to watch the video at least once in fast-forward. I wanted them to pick up on any gestures or hand or body movements that stood out. The intent of the assignment was to have students reflect on what they said and how they moved, and to consider how to refine their delivery. Deliberate practice points us to greater success. The science and art of delivery in public speaking is a field that requires constant study and effort to perfect. Repetition with reflection and refinement help us to achieve that.

Deliberate practice sets a different tone for the way people move from good to great. Duckworth says there are four requirements for deliberate practice: (1) a clearly defined stretch goal, (2) full concentration and effort, (3) immediate and informative feedback, and (4) repetition with reflection and refinement. Let me share a few suggestions that will be helpful to you. First, know the science behind deliberate practice. Study it. Learn it. The time invested produces great dividends. Second, make it a habit. Keep at it over and over until the practice becomes second nature. Third, change the way you experience it. Don't look at deliberate practice as a means to an end but experience it as the fuel that feeds the passion in your life and leadership.

Purpose

I refer you back to the discussion about *why* from chapter 1. Duckworth indicates that interest is one source of passion, but when we understand the true nature of purpose, we find another. Purpose involves an intention to contribute to the well-being of others, but it goes deeper than mere intention. Purpose is not just goal-oriented, but the *nature* of the goal is significant. Purpose involves helping others, or putting the needs of others first. We find similarities behind purpose and the definition of what we call *agape* love. Duckworth says, "At its core, the idea of purpose is the idea that what we do matters to people other than ourselves." The challenge is to distinguish between selfless and selfish. People with grit are people who "see their ultimate aims as deeply connected to the world beyond themselves."

To illustrate the difference when someone has purpose, Duckworth shares a parable: "Three bricklayers are asked: 'What are you doing?' The first says, 'I am laying bricks.' The second says, 'I am building a church.' And the third says, 'I am building the house of God.' The first bricklayer has a job. The second has a career. The third has a calling." Regardless of how we might identify with any one of the three, we can see the value purpose has when it comes to passion and perseverance.

When purpose exists, what we do has a greater meaning for the overall good of others and the society in which we live. We know our efforts make a positive contribution to the world. However we choose to move forward, our passion and perseverance directly relate to the driving purpose in our lives. Find someone with purpose and learn from them, use what you learn to help you discover purpose in your life, and pay it forward by guiding others to discover their own purpose.

Hope

Duckworth defines hope as an "expectation that our own efforts can improve the future. *I have a feeling tomorrow will be better is different from I resolve to make tomorrow better.* The hope that gritty people have has nothing to do with luck and everything to do with getting up again." Without hope, nothing else really matters. The ways in which we speak to others plays a critical role in developing the type of grit that comes with this kind of hope. I appreciate the value of hope that includes the resolve to make tomorrow better. Duckworth says, "Modeling a growth mindset—demonstrating by our *actions* that we truly believe people can learn to learn" may be one of the more important components to this discussion.

While I'm on the subject of mindset, let me suggest a book by Carol Dweck: *Mindset*. Duckworth references the material from this book and how it factors into the power of passion and perseverance. In *Mindset*, Dweck[2] describes a contrast between the characteristics of a "fixed" mindset and a "growth" mindset. A perspective of this contrast is listed below.

Fixed Mindset	*Growth Mindset*
Static	**Dynamic**
Avoid challenges	Embraces challenges
Defensive, gives up easily	Persists in setbacks
Effort is fruitless or worse	Effort, path to mastery
Ignore useful negative feedback	Learn from criticism
Threatened by others' success	Inspired by success

A glance at these lists provides clarity to how one's mindset contributes to the passion and perseverance in life and leadership. Duckworth makes the following connection:

Collectively, the evidence I've presented tells the following story. A fixed mindset about ability leads to pessimistic explanations of adversity, and that, in turn, leads to both giving up on challenges and avoiding them in the first place. In contrast, a growth mindset leads to optimistic ways of explaining adversity, and that, in turn, leads to perseverance and seeking out new challenges that will ultimately make you even stronger.

These four areas provide a foundation for developing a model for Christians to understand the role of passion and perseverance in life and leadership. Consider the following questions to guide the discussion about how grit can be applied to the church:

- How can we create interest within the church and for the community?

- How do we get our community interested in Jesus?

- What does deliberate practice look like to help Christians develop greater strengths in converting their interests into passion and perseverance?

- In a few sentences, how can leaders provide direction for the purpose that drives the passion we have as Christians?

- What can we do to show our purpose in more tangible ways for the church and community?

- Understanding the contrast between biblical hope and worldly hope, how can we communicate the idea of hope to the world?

Answers to these questions give us key pieces to help increase the ways we persevere for the cause of Christ and build up His kingdom.

In the final section of this chapter, I want specifically to look at four ways to make application of what we've learned about conviction, passion, and perseverance. Each of these takes into consideration the material we've discussed throughout the entire section.

We Need a Goal Worth Achieving

People will not persevere through difficulties or obstacles without a goal worth achieving. The attempt to get people involved without a goal before them is an exercise in futility. It simply will not work. However, when leaders place a goal worth achieving before everyone, people see a purpose for their efforts. We increase their motivation when we clarify the *why*. Take the time to go through the exercises in section 2 on goals and planning—it will make a difference. Remember that a goal worth achieving doesn't consist of putting together a calendar full of the same events and activities you've practiced every year for the past one hundred years. Come on, leader! Step up, be challenged, and challenge others with a goal worthy of everyone's time, talent, and energy. I assure you that when you do so, people will follow and great things will occur. The future is before you. What will you do with it? Where will you go? How will you get there?

Keep Your Focus on Jesus

The example Jesus left was intentional. While walking in the footsteps of Jesus is not the easiest path, it's the most rewarding and benefits everyone we influence. Thirty-six years ago, Charles Sheldon introduced the world to a novel called *In His Steps*.[3] The powerful thought behind this title and story are convicting. A small community of business owners and a pastor witness an individual they had all shunned the day before stand before them Sunday morning condemning them for their Christianity. And then he dies. Reflecting on the validity of the accusations against them, these leaders make a decision to take the next twelve months to ask, "What would Jesus do?" before they make any decision. The impact on their lives and leadership is changed from that point forward. They face challenges and receive benefits for the directions they choose.

I can't help but think how different the church today would be if each one of us took the time to stop and truly ask the same question before making decisions. Would Jesus participate in the same activities we do? Would Jesus go to the same places we go? In the heat of the moment, would Jesus use the same words we choose to use? Would Jesus make the same business decisions we do? Would Jesus treat others the way we treat them—including our families and friends? *What would Jesus do?* Four words—and one of the most difficult questions to answer. Maybe we will find it easier to answer the question if we keep our focus on Jesus all the time. Our conviction and perseverance will grow in direct proportion to the way we focus on Jesus.

Realize That Eternity Matters

As I write this thought, I realize the impossibility of the task. We're so bound by time that understanding a realm where time does not exist cannot be comprehended. From the second we are conceived in the womb, the clock begins to tick. The countdown from conception to birth, from birth to adolescence, from adolescence to adulthood, and adulthood to death are all measured within the scope of time. Everything we do is measured by time. We're all given twenty-four hours in the day, with sixty seconds for each minute and sixty minutes for each hour. The days turn into weeks, the weeks into months, and the months into years. We know how much time it takes to get ready for work, the time required for eating our meals, the time from the house to work and back, the time spent on the job, and the time we have with family. We measure the length of time we assemble for worship and even the length of the sermon. There's nothing we do not measure by time in some way. Even when we talk about heaven or hell, we measure it in time. We attempt to use illustrations of impossibility, such as an ant marching around a solid steel ball the size of the earth until it wears a trench one foot deep, and then we say, "We have only experienced the first second in eternity." Even then, our illustration falls short, because you can't measure something that doesn't exist. Therefore, to realize that eternity matters presents the most difficult of situations. The best we can do is acknowledge that we cannot mentally comprehend eternity, but intellectually we can identify what Scripture teaches us. And by faith, we can live out the time we have on the earth in preparation of a glorious event that will unfold in a realm God will share with those who love Him and are called according to His purpose (Romans 8:18, 28).

Help Someone Else in Need

Between now and that final event, the best thing you can do is help someone else in need. I've been told all my life that when everything seems to be against me and is not going my way, I should look around at others. There's always someone who has it worse. In 2010, I made a trip to Kathmandu, Nepal. During my time there, I walked around an area on the opposite side of the Hindu temple.

People lined the pathways, begging for help from anyone who would give it. If there was ever a time I coveted the miraculous gift of healing, it was then. People were maimed, deformed, struggling with diseases, blind, and crippled. The sight was heart-wrenching. Coupled with the smell of burning bodies from across the river, this is a memory embedded deep in my mind. I continue to wrestle with how to help people in those circumstances. A few dollars might fill someone's stomach for a meal or two, but it can't change the long-term outcome of people who live in circumstances hidden far from our view this side of the world. Even though I did not have the ability to change the physical lives of people in Nepal, I can help the lives of those where I live. People have to persevere through challenges in life I will likely never face, but the opportunity to walk alongside them to help where I can may open doors, and these doors may allow me to help them eternally. Are you looking for those opportunities? Will you help when the opportunity is presented? How will you ask God to use you to make a difference in someone else's life? More could be said, but it all comes down to the decisions you and I make as we think about life and leadership.

Throughout this section and chapter, I've focused on concepts associated with passion. While passion can be defined as enthusiasm and excitement, passion really is about suffering. Passion involves sacrifice. What are you willing to give up that others may go up? I used to watch a television show called *Doc*. Billy Ray Cyrus played the part of a country doctor who moved to a big city to work in a major hospital. At the end of each episode, he wrote home to his friend, a retired doctor who encouraged his career. I do not remember anything else about this show, except a thought expressed at the end of one episode: Doc wrote home that night and said, "I've learned that love is not so much what you give; it's what you give up." Passion really boils down to love. When love fills your heart, you will find conviction, passion, and willingness to persevere. Just as enzymes (food) are essential to life, passion is essential to our leadership. As I have stated throughout this section, enzymes are nature's activists, the spark that drives energy into our life, just like passion ignites our leadership, a compelling force to grow, conquer, and achieve.

Conclusion:
Make It Happen!

Aristotle gave us this gem: "Well begun is half done." Well, as I near the end of this book I'm not sure how to describe my emotions. It seems surreal. I never dreamed I would actually accomplish this task—even though I thought about it and threatened to do several times over the past ten years. I just never had the time—at least that's what I told myself. Someone commented that it didn't actually take me that long to write this, to which I reminded them it has taken fifty-eight years.

Poieo is a Greek word used 568 times in the New Testament. We find it translated in a variety of ways: "act," "practice," "perform," "execute," "give," "cause," "produce," "commit," "do," "make," "bear," and more. The basic definition of *poieo* is "to make something happen."[1] Nike's "Just Do It" slogan represents the idea well. Whether you choose to act, practice, execute, produce, do, or anything else, I pray that you will take the material from this book and make it happen! Just do it! The synthesis of life and leadership reminds us how every part of life interconnects with leadership, and leadership interconnects with life. In both life and leadership, action is required.

I've found it powerful to think about the interrelationship of the four essentials to life and leadership. The sun is where it all begins. The air we breathe, water we drink, and food we eat are all possible because of the sun. Yet, each of these essential elements depends on the other to provide the full circle of life. If we remove any one of them, life no longer exists. As each of these essential elements align with components of leadership, we find the same interrelationship. Vision is where it begins. Without vision, there's no purpose for goals and plans, character, and passion—there's no *why*. In the same way, each essential component of leadership depends on the other to provide the full circle of leadership. Leadership involves a variety of components, as does life. These are the essentials we cannot survive without. The sun provides a light to guide each step through life—vision illuminates the future that we can lead others to become something greater. Air is the breath of life and strengthens every facet of our being—goals breathe life into our leadership, strengthening our purpose. Water supplies the foundational building blocks and substance for life—character contributes to the building blocks and substance of our leadership. Enzymes—nature's activists—fuel the energy of life—passion energizes our leadership through conviction and perseverance.

Life and leadership fall into three major categories: home, church, and world. We won't find ourselves in any other realm. When we overlap these three circles, at the heart of it is leadership. Leadership is needed in the home, church, and world. How will you and I make all this happen in these three arenas? The church needs a new culture that focuses on developing leaders. Mark Batterson says, "Too often the church complains about culture instead of creating it. The energy we spend on criticism is being stolen from creativity. It's sideways energy. We need fewer commentators and more innovators."[2] I close with five suggestions on how to move forward from this point.

Urgency

The importance of recognizing the urgency of the situation cannot be overstated. Again, I remind you of the situation that exists. Every time a husband and wife divorce, the family unit crumbles, lives are devastated, the church suffers, and the country begins to deteriorate from the inside. We cannot strengthen the home quickly enough. Every time a church closes their doors, we lose a fortress in the spiritual battle before us. We cannot afford to close another door. Every time we fail to be the salt of the earth and the light of the world, souls continue down the broad path, unaware of their eternal destination.

The struggle for leadership is urgent. John Kotter developed eight steps to leading change. The first step is "establishing a sense of urgency."[3] Kotter begins with the importance of establishing this urgency. Complacency, as Kotter describes, prevents a sense of urgency, and the number one reason for complacency is that "no highly visible crisis existed." I continue to speak with leaders who are unwilling to acknowledge the obstacle before us. But those who do recognize the crisis understand the mountain we must climb. Once we grasp the urgency of the situation, we have to be intentional.

Intentional

Leadership doesn't happen by accident. We must be intentional. I cannot recommend highly enough a book by Eric Geiger and Kevin Peck: *Designed to Lead*.[4] The premise of the book is simple: God designed the church to lead—to produce leaders in every area of life. Geiger and Peck develop three major components of application.

Conviction

The church must have the conviction that it was designed to develop leaders. Without this conviction, nothing is done to develop leaders in the home, church, or world. Geiger and Peck point out, "Developing leaders must be a burning passion, a non-negotiable part of the vision of a local church and her leaders, or it will never become a reality."

Culture

No two cultures are exactly the same. Because this is true, creating a culture of leadership development brings challenges. Geiger and Peck define culture as "the shared beliefs and values that drive the behavior of a group of people. . . . When [leadership] development is in the culture, . . . it is part of the very core identity of the church." They identify two kinds of cultures: a healthy culture develops leaders—an unhealthy culture does not. The cultural component is critical for the next step.

Constructs

By constructs, Geiger and Peck "mean the systems, processes, and programs that help develop leaders. Having a conviction for leadership development without tools to systemize the practices often results in frustration." We understand the necessity of these systems, processes, and programs, but we must back it up by implementing the type of constructs that develop leaders.

The material developed in this book will help you work toward a healthy culture of leadership development. We must be intentional about the direction forward, and if we want leaders in the future, we have to implement a plan now. Leaders don't appear by accident. They are developed with strong and personal intentionality, and a key piece to this intentionality involves prayer.

Prayer

I've been asked why this is not the first suggestion. I strategically placed prayer in the middle for a reason. Yes, prayer should be the first suggestion—and it should be the last suggestion. Prayer should also be in the middle. Therefore, my suggestion is that we bathe every aspect of the situation before us in prayer.

I don't know exactly how many workshops I've conducted over the years. At some point in each presentation, I emphasize the importance of prayer. In all these workshops, I note that I have never heard anyone in the church pray about the development of leadership. With the exception of two where I pointed out the situation, I still have not heard prayers offered in the area of leadership development. If we're not asking God to help us in preparing leaders, then how will it ever happen? In Scripture, we're told, "You do not have because you do not ask" (James 4:2). Is it possible that we do not have leaders today because the church has not asked for them in the past? What will we do about leaders for the future? Perhaps we need to start asking fervently.

I strategically placed prayer in the middle to get your attention. I urge you as strongly as I know how to begin *now*. In every public and private prayer, seek God's help to develop leaders for the future of the church. I know of no other way it will happen. We need to ask! And when we include God in our vision, an abundant future awaits.

Vision

If you cannot envision the future, you'll never go there. Vision is essential. I refer you to the first section of this book. If you don't start with a vision, then all of the activities you participate in are futile. You just do stuff but get nowhere because you have no idea where you're going. I cannot emphasize this point enough: *vision changes everything*.

Vision energizes, challenges, and provides meaning to

everyone involved. Before giving attention to any other area, discover the vision. When you have a vision, people are focused and active. They unite and move forward with an unstoppable obsession. The time invested now to discover your vision will reap rewards in the future that cannot be described in a sentence or paragraph. I said it before, but it's worth repeating here: *vision must incorporate leadership development*. When it does, people are empowered to reach their potential.

Empower

Leadership requires focus on the development of future leaders. The challenge is time. Leaders are busy. The daily demands on a leader are taxing, and to add the responsibility of training someone else to lead only increases stress levels. At best, short-term gains become long-term losses when this approach continues. At worst, the future stability of the church is weakened and the lack of leadership ultimately leads to another closed church. The short- and long-term answer to this dilemma is empowering future leaders.

The future of the church depends on empowering younger leaders to pick up the mantle and the responsibility that goes with it. This only happens when current leaders entrust these younger leaders with the authority to carry out that responsibility. Each section of this book provides pieces to incorporate in this development. I ask you to visit and revisit each section while implementing every component. I pray God will bless you and the kingdom will benefit from your efforts to train leaders.

Let me close with a few words from Mark Batterson to challenge us as leaders:

Quit living as if the purpose of life is to arrive safely at death. Run to the roar. Set God-sized goals. Pursue God-given passions. Go after a dream that is destined to fail without divine intervention. Stop pointing out problems. Become part of the solution. Stop repeating the past. Start creating the future. Face your fears. Fight for your dreams. Grab opportunity by the mane and don't let go! Live like today is the first day and the last day of your life. Burn sinful bridges. Blaze new trails. Live for the applause of nail-scarred hands. Don't let what's wrong with you keep you from worshipping what's right with God. Dare to fail. Dare to be different. Quit holding out. Quit holding back. Quit running away. Chase the lion.[5]

The four essentials of life are sun, air, water, and enzymes (food). The four essentials of leadership are vision, goals, character, and passion. The essential elements of life are intertwined. You can't have one without the other, and so it is with leadership. Each essential element relies on the other working and growing together to make the future a better place.

I've only touched on the tip of the iceberg. The journey cannot end here and now. You must commit to act. You must commit to change. You must commit to make a difference. You must commit to lead as God has called you to lead. You must commit to His greater purpose for life and leadership. I pray that you remember the past, recognize the present, and prepare for the future. Thank you for reading and joining me in the journey ahead.

Acknowledgements

This book would be incomplete without acknowledging the amazing contribution of several special people. Without their love, support, and hard work, this book would not exist. Above all, I am thankful to God for loving me and opening more doors than I can express. Without Him, nothing is possible.

I want to thank my wonderful wife, Sheryl. She has been the rock of our family from the beginning. Her love and support throughout my educational journey was only the beginning. Her continued patience and encouragement makes it possible for me to work in the arena of leadership. This book is due to all she constantly provides to our family and me. TTBOTM

I am also thankful to my children and grandchildren. My two sons and their wives, along with my daughter and her husband, all contributed to the direction of this book in more ways than one. The content, title, design, proofing, counsel, social media advertising, and encouragement pulled it together. I love you all.

I have the best editor. Thank you, Heather Campbell, for working with me on more than one crazy project. You make my crooked sentences straight, and your suggestions have helped me keep the flow of thought together throughout each chapter.

Lastly, I want to thank Dick Brant, my friend and brother in Christ who ignited the fire for leadership in the early 90s as I sat at his feet for the first time. His inspirational teaching has guided me for the last thirty years. Thank you for helping me see the need and value of leadership in the home, world, and church. This book is dedicated to you and your leadership.

Works Cited

Introduction

1 Norman Copeland, *Psychology and the Soldier* (Harrisburg, PA: Military Service Publications, 1942).

2 James MacGregor Burns, *Leadership* (New York: Open Road Integrated Media, 1978).

3 Burns, *Leadership.*

4 Jones, Ken. *"The Heart of Leadership." Beside Still Waters Elder's Workshop* (Mannford, OK, 2019).

Building Block 1
Vision: The Inspiration of Life and Leadership—Lead-In

1 Michael Greshko and National Geographic Staff, "The Sun, Explained," National Geographic Society (September 15, 2018): https://www.nationalgeographic.com/science/space/solar-system/the-sun/.

2 Fraser Cain, "How Does the Sun Produce Energy?" Phys.org. Science X Network. (December 14, 2015): https://phys.org/news/2015-12-sun-energy.html.

3 Wolfgang H. Berger, "Intro to Astronomy: The Life-Giving Sun," University of San Diego, California (2002): http://earthguide.ucsd.edu/virtualmuseum/ita/07_1.shtml.

4 Erie G. Chipman, Donald L. De Vincenzi, Bevan M. French, David Gilman, Stephen P. Maran, and Paul C. Rambaut. "The Sun and Us," NASA.gov, accessed 11 May, 2020, https://history.nasa.gov/EP-177/ch3-1.html.

5 Randy A. Sansone and Lori A Sansone. 2013. "Sunshine, Serotonin, and Skin: A Partial Explanation for Seasonal Patterns in Psychopathology?" *Innovations in Clinical Neuroscience* 10, no. 7–8 (July–August 2013): 20–24, https://www.ncbi.nlm.nih.gov/pmc/articles/

PMC3779905/.

<u>6</u> Timothy J. Legg, "What are the Benefits of the Sun?" Healthline Media (May 25, 2018): https://www.healthline.com/health/depression/benefits-sunlight.

<u>7</u> David Turbert, "More Time Outdoors May Reduce Kids' Risk of Nearsightedness," American Academy of Ophthalmology (August 28, 2104): https://www.aao.org/eye-health/tips-prevention/time-outdoors-reduces-nearsightedness.

<u>8</u> Gretchen Reynolds, "For Better Vision, Let the Sunshine In," *New York Times* (January 19, 2017): https://www.nytimes.com/2017/01/19/well/live/for-better-vision-let-the-sunshine-in.html.

<u>9</u> Phil Maffetone, "Sunlight: Good for the Eyes as Well as the Brain," MAFF Fitness (April 29, 2015): https://philmaffetone.com/sun-and-brain/.

<u>10</u> Kimberly Dumke, "The Power of the Sun," *National Geographic Society* (January 21, 2011): https://www.nationalgeographic.org/article/power-sun/.

Chapter 1 Why Vision?

<u>1</u> "Vision," Merriam-Webster.com Dictionary, accessed April 19, 2020: https://www.merriam-webster.com/dictionary/vision.

<u>2</u> Aubrey Malphurs, *Being Leaders: Nature of Authentic Christian Leadership* (Grand Rapids, MI: Baker Books, 2003).

<u>3</u> Mark Batterson, *Chase the Lion: If Your Dream Doesn't Scare You, It's Too Small* (New York: Multnomah, 2016).

<u>4</u> "Mission," Merriam-Webster.com Dictionary, accessed April 19, 2020: https://www.merriam-webster.com/dictionary/mission.

<u>5</u> "Strategic Planning," Business Dictionary, WebFinance Inc., ac-

cessed April 19, 2020: http://www.businessdictionary.com/definition/strategic-planning.html.

6 Kris Vallotton, *Heavy Rain: How to Flood Your World with God's Transforming Power* (Bloomington, MN: Chosen Books, 2016).

7 "Status Quo Bias," Wikipedia.com, last modified April 18, 2020: https://en.wikipedia.org/wiki/Status_quo_bias.

8 Simon Sinek, *The Infinite Game* (New York: Penguin Random House, 2019).

9 Batterson, *Chase the Lion.*

Chapter 2 Biblical Thoughts about Vision

1 Francis Brown, Samuel Rolles Driver, and Charles Augustus Briggs, *"Hazon," Enhanced Brown-Driver-Briggs Hebrew and English Lexicon* (Oxford, UK: Clarendon Press, 2020).

2 William Arndt, Walter Bauer, Frederick William Danker, *"Blepo," A Greek-English Lexicon of the New Testament and Other Early Christian Literature,* 3rd ed. (Chicago, IL: University of Chicago Press. 2020).

3 William Arndt, Walter Bauer, Frederick William Danker, *"Phaino," A Greek-English Lexicon of the New Testament and Other Early Christian Literature,* 3rd ed. (Chicago, IL: University of Chicago Press, 2020).

4 William Arndt, Walter Bauer, Frederick William Danker, *"Horao," A Greek-English Lexicon of the New Testament and Other Early Christian Literature,* 3rd ed. (Chicago, IL: University of Chicago Press, 2020).

5 William Arndt, Walter Bauer, Frederick William Danker, *"Elenchos," A Greek-English Lexicon of the New Testament and Other Early Christian Literature,* 3rd ed. (Chicago, IL: University of Chica-

go Press, 2020).

Chapter 3 Benefits of Vision

1 John Maxwell, 21 *Irrefutable Laws of Leadership,* (Nashville, TN: Thomas Nelson Publishers, 2007).

Chapter 4 Exercises for Discovering Vision

1 Andy Stanley, *Making Vision Stick* (Grand Rapids, MI: Zondervan, 2007).

2 Simon Sinek, *Start with Why: How Great Leaders Inspire Everyone to Take Action* (New York: The Penguin Group, 2009).

3 Simon Sinek, https://www.ted.com/talks/simon_sinek_how_great_leaders_inspire_action?language=en.

4 Simon Sinek, *The Infinite Game* (New York: Penguin Random House, 2019).

5 Henri Nouwen. "The Beloved of God." https://www.youtube.com/watch?v=dWmeQ9cKRVE.

6 Mark Batterson, *Chase the Lion: If Your Dream Doesn't Scare You, It's Too Small* (New York: Multnomah, 2016).

7 "Success," Merriam-Webster.com Dictionary, accessed April 29, 2020: https://www.merriam-webster.com/dictionary/mission.

8 Andy Stanley, *Next Generation Leader: Five Essentials for Those Who Will Shape the Future* (Oregon: Multnomah, 2003).

9 Mark Batterson, *Chase the Lion: If Your Dream Doesn't Scare You, It's Too Small* (New York: Multnomah, 2016).

10 Derek Swetnam and Ruth Swetnam, *Writing Your Dissertation* (Ox-

ford, UK: How To Books, 2000).

Building Block 2
Goals: The Initiative of Life and Leadership—Lead-In

1 Kim Rutledge, et al., "Air," National Geographic Society (2011), accessed May 12, 2020: https://www.nationalgeographic.org/encyclopedia/air/.

2 Kevin Lee, 2018, "The Importance of Air," Sciencing.com, accessed May 12, 2020: https://sciencing.com/importance-air-6330367.html.

3 Lina Begdache, "Why is Breathing Oxygen Necessary?" Press-Connects.com (2015), accessed May 12, 2020: https://www.press-connects.com/story/news/local/2015/02/12/breathing-oxygen-necessary/23301027/.

4 Burt Camcaster, "Why Your Body Needs Oxygen," VitalityMedical.com, accessed May 12, 2020: https://www.vitalitymedical.com/guides/respiratory-therapy/to-air-is-human-why-your-body-needs-oxygen.

Chapter 5 Goals and Planning

1 Elva Hull-Blanks, Sharon E. Robinson Kurpius, Christie Befort, Sonja Sollenberger, Megan Foley Nicpon, and Laura Huser, "Career Goals and Retention-Related Factors among College Freshmen," *Journal of Career Development 32*, no. 1:16–30 (2005).

2 "Goals," Merriam-Webster.com Dictionary, accessed April 19, 2020: https://www.merriam-webster.com/dictionary/vision.

3 Edwin A. Locke and Gary P. Latham, "Building a Practically Useful Theory of Goal Setting and Task Motivation: A 35-Year Odyssey," *American Psychologist*, 57, 705–717 (2002).

4 Edwin A. Locke and Gary P. Latham, *A Theory of Goal Setting & Task Performance* (Englewood Cliffs, NJ: Prentice Hall, 1990).

5 Heidi Grant and Carol S. Dweck. 2003. "Clarifying Achievement Goals and their Impact." *Journal of Personality and Social Psychology* 85, no. 3: 541.

6 E. S. Elliott and C. S. Dweck, "Goals: An Approach to Motivation and Achievement," *Journal of Personality and Social Psychology*, 54 (1988).

7 J. Robert Clinton, *Building Strategies: Leadership Perspectives for Introducing Change* (self-published) 1992: http://bobbyclinton.com/store/books-manuals/bridging-strategies/.

8 Jim Collins, *Good to Great: Why Some Companies Make the Lead . . . and Others Don't* (New York: HarperCollins Publishers, 2001).

Chapter 6 Achieving Goals

1 Svetlana Whitener, "How to Sustain Your Motivation," *Forbes*, April 1, 2019: https://www.forbes.com/sites/forbescoachescouncil/2019/04/01/how-to-sustain-your-motivation/#6b1af4d85e6e.

2 Kevin Kruse, "The 80/20 Rule and How It Can Change Your Life," *Forbes*, March 7, 2016: https://www.forbes.com/sites/kevinkruse/2016/03/07/80-20-rule/#6da636453814.

3 Stephen R. Covey, *The 7 Habits of Highly Effective People* (New York: Simon and Schuster, 2004).

4 Patricia Thompson, "Self-management vs. Time-management: What you Need to Know," Mission.org, August 14, 2017: https://medium.com/the-mission/self-management-vs-time-management-what-you-need-to-know-67a4063715e6.

5 Mary Morrissey, "The Power of Writing Down your Goals and Dreams," Huffpost.com. September 14, 2016: https://www.huffpost.com/entry/the-power-of-writing-down_b_12002348.

Chapter 7 SWOT, SOAR, and the PERT Chart

<u>1</u> Mike Morrison, "SWOT Analysis Made Simple: History, Definition, Tools, Templates, and Worksheets," RapidBI, accessed April 27, 2020: https://rapidbi.com/swotanalysis/.

<u>2</u> Suresh Srivastva and David L. Cooperrider, *Appreciative Management and Leadership: The Power of Positive Thought and Action in Organizations* (Cleveland, OH: Lakeshore Communications, 1990).

<u>3</u> Jacqueline Stavros, David Cooperrider, and D. Lynn Kelley, "Strategic Inquiry—Appreciative Intent: Inspiration to SOAR A New Framework for Strategic Planning," *Ai Practitioner*, 11 (2003).

<u>4</u> Jay Ekleberry, "Thinking Forward Together: Helping Organizations SOAR," Global Learning Partners, January 7, 2019: https://www.globallearningpartners.com/blog/thinking-forward-together-helping-organizations-soar/.

<u>5</u> Eric Stallsworth, "What Is a PERT Chart in Project Management," Bright Hub PM, August 8, 2008: https://www.brighthubpm.com/project-planning/4997-using-a-pert-chart/.

<u>6</u> James Floyd Kelly and Patrick Hood-Daniel, *Printing in Plastic: Build Your Own 3D Printer* (New York: Springer Science+Business Media, 2011).

<u>7</u> Jacqueline M. Stavros and Gina Hinrichs, *The Thin Book of Soar: Building Strengths-Based Strategy* (Bend, OR: Thin Book Publishing Co, 2009).

<u>8</u> Michele McDonough, "History of the PERT Chart: 5 Little-Known Facts," Bright Hub PM, Accessed April 27, 2020: https://www.brighthubpm.com/project-planning/14025-five-things-you-didnt-know-about-the-pert-chart/.

Chapter 8 Legacy

<u>1</u> "Legacy," Merriam-Webster.com Dictionary, accessed April 19, 2020: https://www.merriam-webster.com/dictionary/vision.

2 John Maxwell, *21 Irrefutable Laws of Leadership* (Nashville, TN: Thomas Nelson Publishers, 2007).

3 Tim Elmore, "How Student Leadership is Morphing in Gen Z," Growing Leaders, accessed 29 April 29, 2020: https://growingleaders.com/blog/how-student-leadership-is-morphing-for-generation-z/?mc_cid=0e9d703245&mc_eid=ea2a4f1ec7.

4 Mac Lake, *The Multiplication Effect: Building a Leadership Pipeline that Solves Your Leadership Shortage* (Nashville, TN: Thomas Nelson Publishers, 2020).

5 Lake, *Multiplication Effect.*

6 Mark Batterson, *Chase the Lion: If Your Dream Doesn't Scare You, It's Too Small* (New York, NY: Multnomah, 2016).

Building Block 3
Character: The Influence of Life and Leadership—Lead-In

1 Charity: Water, Charity Global, Inc., accessed May 8, 2020: https://www.charitywater.org/global-water-crisis.

2 "9-Year-Old Girl's Clean Water Wish Takes Off After Her Death," NBCNews.com, accessed May 8, 2020: http://www.nbcnews.com/id/43898825/ns/us_news-giving/t/-year-old-girls-clean-water-wish-takes-after-her-death/#.XrdYtc41ifB.

3 "The Facts about Water," USGS.gov, accessed May 12, 2020: https://www.usgs.gov/special-topic/water-science-school/science/facts-about-water?qt-science_center_objects=0#qt-science_center_objects.

4 Molly Sargen, "Biological Roles of Water: Why is water necessary for life?" SITNBoston, September 26, 2019: http://sitn.hms.harvard.edu/uncategorized/2019/biological-roles-of-water-why-is-water-necessary-for-life/.

5 Matt J. Weber, "All Life Needs Water. Why?" Medium Space, November 8, 2017: https://medium.com/@mjosefweber/all-life-needs-water-why-8b8301550517.

6 Jonathan Atteberry, "Why is Water Vital to Life?" HowStuffWorks.com, December 31, 1969: https://science.howstuffworks.com/environmental/earth/geophysics/water-vital-to-life.htm.

7 "The Water in You: Water and the Human Body," USGS.gov, accessed May 12, 2020: https://www.usgs.gov/special-topic/water-science-school/science/water-you-water-and-human-body?qt-science_center_objects=0#qt-science_center_objects.

8 Tia Ghose, "What is Water so Essential to Life?" LiveScience.com, September 29, 2015: https://www.livescience.com/52332-why-is-water-needed-for-life.html.

Chapter 9 Godly Character—Psalm 15

1 Jennifer Lee, Namrata Mujumdar, Yiying Lu, and Emojination, "Fortune Cookie Emoji Submission," December 29, 2015: https://unicode.org/L2/L2016/16025-fortune-cookie-emoji.pdf.

2 Francis Brown, Samuel Rolles Driver, and Charles Augustus Briggs, *"yagur," Enhanced Brown-Driver-Briggs Hebrew and English Lexicon* (Oxford, UK: Clarendon Press, 2020).

3 Francis Brown, Samuel Rolles Driver, and Charles Augustus Briggs, "yiskon," *Enhanced Brown-Driver-Briggs Hebrew and English Lexicon* (Oxford, UK: Clarendon Press, 2020).

4 Lawrence Nichols Herman, *Practicing the Presence of God and The Spiritual Maxims* (Digireads.com Publishing, 2016).

5 *"tamim."* 2020. Brown, Francis, Samuel Rolles Driver, and Charles Augustus Briggs. *Enhanced Brown-Driver-Briggs Hebrew and English Lexicon.* Oxford, UK. Clarendon Press.

6 Francis Brown, Samuel Rolles Driver, and Charles Augustus Briggs, "*sedeq*," *Enhanced Brown-Driver-Briggs Hebrew and English Lexicon* (Oxford, UK: Clarendon Press, 2020).

7 "Francis Brown, Samuel Rolles Driver, and Charles Augustus Briggs, *"met,"* *Enhanced Brown-Driver-Briggs Hebrew and English Lexicon* (Oxford, UK: Clarendon Press, 2020).

Chapter 10 Trust

1 Steve Moore, "Three Leadership Topics to Discuss with Your Team," Growing Leaders, October 1, 2019: https://growingleaders.com/blog/three-leadership-topics-to-discuss-with-your-team/.

2 Stephen M. R. Covey, *The Speed of Trust: The One Thing that Changes Everything* (New York: Free Press, 2018).

3 James M. Kouzes and Barry Z. Posner, *The Leaders Legacy* (San Francisco, CA. Josses-Bass, 2006).

Chapter 11 Respect and Credibility

1 John Maxwell, *21 Irrefutable Laws of Leadership* (Nashville, TN: Thomas Nelson Publishers, 2007).

2 Stephen M. R. Covey, *The Speed of Trust: The One Thing that Changes Everything* (New York: Free Press, 2018).

3 William Arndt, Walter Bauer, Frederick William Danker, *"kalos,"* *A Greek-English Lexicon of the New Testament and Other Early Christian Literature,* 3rd ed. (Chicago, IL: University of Chicago Press. 2020).

4 Mac Lake, *The Multiplication Effect: Building a Leadership Pipeline that Solves Your Leadership Shortage* (Nashville, TN: Thomas Nelson Publishers, 2020).

Chapter 12 Improving Character

1 Arbinger Institute, *Leadership and Self-Deception: Getting out of the Box* (Oakland, CA; Berrett-Koehler Publishers, Inc., 2018).

2 Arbinger Institute, *The Anatomy of Peace: Resolving the Heart of Conflict* (Oakland, CA: Berrett-Koehler Publishers, Inc., 2015).

3 Arbinger Institute, *The Outward Mindset: How to Change Lives and Transform Organizations* (Oakland, CA: Berrett-Koehler Publishers, Inc., 2019).

4 Suzie Welch, 10-10-10: *A Life-Transforming Idea* (New York: Scribner Publishers, 2009).

5 "Core Values." YourDictionary.com, accessed April 30, 2020: https://examples.yourdictionary.com/examples-of-core-values.html.

Building Block 4
Passion: The Intentionality of Life and Leadership—Lead-In

1 Olen R. Brown, "Enzymes are Essential for Life; Did they Evolve?" Discovery Institute, August 22, 2018: https://evolutionnews.org/2018/08/enzymes-are-essential-for-life-did-they-evolve/.

2 Kara Rogers, "Enzymes," Brittanica.com, accessed May 12, 2020: https://www.britannica.com/science/enzyme.

3 Ryan Raman, "12 Foods that Contain Digestive Enzymes," Healthline.com, accessed May 12, 2020: https://www.healthline.com/nutrition/natural-digestive-enzymes.

4 Howard F. Loomis Jr., "Why Food Enzymes are Important," Food Enzyme Institute, accessed May 12, 2020: https://www.foodenzymeinstitute.com/content/Why-Food-Enzymes-are-Important.aspx.

Chapter 13 Defining Passion

1 John Maxwell, *21 Indispensable Qualities of a Leader: Becoming the Person Others Will Want Follow* (Nashville, TN: Thomas Nelson

Publishers, 1999).

2 Mark Batterson, *Chase the Lion: If Your Dream Doesn't Scare You, It's Too Small* (New York: Multnomah, 2016).

3 "Passion," Merriam-Webster.com Dictionary, accessed April 19, 2020: https://www.merriam-webster.com/dictionary/vision.

4 "Intensity," Merriam-Webster.com Dictionary, accessed April 19, 2020: https://www.merriam-webster.com/dictionary/vision.

5 *Steve Moore, Who is My Neighbor? Being a Good Samaritan in a Connected World* (Colorado Springs, CO: NavPress, 2011).

6 Steve Moore, "Passion and Leadership," Growing Leaders, February 10, 2019: https://growingleaders.com/blog/passion-and-leadership/.

7 Darren Hardy, *The Entrepreneur Roller Coaster: It's Your Turn to #Join the Ride* (Lake Dallas, TX: Success, 2015).

8 Hardy, *Entrepreneur Roller Coaster.*

9 Tim Elmore, "Power of Passion," Growing Leaders, November 9, 2011: https://growingleaders.com/blog/the-power-of-passion/.

10 Angela Duckworth, *GRIT: The Power of Passion and Perseverance* (New York: Scribner, 2016).

Chapter 14 Passion—Sacrifice

1 Steve Moore, *Who is My Neighbor? Being a Good Samaritan in a Connected World* (Colorado Springs, CO: NavPress, 2011).

2 "Passion," Online Etymology Dictionary, accessed May 1, 2020: http://www.etymonline.com.

3 John Maxwell, *21 Indispensable Qualities of a Leader: Becoming the Person Others Will Want Follow* (Nashville, TN: Thomas Nelson

Publishers, 1999).

4 The Connected Generation, Barna Group, accessed May 8, 2020: https://theconnectedgeneration.com/webcast/.

Chapter 15 Conviction, Passion, and Perseverance

1 Ralph Ingersoll, *Report on England, November 1940* (New York: Simon and Schuster, 1940).

2 Winston Churchill, "Blood, Toil, Tears and Sweat," International Churchill Society, May 13 1940, accessed April 19, 2020: https://winstonchurchill.org/resources/speeches/1940-the-finest-hour/blood-toil-tears-and-sweat-2/.

3 Angela Duckworth, *GRIT: The Power of Passion and Perseverance* (New York: Scribner, 2016).

4 "Passion," Merriam-Webster.com Dictionary, accessed April 19, 2020: https://www.merriam-webster.com/dictionary/vision.

5 Tim Elmore, "What Enables Students to be Resilient," Growing Leaders, October 19 2017: https://growingleaders.com/blog/enables-student-resilient/.

Chapter 16 Biblical Implication and Application

1 Angela Duckworth, *GRIT: The Power of Passion and Perseverance* (New York: Scribner, 2016).

2 Duckworth, *GRIT*.

3 Charles M. Sheldon, *In His Steps* (Grand Rapids, MI: Revell Books, 1984).

Conclusion: Make It Happen!

1 William Arndt, Walter Bauer, Frederick William Danker, *"poieo," A Greek-English Lexicon of the New Testament and Other Early Christian Literature,* 3rd ed. (Chicago, IL: University of Chicago Press. 2020).

2 Mark Batterson, *Chase the Lion: If Your Dream Doesn't Scare You, It's Too Small* (New York: Multnomah, 2016).

3 John Kotter, *Leading Change* (Brighton, MA: Harvard Business Review Press, 2012).

4 Eric Geiger and Kevin Peck, *Designed to Lead: The Church and Leadership Development* (Nashville, TN: B&N, 2016).

5 Batterson, *Chase the Lion.*

Reviews

Don't read this book! Don't read this book if you are just looking for a list of formulaic, proverbial statements about leadership that are best suited for a bumper sticker. However, if you are looking for a "at your desk," daily, go-to resource about leadership, then read this book and read it over and over.

Bob has packed this resource with page after page of real life, relevant, practical leadership advice. Coming from his own study, experience, the expertise of many others and divine wisdom, he looks at leadership from its very heart all the way to its value on Main Street. Bob not only explores the philosophy and concept of leadership, but uses dozens of illustrations, personal stories and gives practical tools for leaders of every kind to lead every day. Although he has designed the book primarily for church leaders it would be of exceptional value to leaders in any field and of any maturity level.

Through what he calls the four essentials of leadership: vision, goals, character and passion, Bob considers the leader as a person, the need for planning, practice and progress. He shows the value of living like a leader, loving like a leader and truly leading like a leader.
There is no single "one stop shop" for leaders, but this book comes very close. A must read for all leaders.

Wayne Roberts
Lead teacher, Metro Church OKC
Marriage Coach with His Shoes, Her Shoes
Director of the TRU Church Conference
Co-Director of the Mighty Men Leadership Conference

For the last two thousand years, every generation of the church has faced various trials. The current generation has been, and will be, no different. The question is, does the church have the leaders she needs to help God's people navigate these trials? Does your congregation have effective leaders and are they equipping future generations to lead? Bob Turner is a leader of leaders and an equipper of equippers. In this book, Turner draws from a deep well of learning and experience on the subject of leadership. Some of the best quotes, studies, and ideas from both secular and religious leadership books are masterfully curated and applied to Christian life and leadership. I hope that elderships, ministers, and other church leaders will read and discuss this book together. The church not only needs strong leaders today, but also strong leaders today who are equipping leaders for tomorrow.

Wes McAdams, Minister
McDermott Road Church of Christ

Vision, Goals, Character, and Passion. Bob Turner's four components of leadership come to life on the pages of this book. I wish that every shepherd and every leader in the world could learn to live out the principles found here. Bob blesses us with outstanding insight from his research, but more importantly, everyone who reads *Essential: Buidling Blocks 4 Life and Leadership* will benefit from Bob's personal perspective as well as what he has gleaned from a lifetime of learning from other leaders. Here is a book that is needed in our day and my prayer is that it will not just be read, but that it will become a rich resource for leaders everywhere.

Jeff A. Jenkins, Minister
Lewisville Church of Christ, Lewisville, TX

In *Esssential: Building Blocks 4 Life and Leadership*, Bob Turner condenses a wealth of knowledge and experience into four essentials (paralleling the four essentials for human life) for Christian leaders to develop and to better implement leadership skills. In this book readers will continuously be called back to Scripture, interact with materials from a number of works in the field, and be given general rules and specific tools to better assess how to come up with a vision, measure success, and continually call themselves back to the best practices for leading others. The illustrations are personal and engaging, the interaction with Scripture and church life is relevant, and the conclusions lead readers to consider how to seek to be motivated to make choices, serve others compassionately, and live with an intentional focus of serving others as Christian leaders. Every reader who engages the material in this book will walk away with a renewed enthusiasm to evaluate his or her own efforts to lead and influence others.

Doug Burleson
Associate Professor of Bible
Director of the Annual Bible Lectureship
Freed-Hardeman University

Bob Turner is my friend, but he's not just a friend. He's a great resource for me when it comes to all things leadership related. This subject has become a passion for Bob and that passion pours forth in his writing. The book is an easy-to-read, practical treatise dissecting the details of leadership. However, the book does not stop there. Just as important is the application of the information, of which Bob does a tremendous job. Each section of the book begins with a historic quote coupled with a story or illustration that serves as a launching pad for that particular section. From determining a vision, to setting and achieving goals, to building character, to developing passion, Essential is a holistic approach that includes the person, the personality, and the performance of an effective leader with God's holy Word being the basis for it all. I highly recommend *Essential: Buildig Blocks 4 Life and Leadership*. I think you will appreciate Bob's insight and intellect as he equips the reader to be a more effective leader.

Chris McCurley, Minister
Oldham Lane Church of Christ, Abilene, TX

Bob Turner's book, *Essential: Building Blocks 4 Life and Leadership*, explores the concepts of effective leadership through a fluid combination of theory, practice, and most importantly, Biblical examples. Each section of the text provides a thoughtful approach to what makes an effective leader, both from the internal motivation to the outward actions that motivates others to follow--and ultimately discover the leadership qualities each has within themselves. While there are many examples that could be used to further explain the concepts set out in the text, perhaps one of the most telling is the statement that there are two types of people—those who have goals and those who do not. Bob then explores the importance of setting goals to accomplish anything, but most importantly to give purpose and direction to our life. Bob had a goal to write an effective, practical text that explores the characteristics of good leadership. *Essential: Building Blocks 4 Life and Leadership* accomplished that goal.

Richard England
Professor of Education and Music
Freed-Hardeman University

About the Author

Bob Turner (MBS, DIS) is the current Director of SALT (Sunset Academy for Leadership Training). He teaches courses in Leadership and Leadership Development around the world. He also conducts workshops in Teaching with Dialogue, Creating Vision, Finding Our Grit, Character Development, Strategic Planning, Communication, Conflict Resolution, and Managing Change. He also serves as an instructor in the Sunset International Bible Institute's master's degree program. Bob is a graduate of the Bear Valley Bible Institute International and holds both a bachelor's and master's degree in Bible. After completing the cohort sequence of 36 units in the Masters of Arts in Global Leadership at the Fuller Theological Seminary (FTS) in Pasadena, CA, Bob went on to earn his Doctorate of Intercultural Studies with an emphasis in Adult Leadership Development at FTS. He and his wife, Sheryl, have been married 38+ years with more than 25 years of ministry experience. They have three children and ten grandchildren. He has preached for several congregations in the US, and his family served as missionaries in Prince Rupert, BC, Canada for five years. Bob also served as the Director of Extension Schools for the Bear Valley Bible Institute for eight years before focusing his attention on developing leaders.